The Gifts of Reading

D1472033

The GIFTS *of* READING

Inspired by
ROBERT MACFARLANE

Curated by
JENNIE ORCHARD

WEIDENFELD & NICOLSON

First published in Great Britain in 2020 by Weidenfeld & Nicolson,
This paperback edition published in Great Britain in 2021 by
Weidenfeld & Nicolson,
an imprint of The Orion Publishing Group Ltd
Carmelite House, 50 Victoria Embankment
London EC4Y 0DZ

An Hachette UK Company

1 3 5 7 9 10 8 6 4 2

A CIP catalogue record for this book is
available from the British Library.

ISBN (Mass Market Paperback) 978 1 4746 2493 0
ISBN (eBook) 978 1 4746 1569 3
ISBN (Audio) 978 1 4746 2244 8

Typeset by Born Group
Printed and bound in Great Britain by Clays Ltd, Elcograf S.p.A.

www.weidenfeldandnicolson.co.uk
www.orionbooks.co.uk

CONTENTS

Preface

ROBERT MACFARLANE

૪ૐ

'The gift moves ...' writes Lewis Hyde again and again in his classic work *The Gift* (1983). It moves in two ways, we might say: the receiver of a gift is emotionally moved by being given something freely, unexpectedly. And the gift itself moves in the sense of moving onwards, of circulating. Having experienced generosity, we are generous to others in turn. The gift 'gives on', as Hyde also puts it, in wild excess of its own original extent.

The book you hold in your hands is proof that 'the gift moves'. Five years ago, I sat down to write an essay about a gift that had changed my life. I realised as I wrote, though, that I wanted the essay to do more than just describe its subject. I wanted it, somehow, to enact its subject; to be itself a *gift that gives on*. So I wrote my essay for free, and I asked my artist friend, Stanley Donwood, to give some of his art for free as the cover of the essay. Penguin, my publisher, agreed to publish the essay for free as a tiny gift book, costing £2. And we all agreed that proceeds from the sale of that book – *The Gifts of Reading*, as it became called – would be given to the Migrant Offshore Aid Station (MOAS), which does vital work saving migrant lives at sea in the Mediterranean and the Bay of Bengal, and which relies on donations for its continued operation.

The Gifts of Reading started to 'move' in strange ways soon after its publication. Stories reached me of people who were buying ten or twenty copies at a time, and giving each copy to a different person, who would in turn give more copies away ... Pat Law – a Scottish artist, sailor and walker – began leaving copies of the book in bothies in the Highlands and Islands. A bothy is a hut or cabin in remote country, maintained by volunteers and left open for whoever needs its use – a sort of gift shelter, as it were, where strangers are kind to strangers. Donations to MOAS via the book reached five figures, and carried on rising.

Among the people to cross paths with *The Gifts of Reading* in its first form were Jennie Orchard, long-term supporter of the inspirational NGO Room to Read, and John Wood, its Founder. This organisation transforms the lives of tens of millions of children, especially girls, by advancing literacy and girls' education in Asia and Africa. Their work is simply astonishing. It is hard proof of the gifts of reading; that books and language can bridge division, grow empathy, change lives from a young age, alter cultures and societies for the better.

It was Jennie Orchard who imagined another way of keeping the gift moving. She had the idea of a collection of essays about reading's gifts, with each essay freely given, and all profits given on in turn to Room to Read. By means of her vision and sheer determination, she brought into being this book – the one you are about to read.

It is a beautiful, tangled skein of stories, filled with surprising echoes and unexpected interlockings. Here books take flight in flocks, migrating around the world, landing in people's hearts and changing them for a day or a year or a lifetime. Here books spark wonder or spark anger; throw open windows into other languages, other cultures, other minds; cause people to fall in love, or to fight for what is right. And here, repeatedly, books and words are given and received as gifts, prompting in turn further generosity – including the giving of each of these essays. Truly, the gift gives on, and on, and on …

Introduction

JENNIE ORCHARD

ℰ

This book has been born out of two defining moments.

The first was in Hong Kong, sometime in the autumn of 2005, when I came across a relatively young non-profit organisation, Room to Read, founded by John Wood, which at the time was building schools, establishing libraries and publishing children's books in seven countries in Asia and Africa. It was also committed to developing and delivering girls' education programs.

The second occurred in London more than a decade later when I chanced upon Robert Macfarlane's essay, 'The Gifts of Reading', and was captivated by his account of the profound joys of giving and sharing books, the story of a friendship cemented through reading.

Almost immediately I began to ponder the possibility of an anthology where a number of writers might write about the books that had so inspired them that they wanted to share them.

And then it occurred to me that Room to Read was approaching its twentieth anniversary and that this anthology might present a perfect way to celebrate the fact that this remarkable organisation had given 'the gifts of reading' to millions of underprivileged children.

Connections are everything.

When I attended my first Room to Read meeting and started to learn more, I found that it was working in Nepal, Vietnam, India, Cambodia, Sri Lanka, Laos and South Africa.

My husband was born in South Africa. Soon after we met (in London), he was posted to Laos and spent several years there running Shell's operations. We visited Laos on our honeymoon and celebrated our marriage with a Buddhist *Baci* ceremony.

In 2008, approaching our twenty-fifth wedding anniversary, we decided to fund one of Room to Read's schools in Laos. We visited Boungkha Incomplete Primary School situated in a remote corner of Xayabouly Province, a bumpy nine-hour car journey from Luang Prabang. What a truly memorable experience it was, both the journey itself and the hours spent at the school enjoying a celebratory *Baci* feast in the well-stocked and colourful library. We were hosted by members of the local community, all overjoyed that their children would now benefit from these vastly improved facilities.

As a teacher in Nepal had said to John Wood: 'We are too poor to afford education. But until we have education, how will we ever not be poor?'

The journey to Laos provided the impetus to commit wholeheartedly to launching a fundraising chapter for Room to Read in Sydney, later Australia as a whole. John Wood had raised this possibility and now I was inspired. We'd been living in Asia by that stage for more than six years and I was ready to embrace a new challenge. Within a very short time of arriving back in Sydney, together with another former Hong Kong colleague, we organised a first information meeting – and then a second and a third. The response to the meetings was so overwhelmingly positive that we quickly started to build a volunteer team and began preparations for the official Sydney launch, a wine gala, to be held in February 2009.

John Wood flew in from the US and international wine writer Jancis Robinson was the much revered guest of honour. In the wake of the global financial crisis, the timing was terrible but the wine flowed and John Wood's passion and optimism won the day. Even on that first occasion, we raised nearly half a million dollars.

And this has been the story of Room to Read all over the world. Fuelled by John's unflagging conviction of the importance of the cause – World Change Starts with Educated Children® – Room to Read has grown in two decades from being a fledgling startup to an impressive global organisation, delivering literacy and girls' education programs in ten countries in Asia and Africa, collaborating elsewhere with partners with similar objectives, transforming the lives of millions of children, their families and their communities.

When he founded Room to Read in 2000, working with Erin Ganju and Dinesh Shrestha, John defined a bold goal – that by 2020 Room to Read would impact ten million children. 'Bold goals attract bold people,' he always said, and he has been proven right. By the end of 2020, Room to Read will have impacted twenty million children, twice as many as he had targeted – and the goal for the next five years is to reach an additional thirty million.

From the very beginning in Australia we were supported by a small group of writers including Susanne Gervay and Markus Zusak. For an organisation focused on literacy, there could be no better ambassadors. This group has grown to around twenty-five writers (all listed in the Acknowledgements at the end of the book). They have raised funds and, more importantly in many ways, they have spread the word through their school presentations, conferences and literary festivals, building trust.

The Gifts of Reading takes this initiative to a new level, drawing in writers from all over the world, many of them with connections to the countries where Room to Read is working, all of them passionate about the power of words, stories, books.

Curating this anthology has been a little bit like organising the most wonderful literary cocktail party. I know of a regular column in one newspaper which asks its subjects which authors they'd invite to a literary dinner – but a gathering of twenty-three authors offers so many more possibilities. We have here people of many nationalities from almost every continent, many age groups, adult and children's authors alike.

The decisive moment came when Robert Macfarlane and his publisher, Simon Prosser at Hamish Hamilton, most generously agreed that Robert's essay could be used as the title piece in this collection. Originally published in a tiny paperback format, with proceeds donated to Migrant Offshore Aid Station, it had been popular – as Robert testifies in his preface – and yet I kept coming across friends and colleagues who weren't aware of it.

It has taken the best part of three years from the seed of an idea to publication but both Robert and John have provided unwavering support along the way. Our 'gifts of reading' community has grown from two to more than twenty, each and every contributor offering a different interpretation of the theme. There are echoes of Chigozie Obioma's childhood in Nigeria and of Alice Pung's Cambodian heritage, hints of Wales from Jackie Morris, scenes from Mumbai thanks to Imtiaz Dharker; and of South Africa, Iran, Ireland and Everest from others.

And there are glorious literary connections running throughout, linking Roddy Doyle and Sisonke Msimang, Jackie Morris with Max Porter, SF Said with Philip Pullman, David Pilling and Dina Nayeri. Some responded precisely to the request to write about the books they loved to give, while others wrote about the 'gifts of reading' they had received.

Andy Miller, SF Said and Salley Vickers all thought back to the extraordinary moment when as children they had started to read, when, in the evocative words of Alberto Manguel, 'the page of a book ... shivered into meaning ... whole universes opened'.

Others, including Candice Carty-Williams and Madeleine Thien, have acknowledged the importance of libraries, so imaginatively defined by Robert in one of his words of the day as 'story-forests, wildwoods of words', and the heart of Room to Read's work since the very beginning.

Many of those who agreed to contribute were admirers of Robert Macfarlane's work and felt privileged to be given the opportunity to feature in an anthology bearing his name. Some of them already knew of Room to Read, others not. Some had been part of my life for a while; others were new to me, encountered through reviews or literary festivals or friends. Pico Iyer was a particularly generous co-conspirator, initially declining the invitation to contribute, then half an hour later saying that he couldn't resist the temptation to write an essay and had already begun work.

Writers are busy people, writing, speaking, teaching, travelling – but this group has been utterly magnanimous in agreeing to write an essay and donate their royalties to Room to Read, in providing reading lists, making valuable suggestions and introductions. Pico encouraged me to write again to Jan Morris and Michael Ondaatje – and these new messages bore fruit.

Jan Morris had been trying to phone me but had trouble with my overseas numbers. She went on to apologise:

… in any case I'm so sorry, but I no longer have it in me to write an essay for you and Mr Macfarlane. I have one rather forlorn suggestion to make, though. My happiest experience of the writing life, one which permanently enriched me, was my participation, purely as a writer, in the first ascent of Everest in 1953. I did write a book about it, but my better short memoir of the reportage was only a talk for the Himalayan Trust. They did print it, for themselves, but the copyright is mine and it has never been published. It's a couple of thousand words, I suppose, and if it would amuse you to have it for your anthology I would adapt it to be a By the Way Gift of Writing!!!! If not, forget it and forgive me.

'If it would amuse me …'? I was simply astonished to hear from the venerable Jan Morris, even more so when she mailed a copy of her speech, 'An Outsider on Everest', and I only wished I could make a pilgrimage to Trefan Morys in north Wales to thank her in person.

I felt equally grateful to William Boyd, who was the first writer (after Robert and John) to agree to contribute an essay, responding almost by return, delivering his perfectly pitched contribution just before Christmas, a sublime 'gift of reading'.

And so, slowly this anthology has grown to become the book that you hold in your hands, representing the intersection of so many lives and stories.

At a time when the world is facing unimaginable challenges, we need to hold on hard to the integrity and the inspiration of the writers, the artists and other creative people in our lives. These essays create an ever-extending web of connections, drawing us all together, extending ever further our libraries, our communities of book lovers. Reading and rereading this smorgasbord of essays has given me so much pleasure, sent me back down many memory lanes of the literary variety but also propelled me into uncharted territory.

In addition to their essays, we asked each of our contributors to create a list of five titles they like to give, and this appears in the final pages of this volume.

Ben Okri wrote about a 'secret trail of books meant to inspire and enlighten you. Find that trail.'

My hope is that this wondrous anthology will spark countless new literary journeys. As Anna Quindlen has written: 'Books are the plane, and the train, and the road. They are the destination, and the journey. They are home.'

ROBERT
MACFARLANE

'A gift can be transformative and ... the act of giving encourages the onwards circulation of generosity.'

Robert Macfarlane's prize-winning and bestselling books about landscape, nature, memory and travel include *Mountains of the Mind: A History of a Fascination*, *The Wild Places*, *The Old Ways*, *Holloway* (with Stanley Donwood and Dan Richards), *Landmarks* and – most recently – *Underland: A Deep Time Journey*. His work has been translated into many languages and widely adapted for screen, stage and musical performance. Copies of his collaboration with artist and author Jackie Morris, *The Lost Words: A Spell Book*, are used in thousands of schools across Britain.

The gifts of reading

ROBERT MACFARLANE

This story, like so many stories, begins with a gift. The gift, like so many gifts, was a book – and the book was given to me by a man called Don, with whom I became friends in Beijing during the autumn and winter of 2000. Don and I were working as English literature teachers in a university on the west side of the city, third ring road out. Our students were mostly the sons and daughters of high-cadre officials: if you mentioned Tibet or Taiwan, thirty faces dipped to their desks. We taught our syllabus from a fat crimson-jacketed anthology of English literature that reframed literary history, Chinese Communist Party style. Literature was functional, and its function was the advancement of the Maoist project. Wordsworth the revolutionary was included, but not Wordsworth the late-life conservative. Oscar Wilde starred as socialist but not as aesthete. Ezra Pound didn't make the cut, for obvious reasons. Thomas Hood's 'The Song of the Shirt' was the most important Victorian poem.

Teaching with The Big Red Book, as we nicknamed it, was hard work. It was easy to forget that literature might be there to thrill, perplex or amaze, rather than only to instruct. What kept me honest was Don. Don turned sixty that year. He was from San Francisco. He was tall, just starting to stoop. He dressed Kerouac-style: black jeans, black leather jackets, white T-shirts. Pebble glasses, short grey hair standing up in spikes. Small, sharp, wonky teeth, which you saw a lot of because Don talked so much and laughed so much. Fast, rat-a-tat questions and answers, or long think-pieces spoken at several words a second, but without ever making you feel like he was taking more than his fair share of airtime.

Don was from a blue-collar background in California, and had met poetry at the City Lights Bookstore in his early twenties. It had changed his life. He'd heard Ginsberg read. He'd hung out with Ferlinghetti. He'd worked night school and then part-time at a state college to get a degree in literature as a mature student. But eventually he couldn't afford to live in California and teach the texts he loved, so he'd switched to Beijing where accommodation came with the job, and the basics were cheap. I don't think I've ever known anyone with a higher-voltage passion for books than Don. Literature *wired* him. When Don read, he crackled.

In the days, Don and I did our best with The Big Red Book and the cadre children. In the evenings, we drank beer laced with formaldehyde, and talked writing. Don introduced me to dozens of authors of whom I cannot now imagine being innocent, among them Ed Abbey, Annie Dillard and Gary Snyder. We shared a love of classical Chinese poetry (Li Bai, Tu Fu), especially in translations by Pound and by David Hinton. Although foreign books were difficult to come by in Beijing at that time, and expensive if you could find them, and although Don didn't have much money, he pressed volume after volume on to me, including his copy of Ferlinghetti's *A Coney Island of the Mind*, with its lit-up monochrome cover. 'Have it,' he told me, 'you'll love it, you *need* to read it, you keep it.'

One day Don didn't show up for his classes. He'd been mugged the night before. He was found in an alley in a pool of blood with a half-brick next to him and his wallet gone. I cut class and went straight to see him. His head had been shaved and there was a linen bandage swaddling half his skull, stained with iodine. But he was smiling, and there was a book open by his bed, and he wanted me to read him Snyder's poem 'Riprap' out loud:

> Lay down these words
> Before your mind like rocks
> placed solid, by hands ...

* * *

I left Beijing after two semesters, and came back to Cambridge to start a PhD in Victorian literature. Don and I wrote often, sometimes by email, mostly by airmail. I missed his intensity. The seminar rooms of Cambridge felt prim and flat in comparison. We arranged that he'd come to England the next summer for a couple of weeks. I couldn't wait to see him.

The visit didn't go to plan. I was struggling with my doctorate, paranoid about time. Don wanted to talk, walk and read *all* day. I needed to study. He wanted to explore the bookshops of Cambridge – G. David's, the Haunted Bookshop, both tucked away on opposite sides of a medieval cemetery. But I felt obliged to put hours in at the University Library, where I was tracking down obscure texts from the 1860s in the huge leather-backed folders that constituted the catalogue in that pre-digitised era. After five days, I suggested that Don head up to Edinburgh for a trip on his own. It was an astonishing city, I said, unmissable, the Paris of the North, etc. I researched bus times for him. I knew I was trying to move him on. I didn't know he knew I was trying to move him on.

On the seventh morning I heard Don get up early and walk around the house. The front door closed. I guessed he was heading to the market. I went to the kitchen to make coffee. There was a neatly wrapped present on the table, with a card. I read the card. He'd gone to Edinburgh, hadn't wanted to wake us before leaving. I felt a quick punch of guilt. He'd loved his stay with us, he said, and had left a few small tokens of thanks.

The present on the table was a copy of Snyder's *Mountains and Rivers Without End*. I walked into the other room. There was another present there, propped up against a lamp: a CD of West Coast jazz. And then in the room in which I worked, on my desk, was the third and last of his presents. It was a paperback copy of a book by Patrick Leigh Fermor that Don and I had talked about once in Beijing, drawn to it by our shared love of walking (which Don mostly did in cities, and I mostly did in mountains). Its title was *A Time of Gifts*.

* * *

If you've never read *A Time of Gifts*, may I urgently suggest that you buy a copy as soon as possible, or better still ask someone to give you one as a present? Together with the two books that follow it – *Between the Woods and the Water* (1986) and

The Broken Road (2013) – it tells the story of Leigh Fermor's legendary walk from the Hook of Holland to Constantinople in the early 1930s, started when he was just eighteen, and constituting what is fondly known by Leigh Fermor's many modern admirers as 'the longest gap year in history'.

Leigh Fermor came up with his plan at 'about lamplighting time at the end of a wet November day' in Mayfair in 1933. Fatigued by his London life and its boozy repetitions, he was suddenly seized by the idea of walking across an entire continent, from Christendom to Islam, passing as he did so through the cultures, tongues and countries of Europe. His aim on setting out was to live like a 'pilgrim' or 'errant scholar': to sleep in ditches and hay barns, and 'only consort with peasants and tramps'. But being who he was – a handsome and charming young man with a few good connections to start him off – he ended up strolling from castle to castle, playing hopschloss across Germany, Hungary and the Carpathians, sipping Tokay from cut-glass goblets and smoking yard-long pipes with archdukes and earls. For a year and a half, he was an aristocratic supertramp, enjoying hospitality along the way, making his rakish progress through the doomed world of *Mitteleuropa*, snatching scenes from a snowglobe – just before it was shattered by the worst war in history.

A Time of Gifts is filled with gifts and acts of giving – it is a book, we might say, that is rich with generosity. Among its gifts is the gift of time: Leigh Fermor did not publish it until 1977, forty-four years after beginning his walk, and a result of that long and thoughtful delay is a narrative voice which possesses both the joyful wonder of youth, and the wisdom and perspective of later age. And among those wisdoms is its reflection on the nature of gift: what it might mean to give without expectation of recompense, and what types of kindness might stand outside the reciprocal binds of the cash economy.

This fascination with gift expresses itself also in Leigh Fermor's famously ornate style, profusely tendrilled as it is with trope and allusion. Almost everything in his prose leads to something else (path to path, culture to culture, word to word) and this abundance of connection is itself a kind of offering up or giving away. You feel, as a reader, passionately – perhaps even at times oppressively – hosted: *Read this! Look here! Listen to that! Walk this way!* His style is gratuitous in the best sense of that word: 'given free of charge; undertaken without necessity or obligation'.

One of the first things Leigh Fermor is given in *A Time of Gifts* is a book: the first volume of the Loeb edition of Horace. His mother ('she was an enormous reader') bought it for him as a farewell present, and on its flyleaf she wrote the prose translation of an exquisite short poem by Petronius, which could hardly have been more appropriate as a valediction to her son, or indeed to anyone setting out on a voyage into adulthood:

> Leave thy home, O youth, and seek out alien shores … Yield not to misfortune: the far-off Danube shall know thee, the cold North-wind and the untroubled kingdom of Canopus and the men who gaze on the new birth of Phoebus or upon his setting.

* * *

The journey of *A Time of Gifts* is set going by the gift of a book – and it is a book that has in turn set going many journeys.

The edition of *A Time of Gifts* that Don gave me that day in Cambridge had as its cover a beautiful painting by John Craxton, commissioned specially for the book, and clearly alluding to Petronius's poem. It shows a young man standing on snowy high ground, puttees on his ankles and a walking stick in his right hand, looking eastwards to where the sun is rising orange over icy mountains, from which runs a mighty river. Black crows fly stark against white trees: there is a sense of huge possibility to the day ahead and to the land beyond.

When I first read *A Time of Gifts* I felt it in my *feet*. It spoke to my soles. It rang with what in German is called *Sehnsucht*: a yearning or wistful longing for the unknown and the mysterious. It made me want to stand up and stride out into adventure. The book's strong magic derives in part from the atmosphere of miracle that attends Leigh Fermor's peregrinations. He marches with the seven-league boots of youth, fatigue barely registering as whole countries roll beneath his heel. The comforting rhythm of his journey – exertion, encounter, rest, food, sleep; exertion, encounter, rest, food, sleep – rocks its readers into feelings of happiness and invulnerability. *I could do this*, you think, *I could just start walking and keep going for a day or two, or three, or four, or more …*

Certainly, I have now walked hundreds of miles under Leigh Fermor's influence, and have carried his books for many of those miles, to read at the day's break or the day's end. One walk in particular was made directly as a result of Don's gift to me of *A Time of Gifts*. That walk happened in the December of 2007, a year when I was living and working back in Beijing. The city was a hard place to be that winter: the 2008 Olympics were imminent, and Beijing was convulsed by demolition and construction. *Hutong*s were being bulldozed by the hundred, compulsory-purchase orders were being served on thousands of poorer homes, and dozens of new stadia and skyscrapers were being built. Migrant labourers toiled on the projects 24/7 in brutal conditions: permanent halogen daylight, with massive speaker-banks blasting out Chinese radio to keep them entertained and educated as they did so.

I was stuck in the seventeenth-storey flat of an eighteen-storey building in a new development, from the windows of which I could count thirty-four cranes, each with a red PRC flag fluttering from its spire. The city's dawn chorus was the gong stroke of rivet on girder, the crump of the piston hammer, the high peal of hit steel. The notorious Beijing smog was choking, thickened by the cement dust raised by the construction. As soon as you stepped outside, you could feel the smog bite the throat and sting the eyes. When snow fell, it was grey. I read Leigh Fermor up in the flat, tried to look after my two young children adequately – and dreamed of getting out of the city and into clean air and white snow.

Then – as if Leigh Fermor himself had conjured it into being – an opportunity appeared: my friend Jon Miceler, a mountaineer and field conservationist, wrote inviting me to join him on a winter journey to the sacred 7,000-metre peak of Minya Konka, which rises between the Dadu and the Yalong rivers in Sichuan Province, south-west China.

I will never forget the days we subsequently spent up in the peaks of the Daxue range: the bright winter sun, the fearsome winter cold, the beaten-earth paths unfurling through oak-woods in the valleys, the high, snow-filled passes with their fluttering prayer flags and cairns of *mani* stones, and at last

Minya Konka itself, a pyramidal mountain of exceptional beauty and danger, its flanks ribbed with huge snow flutes, its ridges running in fine lines up to its sharp summit.

I carried *A Time of Gifts* with me throughout, and I brought the book safely back to sea level, too, its corners knackered from weeks in the rucksack and pannier, sand grains from a river beach stuck in its gutters and a dried leaf of Himalayan oak tucked away between back page and back cover. I would later write about that journey in a walking book of my own called *The Old Ways*, in a chapter that is, I now see, unmistakably Leigh Fermorian in tone. His prose had inspired that journey on foot, and it shaped my subsequent account of it also; he had been my companion on the path, and he was my companion on the page, too. And Don's gift to me had continued to give, in ways neither of us could have foreseen.

* * *

Great art 'offers us images by which to imagine our lives', notes Lewis Hyde in his classic 1983 book, *The Gift*, '[and] once the imagination has been awakened it is procreative: through it we can give more than we were given, say more than we had to say'. This is a beautiful double proposition: that art enlarges our repertoire for being, and that it further enables a giving *onwards* of that enriched utterance, that broadened perception.

I was given a copy of Hyde's *The Gift* – and I don't have that copy any longer, because I gave it to someone else, urging them to read it. Gifts *give on*, says Hyde, this is their logic. They are generous acts that incite generosity. He contrasts two kinds of 'property': the commodity and the gift. The commodity is acquired and then hoarded, or resold. But the gift is kept moving, given onwards in a new form. Whereas the commodity circulates according to the market economy (in which relations are largely impersonal and conducted with the aim of profiting the self), the gift circulates according to the gift economy (in which relations are largely personal and conducted with the aim of profiting the other). In the market economy, value accrues to the individual by means of hoarding or 'saving'. In the gift economy, value accrues between individuals by means of giving and receiving. This, for Hyde, is why gifts possess 'erotic life' as property: when we give a gift, it is an erotic act in the sense of *eros* as meaning 'attraction', 'union', a 'mutual involvement'.

Hyde is not to everyone's taste. His vision of a gift economy is appealing in theory, but not necessarily available to those locked into hard-scrabble lives, gripped vice-tight by the cash economy. Not all gifts are well given, and not all are gladly taken. It is also hard to scale up gift economies from small groups to whole societies (though the internet has made that much more possible since Hyde first wrote). And it's true that the evidence Hyde serves up in support of his gift thesis is one hell of a gumbo: superhero underwear, Scottish folk tales, Walt Whitman, the story of a couple who try to trade in their baby for a Corvette ... But to me at least, it mostly hangs together.

I am particularly moved by his deep interest in what he calls 'the gift that, when it comes, speaks commandingly to the soul and irresistibly moves us'. The outcome of a gift is uncertain at the time of giving, but the fact that it *has been given* charges it with great potential to act upon the recipient for the good. Because of the gratitude we feel, and because the gift is by definition given freely, without obligation, we are encouraged to meet it with openness and with excitement. Unlike commodities, gifts – in Hyde's account and my experience – possess an exceptional power to transform, to heal and to inspire.

That happened to me when Don gave me *A Time of Gifts*. It has happened to me numerous times, in fact – and it has almost always been the case that the gift which has spoken so 'commandingly' to my soul has been a printed book.

* * *

Not all books received as gifts are transformative, of course. Sometimes the only thing a book gives its reader is a paper cut. But having been given so many remarkable books over the years, I now in turn give away as many as I can. Birthdays, Christmases – I give books, and pretty much only books, as presents (always hard copies; I have never given, or been given, an e-book). Once or twice a year, I invite my students at Cambridge to my room and let them take two or three books each from the fifty or sixty that I've laid out on the floor. The pleasure they take in choosing, and their disbelief that the books are *free*, reminds me of how precious books were to me when I was a student. Four years ago, I was given 200 or so books from the working library of my friend Roger Deakin, the great writer and environmentalist (*Waterlog*, *Wildwood*, *Notes from Walnut Tree Farm*), following his too early death in 2006. Now I try to give individual books from that library to writers whose work I know Roger would have loved and wanted to encourage. I gave Roger's copy of Ted Hughes's *Wolfwatching*, for instance, to Rob Cowen, whose *Common Ground* is a wonderful hymn to a Yorkshire edgeland and its inhabitants, and Roger's tattered hardback of Raymond Williams's *The Country and the City* to Melissa Harrison, whose novels and nature notes subtly break down the country/city opposition that Williams also strove to erode.

There are five books that I give away again and again, and they are among the books that have struck me most forcefully. I try to make sure that I always have several copies stockpiled, ready to hand out. When I find a copy of one of them in a bookshop, I buy it to add to the gift pile, knowing that the right recipient will come along sooner or later. The five books are Cormac McCarthy's *Blood Meridian*, Vladimir Nabokov's *Lolita* (care has to be taken with that one), *A Time of Gifts* (of course), J.A. Baker's *The Peregrine* and Nan Shepherd's *The Living Mountain*, her slender masterpiece about the Cairngorm mountains of north-east Scotland. I'm not sure quite what that shortlist reveals of my personality. I think perhaps I shouldn't enquire too deeply.

Shepherd's is the book I have given away most often over the years. Forty copies? Fifty? I couldn't say. I once left a copy on a train, cursed when I realised I'd done so – then took comfort from the knowledge that a book lost by someone is often a book found by someone else (and hoped that Shepherd ended up in the hands of a reader rather than the bottom of a bin).

The giving away of a copy of *The Living Mountain* that I remember most clearly happened in the Lairig Ghru in October 2013. The Lairig Ghru is the vast glacial valley that cuts through the Cairngorm mountains of north-east Scotland from north to south. I was following it up towards the summits when, where the path led through a steep-sided stream-cut, at a stepping-stone ford, I met a young man with a heavy pack. He had stopped to fill his flask and look at his map. We fell into conversation.

He was called Samuel and he was from Singapore. He spoke with distinctive fluency and candour. He had come to the Highlands to escape some kind of problem in his life, the nature of which he did not specify. He was planning to spend two nights out in the Cairngorms, though he had no fixed idea of his route. I gave him some advice about possible bothies he could stay in, and wild-camping spots he could seek out. We exchanged email addresses, and I also gave him the copy of *The Living Mountain* that I had with me, hoping it might keep him good company in hut or tent.

A week or so later, Samuel emailed:

After our meeting, my walk over the hills of the Cairngorms took me the rest of the day and proved to be the hardest thing I had ever done. It was a most humbling experience. Thank you, Robert, for sharing Nan Shepherd's brilliant prose with me and for giving me your copy of the book. I started reading it on the train on my way back to St Andrews, slowly, savouring each word like honey. Every sentence was poignant to a degree that I had never experienced before. I wept as I read. Her sensitivity to the land and its humble creatures, humble forms, glorified through her vision and thoughts, resonated deeply with me. Thank you, thank you.

To receive such an open-hearted email was itself a kind of

gift, further proof of Hyde's propositions that the gift can be transformative and that the act of giving encourages the onwards circulation of generosity. It reminded me also of Shepherd's vision of nature itself as abounding with gifts: offering wonders and beauties but asking nothing of its recipients in return. 'To see the Golden Eagle at close quarters,' she writes in *The Living Mountain*,

> requires knowledge and patience – though sometimes it may be a gift, as when once, just as I reached a summit cairn, an eagle rose from the far side of it and swept up in majestic circles above my head: I have never been nearer to the king of birds.

I recalled Nan's account of that 'gift' again last autumn, when I walked across the Cairngorms with my father, from Braemar to Tomintoul. We camped on the north-eastern shoulder of Ben Avon at around 3,000 feet, tucking our tents into the lee of a group of the granite tors that bulge from the plateau of that mountain. There we were sheltered from the big north-westerly wind that had buffeted us during the day. Just before dusk, Dad was in his tent and I was watching the sunset through the cleft between two tors. Suddenly a golden eagle came sailing past from the north, stiff-winged, its huge primaries trembling in the gale, passing perhaps thirty feet from me at its closest point. 'Dad! DAD! Get out here fast!' But by the time he was out of the tent the eagle was gone, lost in the corries to the west. 'Dad! You missed it! You won't believe it! A golden eagle just flew right past me!' And then, to our amazement, another eagle appeared from the north, sailing past with stiff wings and trembling primaries, passing perhaps thirty feet from us at its closest point. Not one gift but two. *I have never been nearer to the king of birds …*

* * *

During the solitary months and years spent writing a book, it can be easy to forget that it will – if you are lucky – live a social life. That your book might enter the imaginations and memories of its readers and thrive there, that your book might be crammed into pockets or backpacks and carried up mountains or to foreign countries, or that your book might be given by one person to another.

Perhaps the aspects of authorship I cherish most are the glimpses I get of how my books are themselves carried, or are themselves given. When I sign books at readings, people frequently want their copies inscribed as gifts. *Would you make this out to my mother, who loves mountains? … to my brother, who lives in Calcutta? … to my best friend, who is ill? … to my father, who is no longer able to walk as far as he would wish … ?* Several times I've been asked to inscribe books to young children who can't yet read: *We want to give this book to them now, so it's waiting for them when they're ready for it.* These conversations with readers, and the stories that arise from this giving of gifts, are among the strongest of the forces that keep me writing.

* * *

This story began with the gift of a book, and it ends with one too. After three days away in Edinburgh, Don came back to Cambridge to stay with us for another couple of nights. The break had allowed me to catch up with work – and to get my priorities straight. I took two days off from the PhD, and

Don and I *properly* walked and talked: out to Grantchester along the river path, round the colleges, and from bookshop to bookshop. In G. David's I found a cut-price copy of Ezra Pound's *Selected Poems* from Faber, which includes his extraordinary versions of 'The River-Merchant's Wife: A Letter', 'Song of the Bowmen of Shu' and Li Bai's poems of departure, including the 'Exile's Letter':

> *And the wind lifting the song, and interrupting it,*
> *Tossing it up under the clouds.*
>
> *And all this comes to an end.*
> *And is not again to be met with.*

I bought the book and gave it to Don as a farewell present. For two years or so afterwards, we wrote often and sent books to each other, back and forth over the Atlantic. Then one day Don wrote to say that he had been diagnosed with cancer, and that it had been caught late. He'd already begun chemotherapy. 'I have to go into this treatment room, Rob. I call it The Pain Room,' he said. 'It's the worst place in the world.' I wrote more frequently, sent more books, sometimes two or three at a time. Don's replies slowed down, then stopped.

A year or so later, I got an email from an address I didn't recognise. It was from Don's daughter, Rachel, telling me that he had died. He had been glad to get the letters and books I had sent, she told me, even when he was no longer able to write back. 'Reading kept him alive,' she said, 'right till the end.'

WILLIAM
BOYD

'The gift of a book is both a covert search for a like-minded intellect and soul and a curious act of wooing – who knows what the consequences might be.'

William Boyd was born in 1952 in Accra, Ghana, and grew up there and in Nigeria. He is the author of sixteen highly acclaimed bestselling novels and five collections of stories. He is married and divides his time between London and south-west France.

Some observations on the art and practice of giving books

WILLIAM BOYD

Back in 1987, I published my fourth novel, *The New Confessions*. In the novel, the protagonist, John James Todd, is held for weeks in solitary confinement in a German prison camp in 1917. His spirit begins to break until a kindly prison guard volunteers to feed him a few pages of Jean-Jacques Rousseau's astonishing autobiography, *The Confessions*, bit by bit. The word 'feed' is apt. Todd's piecemeal reading of *The Confessions* not only sustains him and keeps him sane but it gives birth to an obsession with Rousseau and his autobiography that lasts for the rest of the novel's 500 pages.

This idea that your sanity, not to mention your very life, can be saved and preserved by the gift of a book, even in the most arduous conditions, was something that I thought I had invented to serve my fictional purposes. Not a bit of it. Annals of prison life testify again and again to the fact that a book can be as precious as food and water, it can even be a substitute for freedom itself. Reading a book allows the mind to escape, if not the body.

In the trenches of the Western Front during the First World War, one of the most popular books in the front line was John Buchan's *The Thirty-Nine Steps*. In the Second World War, the Polish writer and painter Józef Czapski's near-perfect recall of Proust's *À la Recherche du Temps Perdu* allowed him to alleviate the suffering of his fellow officers in a Soviet prison camp by delivering a clandestine series of lectures on Proust's masterpiece. In Reading Gaol, Oscar Wilde comforted himself by reading St Augustine's *Confessions* and *The Renaissance* by Walter Pater. Primo Levi was able to mentally absent himself from the hellish privations of Auschwitz by reciting lines of Dante's *The Divine Comedy* to himself. In the Soviet Gulag, the Russian writer Varlam Shalamov discovered in a package a well-thumbed edition of Proust's *Le Côté de Guermantes*. 'Proust,' he said, became 'more valuable than sleep'. When the Nigerian writer Ken Saro-Wiwa was imprisoned by the Nigerian Military Junta in 1992, he told me that the worst torment amongst many nightmare torments was the absence of something to read. In another corner of the Gulag Archipelago the writer Yevgenia Ginzburg drew strength from her reading of Pushkin. The list goes on and on.

These are extremes. The consolations of reading – its pleasures, its freedoms – need not require such grim circumstances. But all readers, everywhere, will understand exactly what Czapski, Shalamov and Saro-Wiwa and the others are fundamentally talking about. Books can help you survive the most dire and inhuman circumstances – and they can also make a boring, rainy day more tolerable.

* * *

It's an excellent idea to give a gift of any type of book, of course, whether it be a seed catalogue, a repair manual, a dictionary or a biography – but my own feeling is that the gift of a work of fiction is somewhat set apart. Giving a novel to someone, or a book of short stories, or a collection of poetry (to a certain extent) is in a different category, I consider. And I have a theory why.

I believe that our fellow human beings – even those closest to us: spouses, lovers, parents, children, siblings, dear friends – are fundamentally mysterious, almost opaque. We fondly believe we can discern and comprehend what people are feeling and experiencing; we may even convince ourselves that we actually do know what they're thinking; after all, their actions and reactions give broad indications. But we can never be sure. Worse than that: it's very easy to discover how wrong you can be. People are difficult to understand. Come to think of it, even we ourselves are difficult to understand, sometimes. How often have we said to ourselves, 'I've no idea why I behaved/reacted/spoke/felt like that'? And if we are mysteries to ourselves, sometimes, then what mysteries lie concealed and buried in our fellow human beings? The brute fact is that other people are phenomenally difficult to interpret – except in fiction.

Here is the paradox. In fiction – in a novel or a short story – there are no mysteries (except deliberate ones) because the author tells us what is going on in the minds of his or her characters. The author knows exactly what they are thinking, and can swear to its veracity, because the author has made it all up and he or she is the only begetter and progenitor of their inner lives. If we think further about it, amongst the countless pleasures a good novel or a short story offers – beguilement, suspense, amusement, melancholy, empathy, education, style, art, etc., etc. – perhaps the most important and enduring gift is that novels and short stories offer us the *near-miraculous possibility of experiencing other minds and inner lives other than one's own.*

And it is miraculous when you come to think about it. Human behaviour, as depicted in fiction, is comprehensible in a way that it simply isn't in real life. We know exactly what Elizabeth Bennet thinks of Mr Darcy – but, as a counterposing example, I have no real idea what my neighbour thinks of me after thirty years of genial neighbourliness. I have compiled a very few aphorisms in my writing life and one of them that I repeat whenever given the opportunity is this: 'If you want to know what makes people tick – read a novel.'

The older I get, and the more I read and write, the more convinced I become that this idea is fundamental to the novel's power. To put it simply: we read fiction to acquire some kind of sense of other people and why they behave and act like they do. This explains, I am sure, why – as long as there are readers – the novel will flourish, why fiction will flourish. This is the deep source of the novel's abiding allure and potency as an art form. The novel – a complete fiction, paradoxically – makes sense of real people and therefore the real world and the human condition. No other narrative art form – film, TV, strip cartoons, video games, the theatre, dance, mime – has prose fiction's innate, subtle, wonderfully complex and effortless ability to give us this possibility of experiencing the inner lives of others.

And this conviction also explains my choice of book that I

give to others. It's my most frequent literary present, namely, the short stories of Anton Chekhov. I have a particular collection that I persistently give – an omnibus of his mature short stories, written largely in the last ten years of his life (Chekhov died in 1904 aged forty-four) – but any collection of Chekhov will do the same trick, more or less. Chekhov, to refer to my crude aphorism again, seemed to know what made people tick and, even though he was writing about nineteenth-century Russians, his understanding of human nature and the human condition is universal and timeless. His great stories could have been written yesterday. They shine a profound and precise light on the people of his era and they do the same for ours. It's quite remarkable – and of course it's a property that all good writers of fiction exhibit – but it's just that it seems to me that this ability to get into the minds of others is concentrated to perfection in the art of Anton Chekhov.

* * *

There's another aspect of the novel that makes it a powerful art form – and a more meaningful gift, therefore – and that is its intimacy. There is no hierarchy of art form amongst the seven arts but their differences make telling points. The performing arts form one group – theatre, dance, film. Experience of them is a collective one – audiences are the norm – but with literature, painting, sculpture and music the link between artist and consumer (reader, looker, listener) is more one-on-one. But, amongst those four, nothing comes close to the intimacy of writer and reader, I would argue. And by intimacy, I mean infinite complexity, infinite nuance, infinite levels of engagement. Music comes close: I respond to Beethoven's 5th Symphony in a way that is completely personal but compared to the way I respond to, say, *Anna Karenina*, it's comparatively straightforward: the emotions, the responses, generated by the music are broad and I suspect they are shared with many other listeners. But the link between writer and reader is spectacularly individual – almost on a sentence by sentence level. What a novel or a short story does – within the mind of the individual reader – is incalculable. As an author I am repeatedly stunned by astonishing and unimagined particular interpretations and responses to my fictions. Time and again that link, that connection made between the book and the person who reads that book, is confirmed as being entirely one-off. Every reader, as the reading takes place, establishes his or her own distinct relationship with the work. For all the many millions of people who have read *Anna Karenina* there will be correspondingly many millions of unique relationships.

This adds a certain frisson to the gift of a book if it's fiction. It's something of a step into the unknown. The giver is saying, effectively, that my unique response to this novel or short story is so powerful that I want to see, in giving it to you, if you respond in a similar way. It is a particular kind of confidence and contract that is being made. It's saying, in its discreet, diffident way, that I think you are the same sort of person as I am. It can go wrong, of course, and the gifted book is tossed across the room or left unfinished, but when the connection is made a strange bond is formed. The gift of a book is both a covert search for a like-minded intellect and soul and a curious act of wooing – who knows what the consequences might be …

* * *

Some top-five lists. Here are the five fictions that I give most often to other people:

Anton Chekhov – short stories
Vladmir Nabokov – *Pale Fire*
Muriel Spark – *A Far Cry from Kensington*
John Updike – *Couples*
Evelyn Waugh – *Scoop*

I also give works of non-fiction, histories and biographies but they're more random. There are very few repeats. However, there are repeats in other categories I've begun to notice. I also give presents of poetry, journals, books of photography and monographs of painters.

POETS
Philip Larkin
Alice Oswald
Elizabeth Bishop
Jamie McKendrick
Christopher Reid

JOURNAL KEEPERS
Keith Vaughan
James Boswell
Virginia Woolf
Samuel Pepys
Katherine Mansfield

PHOTOGRAPHERS
  Jacques-Henri Lartigue
  Henri Cartier-Bresson
  Saul Leiter
  Ilse Bing
  Lillian Bassman

PAINTERS
  Paul Klee
  Richard Diebenkorn
  Howard Hodgkin
  Georges Braque
  Egon Schiele

Clearly, these lists tell any recipient a certain amount about me but they also send a message to the recipient, namely, 'I think we are on the same wavelength.' It's part of the unspoken one-way traffic of book-giving. It's not just a toothsome present, like a box of chocolates; there are subtexts, implicit messages. It is, in its way, a kind of test.

* * *

But of all the people I've given books to over the years there is one person who is the wholehearted, uncontested beneficiary of my book-giving largesse. Me. I give myself books all the time, almost every day, in moments of book-obsession, book-need. Let's be honest: book-addiction. If I read or hear about a book and it sounds intriguing, I give it to myself. If I spot a reference in a footnote, or an aside in a review, then within days the book is mine. If people are talking about a book, if it's in the zeitgeist, and I feel I should check it out – then I will.

This leads me to consider the only downside to giving books. Book-storage problems leading to book-amplitude leading to book-overkill. There's no doubt that sometimes the gift of a book is unwelcome but that's only because you already have too many books, too many books that you won't read in your lifetime. There is the possibility of a book-purge, of course. You make a gift of several hundred books to your local thrift shop and for a week or so there is some space on the shelves. Then they fill, and then the piles build up on flat surfaces – side tables, coffee tables, kitchen tables, desk tops – and then in corners, small ziggurats of books beginning to colonise rooms in your house. It's a problem – some may say it's a mania, a disease – but in the category of sins it must be a minor one. A sin of omission, perhaps. You have omitted to stop buying books. Or a sin of intent. You intended to reduce your book-buying compulsion but you failed. I say to myself as I look at the exponential growth of books in my house that if there is a circle of hell in a notional literary purgatory where the compulsive book buyer is obliged to dwell for a few millennia, then perhaps I will resign myself to my fate. As long as there's something to read.

* * *

I suppose that maybe giving blood, or an organ, is a more obviously precious gift than giving a book to someone. But there is a similarity, a parallel, and it's worth exploring. The urge to give someone a book that you love or revere is, of course, an act of sharing, but it has more significance. If my argument about the unique one-on-one relationship between writer and reader is conceded, then, in giving a book to someone else, you are making a complicated, multi-layered point. That book you give reflects the kind of person you are because you were so affected by reading it. The gift of a book then becomes a metaphorical symbol of your human nature. In a real sense that book, the present of that book, is a metonym of you, part of the person you are. When you give someone a book you are making a present of part of yourself. Almost like giving blood.

© William Boyd, 2020

CANDICE
CARTY-WILLIAMS

'I adore and am obsessed with books in all their forms, but one of the things that gives me a weird thrill is the look on someone's face when you give them something new to read.'

Candice Carty-Williams is a writer and author of the *Sunday Times* bestselling *Queenie*, which won Debut of the Year and Book of the Year at the British Book Awards, was shortlisted for the Waterstones, Foyles and Goodreads Book of 2019, longlisted for the Women's Prize, as well as selected as the Blackwell's Debut Book of the Year. In 2016, Candice created and launched the *Guardian* 4th Estate BAME Short Story Prize, the first inclusive initiative of its kind in book publishing. Candice is the *Guardian Review* books columnist and has written for the *Guardian, i-D, Vogue International*, every iteration of *The Sunday Times, BEAT* Magazine, *Black Ballad* and more. She also contributed to the anthology *New Daughters of Africa*. She will probably always live in South London.

The best at giving books
(and not just to her nan)

CANDICE CARTY-WILLIAMS

I spend a lot of time wondering if my love for books comes from seeing them as something that my nan took care and time with. Most of the memories from my childhood are either of her dragging me to the shops, or cleaning and then teaching *me* to clean. In the quiet times, though, when she'd finished being a 'housewife', she'd take herself to a quiet corner and read one of her small collection of books. I always observed how peaceful she looked – and so I came to understand the value that books held. And it's probably part of the reason that I so desperately wanted to be a librarian when I grew up. I spent a lot of time in my school library, and then in Lewisham Library, the places where I felt safest. They were always the ports in the storm that was my childhood. It wasn't just escaping into the world of a book, it was going to a place where I could be surrounded by the things I loved the most.

When I was younger, I grew up in a house with very few books. Reading wasn't really the 'in' thing. My mum is dyslexic, so didn't and doesn't really engage with reading at a high level (and still hasn't read my novel, *Queenie*, if you can believe it – but maybe that's for the best). My nan, though, she loved a Catherine Cookson novel, and I'm pretty sure she's the reason I read *Flowers in the Attic* by Virginia Andrews way too young.

I think I've always seen the deep personal value in giving books to others. Obviously, I love books and would be absolutely *overjoyed* to receive one that made someone think of me. Sadly for me (though only in some ways), these days most of the books I receive tend to arrive either in the post, with a press release, or as a PDF, via my agent, with a request to provide a quote.

I adore and am obsessed with books in all their forms, but one of the things that gives me a weird thrill is the look on someone's face when you give them something new to read. It's when their eyes light up and they say, 'I saw this and wanted to buy it' or 'I've heard loads about this!' that really brings me untold joy. I *especially* love when they haven't heard of the book I'm giving them, but then read the blurb and say, 'Candice. This is right up my street.' One of my finest moments was recommending a book to the *mother* of someone I was trying to impress and getting a message to say, 'She really loved it and says thanks.' That made me feel very powerful.

In a way, I think I gift myself books. I love going to bookshops, browsing the shelves and taking it all in. I love looking at the little handwritten notes in which booksellers tell us, the readers, just what they loved about a certain title. One of my greatest satisfactions in life is leaving a bookshop with a fresh, crisp book (or two, three, sometimes even six) packed tightly in a tote bag. I don't really have any vices, but buying books is probably my most serious addiction. My TBR pile is shocking, but sometimes I buy a book just because I love the way it feels in my hands. I always remember walking into the spare room in my dad's old house in East Ham and being amazed by what was inside – a sound system he'd built, which took up one whole wall, and thousands of records. I think it's because of his love of collecting things that I have such a need to harbour hundreds of books at any given time. I have very few records, sadly, but I think it's because books are taking up most of the room.

I take time with what I read. I'm still finding the genre that I love the most, but I think I respond most to stories that I feel are authentic. One of the books that I always go back to, and one that I gift most often, is *The Scholar* by Courttia Newland. It's a retelling of *West Side Story*, set on a council estate in west London, and is one of the truest depictions of estate life, and of human nature, that I've ever had the pleasure of reading. It actually delivers one of the best joys of gifting books, which is being able to discuss it with whoever I've encouraged to read it once they've finished it. And I *am* one of those annoying people who'll be like, 'Okay let me know where you are', 'Okay, what's happening now?' and 'Hi! By my calculations you should be finishing today so let me know when you get there and we can chat.'

As I write this, I'm looking at my bookshelves at the books that I've been given which jump out to me. My eye falls on the *Noughts & Crosses* set by Malorie Blackman which her publisher, Penguin, sent to me to celebrate the release of *Crossfire*, the latest title in that series. A long time ago, I read

Noughts & Crosses. I was probably around twelve years old. I read every one of her other books as soon as it was published, too. I'm a Malorie Blackman superfan obviously, but loved these books so much because I felt seen, in so many ways, for the first time in my life.

Anyway, let's fast-forward a few years. I'm about twenty-five, I have a sister nine years my junior, and we, with our mum, go to my godmother's house. Maybe for Christmas dinner, I can't remember because my memory is so clouded by *rage*: my godmother, when handing us our presents, gave my sister a bag. My sister opened aforementioned bag, and inside were all of the books in the *Noughts & Crosses* series, all signed by Malorie Blackman herself. My sister doesn't care about reading (she hasn't read *Queenie* either, but again, I think that's for the best), so she sort of smiled a thanks. I picked every book out of that bag and checked to see if the books just had Malorie's *signature* in them, or if they had been dedicated to my sister. If they just had a signature, I could steal them for myself and stroke them every day etc. Outrageously, they were all signed specifically for my sister. I don't think that, to this day, I've ever felt a pain akin to the betrayal and sadness I felt in those moments. Obviously, I am being slightly dramatic. But then, actually, I don't think I am. I went to this same godmother's house recently, and I think she still feels bad, because she let me browse her shelves and choose some of the books she's collected over the years. I came away with a first edition of *Beloved* by Toni Morrison, a beautiful Virago Modern Classic, and a copy of *The Prophet* by Kahlil Gibran. So maybe in a way she has gifted me the most important books in my life. I really should stop complaining.

These days, the person that I gift the most books to is, of course, my nan. I think I'm fairly good at recommending books to people. Well, I certainly hope so, considering how many ask me to share a read they'd like, but I definitely do it with care. She's a faster reader than I am, which is impressive, so every few days, she'll call me and ask me to send her a book I think she'd like. This is just as challenging as you'd think. I remember at the beginning, it took us a while to get there. The first book I sent her was *Augustown* by Kei Miller. She said that she really liked it, but that it had a bit too much swearing for her. What she did like was that it was set in Jamaica, where our family are mainly from. So, I had a think about another book set in Jamaica. I would have sent her Marlon James's *A Brief History of Seven Killings*, but that book has … a *lot* of swearing. I went for *Here Comes the Sun* by Nicole Dennis-Benn, which is one of my favourite books of all time. I thought that one might be a bit too sexy for her, but she loved it, which both surprised me, and didn't. The book that she loved the most was *The White Witch of Rosehall* by Herbert G. de Lisser, which tells the myth of Annie Palmer, a young woman who moved from England, by way of Haiti, to Rose Hall, a sugar plantation in Jamaica. She's said to have killed three of her husbands and still haunts the grounds. One day, I'll write a whole essay on how I stayed in a house behind Rose Hall. I don't think I really slept for a whole week.

The major win of gifting last year was taking my nan a copy of *Who Am I, Again?*, Lenny Henry's autobiography. This was such a win because: a) which Caribbean grandparent doesn't love Lenny Henry, or at least highly rate him in the way they rate veteran Trinidadian newsreader Trevor McDonald,

b) she'd 'seen the book everywhere and wanted to read it', and c) I'd reviewed it for *The Sunday Times* and didn't want it in my house afterwards. I have a kind of specific system of categorising books and that just didn't fit.

I think not growing up around books has meant that now I surround myself with as many books as possible. I have books on shelves, books in stacks by my bed, books in the bathroom, books in the hallway, books on the sofa and weirdly, a few in my wardrobe. I very much enjoy, when I have friends round, giving them a book to take away with them. How nice am I? They get dinner, conversation (though I can never bank on that being too spectacular, especially from my side) and then a book to take home! I should patent that somehow and sell the idea. It's not just about giving books away so that I have less to pack up when I eventually move to New York and start my life as some sort of creative writing teacher, it's so that my friends can have a look at all the books I've loved and share in that somehow. I also get to go through the books I've read and talk about why I loved them (probably quite boring for my guests), and not long ago I gave one of my friends a dramatic reading. That in itself was such a special gift for him that he asked me to stop twenty seconds in.

For now, as I try to get over my sister being given signed Malorie Blackman books, I'm mainly happy to be able to give books to people; it's where I feel the most confident in what I can give to others, and it's how I know I can make someone happy; to give them a story that they can completely immerse themselves in, to give them a different life to learn about, and to hopefully pass that story on to someone else. It's what I always think about reading being a total gift; and to be able to keep extending that gift is an honour.

Oh, and I mustn't forget; if you aren't someone who is good at gifting fiction or non-fiction books, let me tell you, a cookery book is JUST as good and, in some cases, better. For every one of my friends who's moved house in the last few years, I've given them a cookery book and have received not *just* friendship points, but also an actual meal later down the line from the book itself. Which suggests that gifting books is a little bit selfish. But that's fine, I think.

IMTIAZ
DHARKER

'When it comes to gifting poetry, I prefer to choose a book with a specific person in mind. Often it is just that a line of a poem reminds me of something else, by another poet, that may be the start of a new conversation between the two.'

Imtiaz Dharker is a poet, artist and video film-maker, awarded the Queen's Gold Medal for Poetry in 2014. Her six collections, all published by Bloodaxe Books, include *Over the Moon* and the latest, *Luck is the Hook*. Her poems have featured widely on BBC radio, television, the London Underground and Mumbai buses. She has had eleven solo exhibitions of drawings and also scripts and directs video films, many of them for non-government organisations working in the area of shelter, education and health for women and children in India.

All spaces change

IMTIAZ DHARKER

Memory is a slippery fish. It is quite difficult to grasp the exact moment when a gift was given or a sentence spoken. I do remember, though, that I was sitting in a South Indian restaurant on New Marine Lines in Bombay, eating steaming idlis and sambar with the poet Nissim Ezekiel, when he said, 'Look at William Blake.'

William Blake was not someone I had thought about at all since school in Glasgow, and that was just 'Jerusalem', sung at full volume by four hundred girls in the Assembly Hall. Now here was Nissim, poet, art critic, wry dry father figure to the hopeful young poets of Bombay, summoning Blake to sit with us in the din of clashing stainless steel and waiters rattling off menus like poems remembered by heart.

I had brought him the manuscript of my first collection and asked if it would be worth including my pen-and-ink drawings with the poems. He said no. The poems should stand alone in their own space, because people didn't take kindly to untried poets crossing over into other art forms. 'Later, if you want to, in the second or third book, you might include the drawings. Maybe then you can afford to slide between worlds. Look at William Blake.'

He casually dropped this in, the possibility of inhabiting different worlds at once, being different things under the skin. He knew something about that himself. He was a rare creature in Bombay, a Maharashtrian Jew of the Bene Israel community which, having sailed from Galilee around 150 BC, was shipwrecked off India and just stayed on. In 1948, Nissim went to London and studied at Birkbeck, published his first book of poems, *Time to Change*, in 1952, and paid his way back to India as a deck-scrubber on a cargo ship. Having read Philip Larkin and Ted Hughes among others in post-war Britain, he carried back to India an idea of poetry written in a more modern idiom. He was always willing to shift between forms, writing plays, translating from the Marathi, putting poems on posters, often using an ironic Indian English, as he did in 'The Professor'.

> *If you are coming again this side by chance,*
> *Visit please my humble residence also.*
> *I am living just on opposite house's backside.*

Watchful and sardonic, he often stood at the edges and spoke as an outsider, yet in his book *Latter-Day Psalms*, he says,

> *I have made my commitments now.*
> *This is one: to stay where I am,*
> *As others choose to give themselves*
> *In some remote place.*
> *My backward place is where I am.*

Nissim didn't gift me a copy of Blake's *Songs of Innocence and of Experience* because he couldn't afford to give books away. He had just the dusty books on the shelves of his office in the Theosophy Hall across the way. He had reminded me of something that kindled a forgotten spark, so I went to the second-hand bookseller on the roadside by Victoria Terminus and found a paperback copy with some small badly printed illustrations. The quality of it didn't matter. Blake's lines blazed off the pages all the more powerfully for the crude reproduction. Of course I had seen some of the illustrations in my Scottish childhood, images of 'The Ancient of Days' or 'The Tyger'. When I first heard the poem, I had not understood the depths of its mystery and violence. Now, with all of Bombay roaring at my back, I understood the references to rebellion, Satan rising up against God, Prometheus flying in the face of Zeus. It was the most powerful expression I could imagine of someone balancing on the knife-edge of faith.

Blake began to walk with me down every Bombay street, through all the daily shocks and revelations of India. In my ear, there was always that voice questioning the religious and political certainties of his own time, and mine. Later, when I came to London, he was even more present: Blake the child, in Soho, seeing God at the window and angels in the trees of Peckham Rye; Blake whose filthy London streets were veined with splendour; who invented his own painstaking process of etching to print poems with illustrations; the radical who championed women and slaves (even if he never did question the association of whiteness with virtue); whose 'infernal wisdom' included words like 'Some see nature all ridicule and deformity ... and some scarce see nature at all. But to the eyes of the man of imagination, nature is imagination itself;' Blake the dissident outsider, ridiculed and ignored in his time, buried in an unmarked grave in Bunhill Fields.

Now I have all his work in beautiful illuminated books and when I come across exceptional young artist poets, or poet dancers, or performer poets, or poet doctors, or singer poets, or poet film-makers, I gift them a volume if I can.

Just as often, though, I might hand them A.K. Ramanujan's magnificent translations from the classical Tamil, *Poems of Love and War*, *Selected Poems* by Kamala Das (who was a contemporary of Nissim's, belittled and dismissed by all the male poets of her time), Carol Ann Duffy's *Rapture*, Jackie Kay's *Darling*, Neil Astley's anthology, *Staying Alive*, a volume of *Poems on the Underground* edited by Judith Chernaik, Cicely Herbert and Gerard Benson; or books by poets whose work has come into my hands more recently, like Ocean Vuong's *Night Sky with Exit Wounds*, Shivanee Ramlochan's *Everyone Knows I Am a Haunting*, Andrew McMillan's *Physical*, Liz Berry's *Black Country* or Raymond Antrobus's *The Perseverance*. The list may change from week to week as new collections fall into my lap. When it comes to gifting poetry, I prefer to choose a book with a specific person in mind. Often it is just that a line of a poem reminds me of something else, by another poet, that may be the start of a new conversation between the two.

* * *

When I lived in Bombay, after its name changed to Mumbai, a ceiling in my house fell down. There had been a slow leak from above, causing ancient wooden beams to swell and burst through the plaster. After the rubble cleared, I decided the house was telling me something I had known all along, and that it was time to release all the things I thought I owned there: tables, chairs, clothes, jewellery, rings, wedding ring. I packed away the books that mattered to me and donated the remainder to the meagre library of The Poetry Circle, housed in Nissim's old office in the Theosophy Hall. This was the most unsatisfactory giving I have ever done, because I prefer to gift books I love rather than the ones I am indifferent to. But it did start a habit of letting go, travelling lighter, trusting clear space over structure.

One of the books I have kept and carried from country to country was gifted to me by my daughter, Ayesha. She has always been a reader, her bedroom walls graffitied from the age of eleven with lines from MacNeice and Hopkins, immersed in *The Thousand and One Nights*, lost in labyrinthine stories within stories. The book she gave me, *Angela Carter's Book of Fairy Tales*, is populated with women from all over the world, who kick through the usual conventions of folk tales. There is the princess who wears a suit of leather, the old woman who no longer wishes to live in a vinegar bottle, there are witches and 'sillies', resourceful girls, women who are brave, bold and wilful, two who escape an abusive husband by living in a whale, and even one whose vagina turns into a sledge. They slide through the membrane that separates fantasy from reality and back again, living in worlds that are richly imagined but just as harsh as the storytellers' own lives.

These women may be good or evil, cunning, cruel or gullible, but they are out there, larger than life, filling the space of the story with their own light.

I have often gifted this *Book of Fairy Tales*, as well as Naguib Mahfouz's *Arabian Nights and Days* and Marina Warner's

Stranger Magic: Charmed States & the Arabian Nights to young people across the world. Sometimes they send me an email saying they have read and enjoyed the books. Often, in the way of the young, they never mention either receiving or reading the gifts.

* * *

In a signing queue in St Andrews one day, a man I did not know offered me a book. He said, 'I read your last collection and thought you might like this.' I signed for his wife and never took his name, so I don't know who gave me the gift of a lifetime, Italo Calvino's *Invisible Cities*.

On the long train journey to Glasgow and then onward to London, I opened to a page at random and began to read:

'Journeys to relive your past?' was the Khan's question at this point, a question which could also have been formulated: 'Journeys to recover your future?'

And Marco's answer was: 'Elsewhere is a negative mirror. The traveller recognises the little that is his, discovering the much he has not had and will never have.'

Those lines pulled me into Calvino's imagined conversations between Marco Polo and the occasionally sceptical emperor Kublai Khan, and have kept me reading him ever since. In every city I go to, Mumbai, New York, Edinburgh, Hong Kong, Venice, these lines wait for me round street corners:

... when you least expect it, you see a crack open and a different city appear. Then, in an instant, it has already vanished. Perhaps everything lies in knowing what words to speak, what actions to perform, and in what order and rhythm; or else someone's gaze, answer, gesture is enough; it is enough for someone to do something for the sheer pleasure of doing it, and for his pleasure to become the pleasure of others: at that moment, all spaces change, all heights, distances; the city is transfigured, becomes crystalline, transparent as a dragonfly.

With Calvino, it is possible to walk many streets at once, sliding between fable and memory, meeting mythical characters as well as real people; to recognise that there may be gods at the windows, trees bespangled with angels' wings, and that behind the walls, the hard graft of making still continues, turning copper plate and acid to visions, our own cities to crystal.

* * *

Once, in the later part of Nissim Ezekiel's life, and the earlier stages of his Alzheimer's, I found him standing outside Churchgate Station, a bag of books under his arm, lost in the rush-hour frenzy with no knowledge of where he was going. He had managed to conceal the slippage of his memory for years by employing various stratagems. After poetry readings he would sometimes ask to be dropped off at his flat in Bombay's red-light district, because he felt threatened, he said, by thugs in his area and 'bad elements' outside his building. On one of these journeys he showed me the books in his satchel. Among them was *The Book of Questions* by Pablo Neruda and Nissim read out the lines:

> *And does the father who lives in your dreams*
> *die again when you awaken?*

I don't remember the other titles in the bag now. It was a long time ago, in another country and a life I left behind.

When we arrived at the entrance to his building, Nissim said, 'Thank you, Daisy will look after things now.' Daisy was his wife, separated from him and gone many years earlier. I asked the taxi driver to help him up the stairs. There was not a thug in sight, and the women in the area seemed protective rather than hostile. With *The Book of Questions* under his arm, he disappeared into the dark mouth of the building. All he really wanted was to be shown the way home.

© Imtiaz Dharker, 2020

RODDY DOYLE

'I've given 'Broadsword Calling Danny Boy' to men I grew up with, men I shared time with when I was a child. I don't know if they've all read it. It doesn't matter. It's a gift, a pocket-sized token of my love and gratitude. The book means a lot to me. That's what matters. I don't have a copy of my own. I keep giving it away.'

৪৯

Roddy Doyle was born in Dublin. He is the author of twelve acclaimed novels, including *The Commitments*, *The Van*, *Paddy Clarke Ha Ha Ha* (winner of the Booker Prize) and, most recently, *Love*. In addition to his fiction, Roddy has written several collections of stories, as well as the *Two Pints* collection of dialogues, a memoir of his parents, and several works for children and young adults. He has also written for the stage, and for big and small screens. He lives and works in Dublin where he is Chair and co-founder of Fighting Words, an organisation dedicated to using the creative practice of writing and storytelling to strengthen children and teenagers to be resilient, creative and successful shapers of their own lives.

I kept the piano

RODDY DOYLE

I was in the Crown, a pub in Belfast. The shop was packed but I was alone in a snug at the back, with a pint of Guinness and a book. The book, 'Broadsword Calling Danny Boy', was new; I hadn't started it. I'd read other books by Geoff Dyer – But Beautiful, and Another Great Day at Sea. I'd loved both but I'd brought this one with me from Dublin for one real reason: it fit in my coat pocket. I let my pint settle and opened the book. A minute later I was laughing. Laughing alone is often a decision. On this occasion, though, I had no choice. The book demanded that I laugh. And I obeyed.

'Broadsword calling Danny Boy' is a line from Where Eagles Dare, one of those great, daft Second World War films that were made in the 1960s. I wasn't sure which daft film it was when I started to read but it came back to me, vividly, very quickly. The book is a scene-by-scene stroll through the film with a very funny, very clever man who loved the film when he was a child, and still loves it. It becomes two films, the brilliant film of Dyer's childhood, and the very differently brilliant film of his late middle years. I didn't know this as I started. I was just enjoying myself.

And something happened. I began to feel that what I was reading was important – to me. The book was permitting me to re-enter my own childhood, and laugh. It's a wonderfully funny, very short book. But slightly more than a year after I started to read it, it has become the moment when I began to feel better – when I could start to look back without delicate, worried care.

My mother had died earlier in the year. One of my closest friends, a man I'd known since we were both boys starting secondary school, died two months after my mother. My mother was ninety-two when she died; I was almost sixty. I was too old to be an orphan but that was what I was. Alone. Surrounded by family and friends, but alone. My friend's name was Ronnie Caraher, and his death is still a shock. I was alone and now frightened too. Not of my own mortality, I think, but of the rest of my life. I wasn't sure what to do with it, how to approach it – if I even wanted it. I was grieving. I'd written a novel; I'd watched a film I scripted being made; I'd gone to New York, Ljubljana, Toronto; I'd gone to gigs and football matches; I'd read; I'd watched box sets; I'd been living my usual life. But the word 'hauling' had real, physical meaning. I was hauling myself through the days.

Reading 'Broadsword Calling Danny Boy' seemed to show me how to be adult with my childhood, and how to look at it, to use it. Honestly. Fondly. Complicatedly. I'd been laughing all year, in the company of other people. But this time, in the Crown, I was laughing with myself. I was happy in my own company. It seemed like a long time since I'd felt that bit of joy. And I felt it now, reading.

I've given 'Broadsword Calling Danny Boy' to men I grew up with, men I shared time with when I was a child. I don't know if they've all read it. It doesn't matter. It's a gift, a pocket-sized token of my love and gratitude. The book means a lot to me. That's what matters. I don't have a copy of my own. I keep giving it away.

* * *

I've loved books since my mother taught me how to read, several years after I started school. She used comics – the *Beano*, the *Dandy*, *Sparky*. I remember the day, sitting at the kitchen table, when I put my finger under the first word in Desperate Dan's speech bubble, and I knew the word – and the next one. I was reading without help for the first time. I think I started reading my first book that same day. The house was full of them and now they were mine too, like the records stacked against the wall beside the record player. I read *The Famous Five* books and the *William* books. I read a biography of Daniel O'Connell. I didn't understand it but that didn't matter; I was going to read every book in the house.

But books weren't presents.

I remember – I think it was my tenth birthday – I was handed a book, gift-wrapped. I knew it was a book – the shape and the weight of it – but I hoped it was an Airfix. I didn't shake or squeeze the package, so the improbable could remain possible. But I had to open it, and I did, and saw what I knew I'd see. A book; *Oliver Twist*. I started reading it that night and loved it. But it was still a shite present. Books weren't toys or footballs. They were the vegetables, really – good for you.

Then they became deeply personal. Flann O'Brien became my writer. E.L. Doctorow was my writer too. They were my writers in the same way that Steely Dan and Crosby, Stills,

Nash and Young were my bands, and Dylan was my personal singer-songwriter. I'd found them, myself. My friends could tell me, 'You should read this.' Everyone else could get lost.

I can think of only two times when I haven't read. The first was when I was in Palestine in May 2008. I'd brought *A Tale of Two Cities* with me but my head was so full of what I'd seen and heard each day – the daily outrages that I witnessed, the checkpoints, the Wall – I couldn't concentrate on the words at night or when I woke. I didn't read a page until a week after I got back to Dublin. The other time was during a short stay in hospital. I had a book – I can't remember the title or if I ever finished it – but I didn't want to open it; I didn't care. A week or so after I got out of hospital, I went to see Raoul Peck's film on James Baldwin, *I Am Not Your Negro.* I came out of the IFI – the Irish Film Institute – thinking I'd just been to the best documentary I'd ever seen. Baldwin's words, the way he spoke, the way the film was structured, Kendrick Lamar's howl over the end credits; everything about the film was glorious and invigorating. I was going to make my own film: *I Am Not Your Catholic!*

I was walking out to the street, past the IFI shop, when I saw Peck's *I Am Not Your Negro* screenplay, published by Penguin, in the shop window. I went in and bought it. A cup of coffee and the bus home later, I'd read it. It was a great way to discover Baldwin's non-fiction prose, so soon after hearing his voice and seeing him. The screenplay was like a doll's house; the doors opened to bigger rooms – *Notes of a Native Son, The Devil Finds Work* and, especially, *The Fire Next Time.* I felt like a teenager again, finding another of my writers. I bought more copies of *I Am Not Your Negro* and gave them to friends. Again, the little book meant a lot to me. I loved giving it away.

I was walking past a charity shop on the North Strand, not far from where I live, about a year ago. There was a table outside it, and two boxes full of books on the table. Without slowing down, I looked into the boxes, and saw *The Shooting Party* by Isabel Colegate. I stopped, took the book – an old Penguin – into the shop, and bought it for €3. I gave it to my wife. She'd worked in a bookshop in London in the early 80s.

–Do you remember this one?

She did, fondly, and so did I. I remembered it vividly – the characters, the tension. My wife started reading it again that night.

–Is it as good as you remembered it? I asked her a few days later.

Yes, she said. Did I remember the ending? I did, I told her, and I recalled that I'd known how the book would end – who'd get shot – before I got there, back when I'd read it the first time. Meanwhile, I found the copy I'd bought – another old Penguin – in 1982. I bought it in London, where I'd gone for the summer, to get myself into the habit of writing every day. I associate the book with that summer, when I began to become a writer. I started to read it again. It's set just before the outbreak of the Great War, and a group of men gather on an estate to shoot everything that flies. The women are there to watch and admire, the servants are there to serve and groundsmen are there to make sure the unfortunate birds fly towards the guns. But it's so much more complicated and entertaining than that; it's even better than I remembered it. And the ending I recalled so vividly; I'd got that completely wrong, which makes the book better still. I saw another copy in a secondhand bookshop and bought it. I gave it to my sister. I look for the book whenever I'm in a bookshop. The copies I find and buy, I'll give away.

My children's books' publisher, Marion Lloyd, suggested to me that I write a series of books about a gang of boys. This was about ten years ago. I liked the idea and took down a few notes which I now can't find. I never got around to writing anything but I did read *Just William* again. I started and couldn't stop; it was brilliant. Soon after I finished it, I was asked to write something short about a favourite book from my childhood. Here is what I wrote:

> *Just William* made complete sense when I was a child. The boys wandering the fields – that was me and my friends, before the building started and the fields became rows of houses. The pecking order and politics of the gang were very familiar, although 'politics' back then meant my father shouting at men smoking pipes on the television. Big sisters tyrannised the neighbourhood, and getting into trouble was inevitable, one big commandment: *Thou shalt get into trouble*. We were like William when we were outside the house, and this was where William became heroic: he was still William when he went back inside. He fought for the right to be William, and he always won. More importantly, he was always right. *Just William* was a manifesto. I read it again recently. It's still very, very funny and William is still heroic.

There's a character in *Just William* that I hadn't remembered. She's called Cook. 'Cook was uttering horrible imprecations and hurling lumps of coal at the door. She was Irish and longed to return to the fray.' The racism – she's Irish, therefore wants to fight – was a shock. So was the fact that she doesn't have a name. Her name is her occupation, her worth in the household. The kitchen maid is 'the kitchen maid'. I looked up several lists of characters in the *Just William* series, online. (Richmal Crompton wrote thirty-nine of them. I remember, when I was a child, being surprised when I discovered that Richmal Crompton was a woman, but that's for a different essay.) Cook isn't on the lists, and neither are the other servants – because they don't have names. They live in a Jane Austen world, although *Just William* was published in 1922. I wondered if *Just William* and Cook were somewhere at the back of John Cleese's mind when he and Connie Booth created O'Reilly, the Irish builder, in *Fawlty Towers*. (The back of Cleese's mind because Booth is American and I'm not sure if William made it to the back of American minds.) O'Reilly, played by David Kelly, is hilarious and – today – quite unsettling, and still hilarious. And Sybil's attack on him; there's no doubt at all that her antipathy to the Irish pre-dates any encounter with O'Reilly. Reading *Just William* again reminded me of the Ireland I grew up in in the 1960s. It was still newly independent; De Valera was the President and Seán Lemass, a veteran of the 1916 Rising, was the Taoiseach, or Prime Minister. The country was just starting to become the European state it is today, while across the water, on the telly, we, the Irish, were supposed to be feckless and a bit thick, and sometimes charming. I felt grateful reading the book. Times, of course, change – and they don't. Boris Johnson, about to meet the Taoiseach, Leo Varadkar, is reported to have said, 'Why can't he be called Murphy like the rest of them?'

I was asked to write a foreword to a new edition of *Just William*. I quickly agreed to do it; it's such a rich book. 'William was bored.' Has a better line been written about the state of being a boy? I was sent another copy of the book. I now had two, and gave one to my mother. There must have been a mix-up at the publishing house, because a week later another copy arrived, which I gave to a friend.

I asked my mother if she'd read the book.

–I did.

–Did you enjoy it?

–I did.

–Did you like Cook? I asked her.

–She's great, she said. –She loves to return to the fray.

There are books I read that made me want to be a writer. There are also the books that fooled me into thinking I could be one. E.L. Doctorow's novel, *Ragtime*, is one of them.

There was a books programme on BBC on Sunday nights, when I was sixteen or seventeen. I think it was called *Read All About It*. The opening credits featured paperbacks that started to open and fly, and the Beatles' song, 'Paperback Writer'. The show was presented by Robert Kee, who was approved of in our house. That is, my father liked him. Robert Kee was one of the few Englishmen on British telly who knew where Ireland was and what went on here. If I'm remembering right, the programme featured only paperbacks. The Beatles, Robert Kee, paperbacks: it seemed – and still does seem – perfect. Quite often, a book that was enthusiastically reviewed on Sunday night was brought home by my father a few days later. I remember Isaac Bashevis Singer's *The Slave* coming into the house and doing the rounds – my father to my mother, to my sisters, to me. *Ragtime* was another of the books my father brought home in his briefcase.

It was the book that invited me to think that I could write. I read it again a few years ago. I've been doing that, reading books I loved when I was a very young man. I couldn't get past the first twenty pages of *Catch 22*; it was unbearable. *1984* was boring; I had to accept that after a couple of pages. *At Swim-Two-Birds* is still mad and wonderful, and much darker than the book I read when I was sixteen. *Ragtime* is glorious. The mix of real and fictional characters is exhilarating and still seems a bit illegal. The racism of the Irish firemen still makes me uncomfortable. The actuality of the musical notes – they're in the air – as Coalhouse Walker plays ragtime on the family's piano; the words capture the glory of music being performed better than anything else I've read. And that's it; that is why I thought there was a writer in me: the words. I knew every word in the book; I'd used them all, myself, talking and writing. Doctorow had created this magic using things – words – that also belonged to me.

Some years ago, I was asked to recommend a book written in English that Brazilian readers might not have read. *Ragtime* was my choice. I'm not sure if it had already been translated into Portuguese, but a special edition was printed and distributed, free, to – I think – thirty thousand people. That was me saying thank you to E.L. Doctorow, shortly after he died. I was sent a copy of the book. It came in a box, with a little bronze upright piano. I gave the book to a Brazilian woman who works near where I live. But I kept the piano.

© Roddy Doyle, 2020

PICO IYER

'None of us can give voice to what is deepest inside us, but our writings are an attempt. And when we hand over a book to a friend, we're in effect giving her what we cannot put into words. Reading is the richest conversation I know, and the books I press on fellow travellers … become the confessions I long to whisper to those I care for deepest.'

Pico Iyer has spent the past forty-six years essentially just reading and writing, resulting in fifteen published books, on topics ranging from globalism to the 14th Dalai Lama, and from the Cuban Revolution to Islamic mysticism. His books have been translated into twenty-three languages and for more than a quarter-century he has also been a constant contributor to the *New York Review of Books*, *Harper's*, the *New York Times* and more than 250 other periodicals worldwide, while writing introductions to more than seventy other works. His four talks for TED have received more than ten million views so far.

The best conversations of my life

PICO IYER

Very young, I decided that there were two things I should try to do before anything else: strive to understand the world around me, and strive to understand the self who was observing that world. A mischievous teenage friend in my fifteenth-century English boarding school had slipped me an unpromising-looking grey paperback by a German author, entitled *Narziss and Goldmund*, about two friends, in what sounded very close to a fifteenth-century English boarding school: one, Narziss, remains a monk all his life, committed to selflessness and prayer; the other, Goldmund, becomes a lifelong wanderer and lover of the world, an artist committed to making beautiful works. It struck me then that each represented something as deep inside me as a forgotten home; and I realised at some intuitive level that the planet was open to me, as someone fortunate enough to be born in England to professor parents, as it had never been before in human history. It would be a shame – even a sin – not to get to know my global neighbours as my grandparents, in the age of ships and trains, could seldom have done.

But understanding the outer world is only as rich as one's command of the inner world. And I could see, even at fifteen, that Narziss and Goldmund were in certain respects the same person, and lived inside us all. One couldn't really give up the world until one had come to know it; and coming to know the world and its surfaces can only be as useful as one's commitment to the depths that lie beneath. I had devoured the book in almost one sitting, in a little room above the oldest classroom in the world, from which few things could offer escape and in which almost everything (women, travel, loitering) was forbidden.

Books, I was beginning to see, were an escape route – and a medicine and an education and a companion and a secular scripture all at once. Almost half a century later, I live with my wife in a tiny, rented, two-room apartment in suburban Japan that doesn't look so different from my boyhood quarters. We have no car there, no television I can understand, no cellphone. But every afternoon I make a strong cup of tea, gather some tiny, sweet Japanese tangerines and walk out onto our thirty-inch terrace to engage in a deep conversation in the sun.

Suddenly Edith Wharton or Marcel Proust – or Akhil Sharma or Dinaw Mengestu – is whispering rich, endlessly surprising, funny, warm and penetrating secrets to me, as even my best friends seldom could. Suddenly I'm being released from the tyrannical moment into something as large, as immortal, as the sky. Suddenly, I'm freed of my passing thoughts and brought into a space that feels as large as Notre Dame. By the time I return to my room, an hour later, I can feel myself deeper, more attentive, more nuanced than I was before; reading speaks to the best in me and invites me to offer the best of myself in return.

I've never forgotten the gift of the Hesse book, not least because, almost fifty years later, my benefactor is a distinguished biographer and editor who somehow ended up with the same American editor that I enjoy; it hardly matters that he was urging it upon me only because of its love-scenes. And I've never forgotten the gift of Somerset Maugham's *The Summing Up* which my late father conferred upon me, from his enormous library, realising that Maugham was a counter-cultural explorer in disguise, who knew as much about East and West and the mingling of the two as any secret seeker I might meet.

The books others have given me make up, in truth, the story of my life, and the self that other people discern; I will always cherish every volume my mother has handed me, carefully wrapped, for Christmas or a birthday because it's a register of how she views – or intuits – her only son. I will always recoil a little from the books a predator kept sending me when I was in high school, even though the works themselves were innocent affirmations of young love. The kind readers who've sent me books, though we've never met, cannot always understand my tastes because they've met me only on the page; yet just as I was writing this, a stranger in a crowded auditorium in Nashville handed me a soulful and intimate book because, she said, she loves to pass on every work she's enjoyed.

And the books I've given in turn? They are a perfect reflection of who I am beneath the surface, and how I try to read my friends. Giving a book to someone is such a presentation of one's secret self that, to me, it reveals more than any bracelet or necklace this clumsy male might alight upon; I've always been wary of giving books to women friends with whom my relations are uncertain because a copy of Keats (or of Anne Michaels's *Fugitive Pieces*) can so easily be misread, and taken to mean more, or less, than I intended.

But every year I delight in sifting through my memory bank to find a book to send on a birthday to my old pals Mark and Michael and Steve, trying to gauge not just who they are but who they might wish to become. One year I might send one of them *The Conversations*, the richest work on creativity I've read, as the masterful novelist Michael Ondaatje talks with the Renaissance man film editor Walter Murch about leaping poetry and how to structure scenes so the audience can stitch them all together. Another year it is *The All of It*, a forgotten novel by Jeannette Haien that, in fact, Michael Ondaatje, also the most enthusiastic champion of overlooked books I know, pressed on me (as earlier he had urged me to read Sebald, Sue Miller – and *Commonwealth* by that great other contemporary friend of fellow writers, Ann Patchett).

At one point, to my literary pals, I sent copies of James Wood's impenitently brilliant first book of essays, *The Broken Estate* – literature itself as our answer to religion! – and to one friend I sent a subscription to the redeemingly whimsical and unpredictably learned *Lapham's Quarterly*. The art of giving books has something to do with finding works that are not well-known enough, but not ostentatiously obscure; I want to open a door through which a friend can pass so as to open fresh doors for himself.

On my zany and high-born English friend Louis I confer

deliciously pulpy – and brilliantly reported – *narcotraficante* novels by Don Winslow, precisely what he would never otherwise find in Holland Park, and when my mother was uncharacteristically complaining of excruciating pain after back surgery, I knew that the only medicine to prescribe was P.G. Wodehouse, even if she'd read the stories a dozen times before. To anyone sorting through the England and counter-England inside himself, I hand out James Hamilton-Paterson's eerily soulful and overlooked *Playing with Water*, and to anyone on her way to Japan I have to give *The Donald Richie Reader*.

And then, of a sudden, my old schoolfriend, James – I've known him since the age of nine – will send me a book about a record producer from the 1970s: what strange memory is he dredging up now? And a bookstore clerk and friend at beloved Chaucer's, in Santa Barbara, will hand me a startling and completely unknown set of conversations between Haruki Murakami and the Japanese Jungian Hayao Kawai, thoughtfully inscribed. The only crime when it comes to the free exchange of books, I feel, is to give someone a book written by yourself (when you could be offering Alice Munro or *The Buried Giant* or *Leonard Cohen on Leonard Cohen*).

As I think of the five books I most love to pass on, I realise that the list may be the truest memoir I'll ever compose. Every one of them represents a chamber deep inside me, and if you put them all together on a shelf – well, maybe they'd add up to something like a portrait of the caretaker of that shelf.

* * *

I knew I had to avoid Graham Greene when I was growing up because my mother adored him and – a double whammy! –

he was the author foisted on fourteen-year-olds in our English classes. I turned my back on him, therefore, as I would on Alan Paton and Huxley and Pinter and all the other contemporary authors on our syllabus until I was out of the classroom and came to see that these authors are essential precisely because they are teaching us how to live.

As soon as I began to travel alone to foreign places, in my twenties, I recognised that there was only one companion who knew exactly what it was to be a foreigner by himself in a very foreign place, unable to tell right from left – or right from wrong – and reduced to mouthing silent prayers to a God he didn't believe in, and that was this unmet godfather. He'd grown up in the boarding-school England I recalled, which meant he was well defended and knew how to throw up urbane covers.

But on the page he rendered himself naked, in all his frailty, and gave the benefit of the doubt always and only to those who weren't himself. Greene became a kind of secret Bible for me – the human, fallen doubter's gospel that I turn to every year – in part because he knew that a drunken, fornicating, terrified whisky priest could rise to a compassion that any cardinal might envy. His was the sacred text for all of us who believe mostly in humanity, and feel that what we do is more important than what we believe. He will always be the champion of those who intuit at some level that kindness should trump doctrine in every right-thinking being's heart.

As my life took me to many of his places (Vietnam, Paraguay, Cuba, South Africa, Haiti), *The Comedians*, *The Honorary Consul*, *The Power and the Glory*, all at times became overwhelming; these were books given me by the world, it seemed, and by experience. And it was *Our Man in Havana* I devoured, for the sixth or seventh time, chuckling hysterically, as my wife and I took off on our honeymoon. But *The Quiet American* will always be for me his deepest work, because it can squeeze so much emotion out of the simple word 'home' and show us the agony of pretending not to love that which you've lost your heart to.

If you want to understand what's happening in Afghanistan or Iraq tomorrow, I tell friends as I give them the book, this novel about Vietnam from 1955 will tell you more than any newspaper or 'breaking news' broadcast ever could; but if you want, in the same breath, to see what it is to lose your only friend, to gain a love you feel you've won by treachery, to realise that you're doomed if you give up your rival to the authorities – and if you don't – please take this emotional explosive and handle it with care.

* * *

Zadie Smith's essays came to me, delightfully, through her pieces in the *New York Review of Books*, but this wasn't an entirely impersonal gift because the editor of that paper, Bob Silvers, magisterial fount of curiosity and enthusiasm well into his eighty-eighth year, became for me a great sponsor, an editor who read my interests better than I could – getting me to write on Maugham and sherpas and solitude and Sri Lanka – as well as the host of a magazine that was concerned only to lavish new discoveries upon readers, whom it treated as the most discerning friends.

Growing up in England, I felt myself well prepared for the divisions that now convulse most of the globe. In Oxford, when I was a boy, you had only to open your mouth and you were condemning yourself to being seen as too educated or not educated enough, too rural or too urban, too dark-skinned or too fair. Sometimes I think I fell in love with D.H. Lawrence precisely because he exploded every surface distinction, by being not really male or female, working-class or privileged, English or not English. He lived in his own sphere, a ball of fire, and threw off sparks unstoppably until he flared out at forty-four.

Seventy years later, suddenly another writer appeared who made a mockery of all the either/ors we hide behind. Zadie Smith was neither black nor white, as the daughter of a Jamaican mother and a much older English father; she grew up in modest circumstances, but thanks to her intelligence became a star at Cambridge, so she could see both sides of that divide, too. Soon she was writing searching, open-ended, humble (and brilliant) essays on E.M. Forster and Jay Z, on the movie *Get Out* and the works of George Eliot. She was so various that there was nothing, it seemed, that didn't feel like home to her.

In her greatest essay, this became her very subject. Delivering a lecture for Bob Silvers in 2008, she wrote 'Speaking in Tongues', in which – only she could do this – she braided together Shakespeare's gift for stealing into every kind of heart and the newly elected president Barack Obama's talent for working high and low, all in the context of her own life, on every side of every polarity. It was a typically vulnerable, dazzling, unique piece on the predicament, the fresh possibilities of the twenty-first century: having many voices (which is to say, many homes).

And the book in which her piece appeared, *Changing My Mind*, is itself a coat of many colours, in which she mixes literary criticism, reportage, writing tips and personal testimony, so that one can never predict what will be coming next and which of the many Zadies she has inside her will modestly share her rare mind and heart.

* * *

If Bob Silvers was the most capacious and infectiously invigorating magazine editor I've run across, the man who was head of my publishing home for all of my first thirty-four years of writing books, Sonny Mehta, was perhaps the soul with the most exquisite taste (what a delight that a man who loved reading and did it with such intuitive grace should also be the boss for so long of perhaps the leading publishing house in America). Sonny's gift was for reading everything and delivering one word on each book, which always turned out to be the last word.

When, in 1991, he sent me Rohinton Mistry's *Such a Long Journey*, he knew he was giving me a slice of the Bombay where both my parents had grown up, but he pointed out, too, that unlike many polymorphous books on that big city, this one had heart. His gift – and the further gift he offered, of sending me to do an event with the author four years later – meant that I devoured Rohinton's next book, and masterpiece, *A Fine Balance*, as soon as it came out.

I have never read a book written in my lifetime that so deserves to be cherished, for centuries, in the way we cherish Dickens or Hardy. And, happily, I'm not the only one who was moved to tears by the deeply compassionate story of four regular souls struggling to get by in the India of the Emergency when everything is set against them.

Indeed, when Oprah Winfrey – whose talent for highlighting books of open-hearted beauty is often remarkable – chose to share this gift with millions of readers, she took the onus of handing it out, one by one, off me and many others. But still I want to bequeath Rohinton's book to everyone I meet because it simply explains the human condition, especially in our overcrowded and inequity-haunted megacities, with as much warm precision as any work I know.

Having lived in Toronto for almost forty-five years now, Rohinton has kept intact the heart of his boyhood Bombay as perhaps he could not have done if dwelling in the midst of the city's many changes. And living quietly with his wife in a state of shy reserve, he has kept every channel in his heart open to experience.

Bombay to me has become the centre of English-language literature in the twenty-first century – as London was in the nineteenth and New York in the twentieth. A friend and I recently counted fourteen great works set there, not least Katherine Boo's impeccable work of non-fiction, *Beyond the Beautiful Forevers*. Behind them all for me lies Rohinton's universal, bleeding tale of hope and humour and devastation.

* * *

Zen Mind, Beginner's Mind has a title that I was happy to avoid for decades. Besides, I didn't know much about Zen practice, but what I did know was that it was mostly about putting all words and texts behind you and simply grounding yourself in physical discipline. So it was twenty-five years after I moved to Japan – to try to spend time in a Buddhist temple, as it happened – that finally, reluctantly, I picked up this short series of crystal-clear lectures delivered by the founder of the first Zen monastery in the West, shortly before his death in San Francisco in 1971.

The less I say about this book, the better, but it is the prescription I write for every friend in need. If you're confused or at a loss, if you're grieving or in a tangle, most books won't help. Philosophy cannot cure a toothache. But this one could be a friend, and the kind of wise, clear friend whose simple sentences unlock some truth within you.

One's best friend gets one to say and see things one didn't know one had inside one. That's why Suzuki Roshi is such a great friend to so many.

* * *

When I was young – soon after reading *Narziss and Goldmund* – I, like many of my friends, became transfixed by *Rolling Stone* magazine, the remarkable young periodical out of San Francisco that offered all the sense of liberation, exploration, delight that didn't seem available in our dusty medieval classrooms. Anything went in *Rolling Stone*, and its youthful editor saw fit to let loose writers – Hunter S. Thompson, Tom Wolfe, even Wales's own Jan Morris – on any theme at any length, true to the spirit of the times.

Very soon, many of us grew fascinated by a writer for the magazine called Jonathan Cott, who seemed to be the house intellectual, the one Jann Wenner sent to talk to Peter Brook or Werner Herzog or Susan Sontag, as well as to Bob Dylan and John Lennon. His name became a kind of talisman to us, as he would somehow quote an obscure rabbi to a film-maker, breaking the film-maker's mind wide open, or locate some Japanese poem that could illuminate Schoenberg.

I suppose he was the person we wanted to become.

Thirty-five years later, I was backstage in Town Hall in New York City, when a few people drifted in, and I was introduced to a small, quiet man in his late sixties, full of shy excitement, whose name, I was told, was Jonathan Cott. He started – as is his way – offering extravagant praise of a piece that I had written eight years before, and I asked him if he'd be free for lunch.

Weeks later I was back in Japan, and this person whom I had scarcely met, except on the page, began sending me, out of the blue, books he thought I might enjoy. They were always books I'd never have heard of otherwise – the aphorisms of Joseph Joubert, the poems of a seventeenth-century Japanese master, the thoughts of Max Picard – and I pored over them because I knew there would be treasures there, pulled up from some deep, deep well.

Jonathan sent me a rare signed edition of *The Henry Miller Reader*. He told me about Jack Gilbert's poems and Kiarostami's collection of haiku. It didn't matter whether he mentioned the books or actually transmitted them; whatever topic I happened to invoke, he knew some memorable work on it.

One day I went to my mailbox, to be greeted by a large hardbound edition of the poems of Emily Dickinson, edited with painstaking devotion by Helen Vendler. Emily Dickinson had been my secret hymnist for decades, especially as I'd plunged deeper into her secret brothers, Leonard Cohen and Thomas Merton. I'd first encountered her while studying American literature just thirty minutes by car from Concord and began to watch the devils and the angels have it out on the battlefield of the hearts of Emerson, Melville, Whitman and Thoreau.

But here was all of Emily, radiantly annotated. And then, when I met him next and thanked him for the present – Jonathan didn't want to talk, he wanted to share with me a collection of handwritten Proust letters in the Pierpont Morgan Museum – he let me in on an even better secret.

'You know the letters of Dickinson?'

'I don't.'

'You might enjoy them.'

When I acquired a copy of her passionate, terrifying, lightning-lit missives, often almost shockingly unbuttoned in their openness and need, I knew I had found the book, hidden in plain sight, that now I would be passing on to my most deserving (ardent and retiring) friends. That it had come to me through a boyhood hero was another grace.

And that it was about nothing more than what one person writes to her loved ones was the final blessing. None of us can give voice to what is deepest inside us, but our writings are an attempt. And when we hand over a book to a friend, we're in effect giving her what we cannot put into words.

Reading is the richest conversation I know, and the books I press on fellow travellers on the shelf (much like the books I write) become the confessions I long to whisper to those I care for deepest.

ANDY
MILLER

'If for some reason you don't know what the Blinovitch Limitation Effect is, may I suggest you read Doctor Who and the Day of the Daleks by Terrance Dicks?
'My gift to you.'

৯৯

Andy Miller is a reader, author and editor of books, including *The Year of Reading Dangerously* (4th Estate). He has also written books about how much he likes the Kinks and how much he dislikes sport. His work has appeared in numerous publications, including *The Times*, the *Telegraph*, the *Guardian*, the *Spectator*, *Esquire*, *Mojo* and *Sight and Sound*. He has toured the UK with his motivational lecture 'Read Y'Self Fitter' and appears regularly on BBC radio programmes such as *The Verb* (Radio 3) and *The Museum of Curiosity* (Radio 4). He is also the co-host of *Backlisted*, the award-winning literary podcast which gives new life to old books.

Andy Miller and the
Brain of Terrance Dicks

ANDY MILLER

'I think if you can get a kid reading for pleasure, not because it's work, but actually reading for pleasure, it's a great step forward. It can start with me, you know, start with Dicks and work its way up to Dickens – as long as you get them reading.'

– Terrance Dicks, writer

I am not one of those bookish people who grew up in a house without a TV; and when I think about who or what gave me the gift of reading – approximately fifty years ago in a Surrey dormitory town – I judge it to have been a combined effort between Mum and Dad, our local library and the three available television channels. My childhood love of reading is indivisible from my childhood love of watching the telly.

In this regard, I am fortunate to have had Terrance Dicks looking out for me, me and thousands of other young readers. Dicks, who died in 2019, is best known for his contributions to *Doctor Who*, both as a screenwriter and as the programme's script editor from 1968 to 1974. This was a golden era encompassing the tenures of the second, third and fourth Doctors, incarnated by Patrick Troughton, Jon Pertwee and

Tom Baker respectively; I hero-worshipped all three. Tens of thousands of words have been written about Dicks's time on the show, many of them by Terrance himself – and quite right too. But I would like to focus on the author's life before *Doctor Who* and his career after it; to say something about his attitude to culture, which I continue to be inspired by; and to note that hero worship is transferable.

Terrance Dicks was born in East Ham, London, in 1935, the only child of working-class parents. His father was a tailor's salesman and his mother was a waitress; later they ran a pub in Forest Gate called the Fox and Hounds. Terrance was a bright lad and an omnivorous reader: *Boys' Own* adventure stories, poetry, pulp magazines, crime thrillers, and classics – Dickens, the Brontës, H.G. Wells. He passed the eleven-plus examination and went to grammar school, where he excelled at English; so much so that in 1954 he was awarded a scholarship to read English Literature at Downing College, Cambridge. It was here that he studied under F.R. Leavis.

In 1954, Professor Leavis was arguably at the height of his influence in how literature was defined and discussed in British intellectual circles. He sought to divide opinion and succeeded triumphantly. Six years earlier he had published *The Great Tradition*, the work in which he propounded a canon of 'great literature' which included novelists such as George Eliot, Jane Austen and Henry James but excluded major figures like Laurence Sterne, Thomas Hardy and Charles Dickens, the last of whom he characterised, notoriously, as a 'mere entertainer'. For all his pre-eminence and fearsome reputation, it seems reasonable to suggest that Leavis had not read as widely, or with the same enthusiasm, as his new working-class pupil. Certainly there was to be little meeting of minds.

'Leavis and I did not get on well,' Dicks told an interviewer many years later. 'He was a mad old paranoid and he'd completely lost it by the time I was there. He had letters and replies pinned up outside his office of people he had academic controversies with and sent crushing replies to. For years and years and years he said Dickens was a minor novelist, not really a novelist to be reckoned with; he did backtrack later on. But he said there is one good Dickens, which is the only exception, and that's *Hard Times*. That's the one Dickens which is pretty bloody well unreadable and utterly miserable at the same time! That was typical Leavis: "You've all got it wrong, I've got it right."'

Many of those who studied English literature under Leavis at Cambridge went on to pursue careers in academia or the arts; but his approach to the subject did not so much galvanise his students as radicalise them. Dicks's near-contemporary Karl Miller, for instance, would go on to found the *London Review of Books* and to edit the *Listener* magazine, where he dismayed certain parties by pioneering serious TV reviewing; 'I was disliked by members of the London literary world as a Leavisite zealot,' Miller recalled, 'and disliked by Leavisite zealots as a renegade who had sold out to the London literary world.' Dicks swerved this twin dilemma by opting out of the London literary world entirely, first by doing two years of National Service with the Royal Fusiliers, and then by pursuing a career as an advertising copywriter. He penned scripts for BBC radio in his spare time, eventually graduating to popular TV series like *The Avengers* and *Crossroads*. In 1968, he was hired as assistant script-editor on *Doctor Who*.

* * *

Like Terrance Dicks, I did not grow up in a classically bookish home. While my parents enjoyed reading, they did not subscribe to the *TLS* or concern themselves with the Great Tradition. As I wrote in my memoir *The Year of Reading Dangerously*, 'there was no one in my life pushing the canon of children's literature … No one tried to improve me with C.S. Lewis or *A Child's Garden of Verses*. Though I grew to appreciate it later, I can remember trying to read *Alice's Adventures in Wonderland* at the age of eight and being tremendously disappointed; it was *so* much better on TV.'

It was television which had the biggest influence on my burgeoning literary taste. This might have been a bad thing had I not had the good fortune to be growing up in Britain during the 1970s. There may have been three-day weeks and Dutch elm disease but there were also two national broadcasters with the same public service remit, broadly speaking: to inform, educate and entertain potentially huge audiences. And there were hours of screen time to fill. Programme makers often turned to books.

Take *Jackanory*. It was via *Jackanory* that I discovered the Moomin books and thus a love for Tove Jansson's writing which has sustained me for forty years and counting. *Jackanory* gave me Betsy Byars's *The Eighteenth Emergency*, a wonderful, funny, melancholy little novel about being bullied which helped me deal with being bullied myself. And there were all those Roald Dahls, and the adventures of Littlenose the Hunter by John Grant, and stories as captivating as *The Eagle of the Ninth* by Rosemary Sutcliff, *Ludo and the Star Horse* by Mary

Stewart, *Black Jack* by Leon Garfield ... As Nigel Molesworth notes in *Whizz For Atomms*, 'Aktually t.v. is v. cultural for boys and improving to the mind. You learn so many things that when you go back to school all are quite surprised.'

Then there were the frequent adaptations and serials of children's classics, such as *The Secret Garden* by Frances Hodgson Burnett or John Masefield's *The Box of Delights*. You didn't need to have read E. Nesbit to be familiar with *The Railway Children* or *The Phoenix and the Carpet* or *Five Children and It* but there was a good chance, having been introduced to them on TV, you might borrow the book from the library. *The Owl Service*, *Flambards*, *The Bagthorpe Saga* ... the list goes on. We are habituated to thinking of books and television as alternatives to one another but as a young reader-viewer I had almost no sense of this divide. In the 1970s, books were entwined with the fabric of a child's daily life: in the library, at school, in the shops and on TV. (We no longer live in such a country; I leave you to draw your own political conclusions.)

My parents gave me an enjoyment of reading; but I think this democratic approach to culture came from them too. They were not snobs and there were few cultural neighbourhoods that were *not for the likes of us*; we watched *Coronation Street* and *3-2-1* like everyone else – except perhaps that dwindling band of Leavisites who refused to have a TV set in the house. Which is where, unbeknownst to him, Terrance Dicks enters the picture.

It was television which also provided me with the biggest weekly thrill of my young life: *Doctor Who*. From the first episode I ever saw – part three of *Invasion of the Dinosaurs*, starring Jon Pertwee – I was completely hooked. Every

Saturday, I would sit in front of the TV and be scared out of my developing wits by Daleks, Zygons, Wirrn or the Peking Homunculus, to name but four. Even today, typing the words Peking Homunculus gives me a shiver of pleasure. Because there were no videos and DVDs, no internet and few repeats, the only way a fan could access the Doctor's earlier adventures was through the hugely successful range of novelisations published by Target Books. In due course, I would become completely hooked on them too. And more often than not, these books were written by Terrance Dicks.

I mention this because in terms of my reading habits, *Doctor Who* represented an uncharacteristic reversal of polarity. Not only were the books adaptations of TV scripts, rather than the other way round, but they also offered a contrasting experience to anything else I was reading at the time. They were incomparably, straightforwardly exciting. There was humour in them, and a bit of pathos, but mostly it was adventure in time and space all the way. Dicks's style is pacy, economical and precise but he is not afraid to use a long word or pause briefly for an arresting image. They are amongst the only books I have ever found to be authentically 'unputdownable' – I am certain *Doctor Who and the Brain of Morbius* by Terrance Dicks was the first book I ever read from cover to cover in one go, sitting in the back seat of the car outside Coulsdon South station one evening, while Mum and I waited for Dad's much delayed train ...

Chapter One: A Graveyard of Spaceships

Kriz was dying.

Painfully he dragged his insect-like body away from the

blazing ruins of the shattered spaceship. Only a powerful survival instinct kept him alive and moving. Two of his legs were broken, and he scrabbled painfully across the razor-sharp rocks with the remaining four. The tough, chitinous carapace that covered his body was cracked clear across, and thick purplish blood welled sluggishly from the wound, leaving a glistening trail across the rocks behind him …'

[SEVERAL HOURS LATER]

Sorry, where was I?

For *Doctor Who* fans of a certain age, including those who now script and produce the programme, the enchantment of the Target books has never worn off. Writer and actor Mark Gatiss recounts a similar story to mine and thousands of others:

'I remember going into a shop in 1975 and seeing the novelisation of the series' tenth-anniversary story *The Three Doctors*, which had been on TV a couple of years before. The cover illustration showed the power-crazed Omega crackling cosmic energy over all three incarnations of the Doctor, and I just had to have it. I bought it for 35p, and while my parents went shopping at a garden centre in Darlington, I sat in the back seat of a Hillman Minx and read it straight through; my first Target book. I read it; I reread it; I think I knew every word …'

Now we have *Doctor Who* back on British and American screens, being wildly popular and successful – and good – it is possible to look back at the Target books and acknowledge their importance to that first generation of junior devotees. Firstly, they unquestionably bolstered the reputation of the

TV series. Stories which would have looked cheap and silly had one actually been able to re-watch them – I am looking at you, *Invasion of the Dinosaurs* – were, on the page, convincing in every respect. Young imaginations were able to produce a gargantuan T-Rex or an orbiting space-liner on a far grander scale than anything the cash-strapped BBC props and make-up department could manage. This was only confirmed when BBC Enterprises began to issue old episodes on VCR in the 1980s; the papier-mâché reality rarely measured up to the version you had been carrying round in your mind's eye for years – they were *so* much better in the books. And when the programme returned triumphantly in the 2000s, it may be that it was this vision of *Doctor Who* – one seen through the prism of these novelisations and never forgotten – that writers like Gatiss, Russell T. Davies and Steven Moffat were hoping to serve.

However, the uplifting effect of the Target series was not confined to journeys in the TARDIS. The broader achievement of these little paperbacks was to show thousands of children, as Russell T. Davies says, 'how vital a book can be, how powerful, how forever'. They were neither hard work nor homework; they proved to the doubtful or reluctant reader that a book could be much bigger on the inside. For young *Doctor Who* fans, the books were an introduction to the pleasure of reading for its own sake; in Mark Gatiss's words, 'their introduction to literature'.

Between them, Terrance Dicks's sixty-seven *Doctor Who* novelisations are estimated to have sold approximately three and a half million copies; sales figures for F.R. Leavis's *The Great Tradition* in the same period are not recorded. 'Large cheques seemed to arrive by every post,' Dicks reminisced. 'Later, the tax bills arrived ... Still, it was a great time while it lasted.'

When Dicks died, what really struck me were not the well-known authors such as Neil Gaiman and Frank Cottrell Boyce who lined up to pay tribute to him but all the grown men – usually men, though not exclusively – who said something like: 'When I was a kid, I was a reluctant reader. If it hadn't been for Terrance Dicks I probably would have remained one. Thank you for a lifetime of pleasure.'

What a legacy; what a gift.

Now, by no stretch of the imagination could I be described as having been a reluctant reader. I was lucky; I didn't need anyone to demonstrate 'how vital a book can be, how powerful, how forever'. But I owe Terrance Dicks a debt of gratitude regardless, partly for all the pleasure his work has given me over the years and partly for what he did after he left *Doctor Who*. After five years as a freelancer, in 1979 Dicks rejoined the BBC, first as script editor and then producer of the Sunday afternoon *Classic Serial* on BBC1, a position he held for eight years, during which time he oversaw adaptations of *The Hound of the Baskervilles* (with Tom Baker as Sherlock Holmes), *Jane Eyre* (script by the novelist Alexander Baron), *The Invisible Man*, *Vanity Fair* and several novels by the 'mere entertainer' himself, Charles Dickens: *The Pickwick Papers*, *Oliver Twist* and *Great Expectations*. 'Dickens was our bread and butter,' he later observed.

'It was curiously similar in format to *Doctor Who*,' Dicks told an audience in 2015, 'in that it was a series of serials, which practically no one else did, I think, before or since.

And it had been around for quite a while … It was called the children's classic, and I think the Children's Department always thought they should be doing it, not Series and Serials. It was not much loved or much thought of at the BBC – partly, of course, because it was expensive. Both the genres I'd worked in, science fiction and historical period fiction, are expensive by definition. I didn't realise until I became a producer – you have to blank out the telephone lines and paint over the white lines on the road and God knows what. It's a hell of a business, as well as the costumes and the horses and carriages and everything else.'

The 1980s would transform the BBC. As the decade wore on, the idea of adapting classic literature for a family audience came to seem old-fashioned and patrician. 'What happened with the *Classic Serial* is that the BBC eventually decided they couldn't afford it in the end,' explained Dicks. 'People were saying, "Oh God, every time you switch on the BBC it's hats and bonnets and horses and carriages and 'Gadzooks oh!' and all that kind of thing. Can't they do anything else?" So gradually they faded away … Then people started saying, "What happened to those wonderful old BBC *Classic Serials* we all loved so much?" In fact they came back with *Middlemarch* many years later, which suddenly was a huge success. Then they came back in that form, which is the annual or biannual big prestige production.'

I did not watch all these serials; almost certainly I took it for granted they would always be there; I was wrong of course. But with the benefit of hindsight, how fortunate we were that Terrance Dicks believed culture could move from one medium to another – from sci-fi serial to novelisation or from classic novel to TV screen – and enrich the reader and/ or viewer in the process; and that he had the will, the talent and the brains to make it work.

Let me put it another way. How fortunate we were that Terrance Dicks believed culture was for everyone.

I met Terrance Dicks only once, at an event in an upstairs room in a pub in the City of London. He signed a copy of *Doctor Who and the Brain of Morbius* for me ('yes, people do seem to like this one') – not my original copy sadly, that had gone back to the library in 1977. But I took the opportunity to thank him in person, as I do now in print, for giving me so much to read and watch and enjoy; for popularising great books while retaining their essence; and for being a cultural democrat.

'Goodness!' said Terrance. 'Is that a good thing?'

I reckon so, I said.

'Excellent,' he said and shook my hand. 'Well, thank you very much! Fans usually just want to thank me for the Blinovitch Limitation Effect or that sort of thing, you know.'

And if for some reason you don't know what the Blinovitch Limitation Effect is, may I suggest you read *Doctor Who and the Day of the Daleks* by Terrance Dicks (Target Books, 1974)?

My gift to you.

© Andy Miller, 2020

JACKIE MORRIS

'If you really want to give the gift of reading, then buy books for friends ... If you REALLY want to give the gift of reading, then support libraries ... That is a real gift of reading.'

Jackie Morris is an award-winning, internationally bestselling illustrator, artist and author. As a child she was told that she couldn't be an artist but inspired by her father, she nevertheless decided to throw caution to the wind and learn to paint. She moved to Wales just before the publication of her first book and now lives in a small house by the sea, with numerous cats and dogs for company, painting and writing and dreaming and proving her teachers wrong. Jackie has a cornucopia of books to her credit but her most successful book to date has been her stunning collaboration with Robert Macfarlane, *The Lost Words*, recipient of numerous accolades and awards, including the 2019 Kate Greenaway Award. Her most recent works are *The Lost Spells*, another collaboration with Robert Macfarlane, and *The Unwinding*, a beautiful new 'pillow book'.

Intimate relations

JACKIE MORRIS

INTRODUCTION

Reading is such an intimate experience. A book shared, read aloud, passed around, connects each to the other and to ideas.

Alone, when we read, we form intimate connections with the author, seeing as far into their minds as they will allow, as we feel we can travel, touching thoughts, building images, finding pathways.

When we give books as gifts, if the book chosen is one that we have loved, wish to share, it's like sharing time with someone.

CHAPTER 1

I grew up with few books in the house. My great-grandparents were illiterate, signed their wedding certificates with an 'x'. My grandmother, a nail and chain maker from Blackheath, thought reading was a pursuit for the idle. Always bustling about the house, her home was immaculate, grate always blacked, doorstep chalked white. I never once saw her with a book in her hand. She was given to saying, 'Them that reads books has got dirty houses.' I grew up with that mantra in mind and fulfilled her prophecy.

Books were expensive, a luxury. But my mum enrolled us in the library, me and my sister.

I loved to draw, and would often listen to the radio while I worked. One afternoon I heard on the radio the most marvellous tale. 'The Sea Woman' by Kevin Crossley-Holland. It set my heart ablaze. Days later my dad handed me a heavy parcel in a manila paper bag. It was *The Orchard Book of British Folk Tales* by Kevin Crossley-Holland and there inside was 'The Sea Woman'. I still have the book, can remember the weight of it in my hands, the colours of the cover, the smile on my dad's face, the feeling of being loved. It wasn't even my birthday! The story led to a life-long love of selkies and a searching for stories of the 'people of the sea'. I'm sure the fact that I live now just a sea-smoothed stone's throw away from a seal colony is connected to the unexpected gift of this book to a child who ached to be something other than human.

CHAPTER 2

My own children grew up in a house made from books. Always the bookcases overflowed onto stairs, under beds, into corners.

When they were tiny breast-feeding babes I would balance books on them, taking that peaceful time to read, and as they grew I would read to them, even before they could understand the words. They loved the rhythms of the language of poetry.

I would read the texts of picture books over and over again. These were the best of times, intimate, cwtched close, sharing language, finding new things in repetition. I read *Where the Wild Things Are* so many times, I knew each word by heart – and when they woke in the night, fretful of dreams, I would lie beside them and recite the words into the dark until they slipped back into sleep. Of all the gifts reading gives, this intimacy with our children is the best of things.

We had little money when they were young, but we had the library and also a good friend, Catherine Davies, who gave us box after box of beautiful picture books.

At some point Tom overheard someone say that boys don't read fiction. Luckily I pulled him back into the understanding that grown-ups are often ill-informed and talk nonsense, with the help of *Stormbreaker* by Anthony Horowitz. He stayed up all night the night I gave him that book. I never had the heart to tell my children to turn their lights out and go to sleep if they were reading.

I would love to say that I gave my daughter *Northern Lights* by Philip Pullman, her favourite book. The truth is, she had a habit of picking up the books I was reading and then reading aloud from them (which could be hilariously inappropriate - one time when she was about eight the book in question was A *Widow for One Year* by John Irving!! Highly inappropriate but also hilarious). She found my copy of *Northern Lights*, had seen me lost in the book and so entered the curious world of Oxford, the Panserbjørn, Lyra and Pan. She's read it so many times now. I still remember her, half asleep, half awake, asking me what her daemon would be when she grew up.

My children's world was rich with books. One summer they spent days in the sunshine, like peas in pods, hanging in hammocks in the tree in the garden, reading.

I was a neglectful mother, always working at the next book, always happy when my children were reading.

CHAPTER 3

Being a parent doesn't come with a handbook, but neither does being a child. Growing up I struggled, wanting to be accepted for who I was and not who I felt my family thought I should be, what they wanted me to be. At the age of twenty-five I realised this was a two-way street – that I should accept my parents for who they were and understand that they, like me, like most parents, were just trying to do the best they could. It was a good lesson to learn.

I have always felt that as a mother I have never really been as focused on my children as I have on paper – reading, painting or writing.

I've never been a great one for reading graphic novels. In retrospect this is ridiculous, as I love images. The way pictures work together with words in the best graphic novels is a curious deep alchemy.

In a bookshop in Edinburgh called The Golden Hare, a graphic novel ambushed me from the shelves. *The Best We Could Do* by Thi Bui is a heart-song, a soul-song. Years in the making, it's a beautiful triumph of a book, which tells in few words and many beautifully drawn images a family saga. It's about being a child, becoming a mother, relationships, understanding. Even when I was reading it I knew that I wanted to pass it on to my beautiful friend Claire, who is the daughter of her mother and the mother of her daughter. I knew it would make her cry. I hoped it would help her heart. Books can do that. And this, at the time, was the best I could do.

CHAPTER 4

The past few years have brought changes to my life. One change has been that publishers send me review copies of books. I am a slow reader. I know how hard it is to make a book. When the review copies pile up unread, I begin to feel a weight of guilt. But sometimes one will leap out from the pile. It happened with Raynor Winn's *The Salt Path*. And also with another book which came to me like such a gift.

Chloe Currens at Penguin Books had seen a tweet I had written about Wendell Berry's *The Peace of Wild Things*. It's a place I often revisit to remind me that the deluge of nonsense that comes out of the Westminster news monster is almost meaningless, to take me back to the centre of what is really important, and where truth lives. Chloe sent me a proof copy of Wendell Berry's new book, *Stand By Me*.

The book is a collection of interconnected short stories built around an imagined small town in America. It is beautiful. It shines with love and a quiet kindness. Everything about this book restores the soul. I have bought so many copies now and given them to friends.

The book came to me at a time when I needed the uplifting healing song of it in my life and so rather than tweeting or writing an email, I sent Chloe a handwritten postcard to say thank you for this absolute gift of a book. She emailed back, thanking me, and asking if she could quote part of my note to her on the cover of the book.

Many marvellous things have happened to me in my career. Having a quote on the front of this book is right up there at the top of everything. Lost for words I managed to say, 'Yes, please, do.'

CHAPTER 5

I was invited to become a small part of a project in which representatives of our creative community were asked to write letters to our fragile planet. The aim was to read these letters out in theatre foyers, galleries, on streets, and try to help, through creativity, to focus people's minds on the greatest problem of our age – climate emergency. It was also to focus on the fact that creativity is the antidote to despair, and only through creative thinking can we move forward to a better future.

I took pen and notebook to the beach, thought, walked, swam and then wrote about swallows. I wanted to try to capture something of love and loss and time on the wings of a bird.

Later my piece was read from the pink boat in Oxford Circus during the Extinction Rebellion gathering.

Later still the letters became a book. I was asked to illustrate it, and a swallow became a flock, became a book.

The book is a collection of the writings of actors, poets, artists, writers, lawyers, thinkers, musicians and children – and the words of the children are often the most powerful. Jenny Ngogi's letter sings with a rhythm that would make any adult author proud. Simple, spare, straight to the heart. Genius.

Over the past few weeks, I have gathered with small groups of people, in St Davids, and in Crickhowell. There are times when I feel shattered, filled with doubts, and hopeless, and these gatherings have lifted me. We have passed the book around, read aloud, spoken and shared hopes and fears.

The book is a song of hope. Not 'head in the sand hope' but 'active hope', that through creativity we can find better ways to live, dream better ways to face the future, 'eye to eye and face to face'.

Through the book I already felt more connected to the community of my peers. Now it connects me to the community I live in, work in. I'm trying to make this a protest through poetry. On the first day there was a family from Australia, who said they would take the idea home with them. What a reach for the first day, with a handful of people reading while someone sucked up autumn leaves with a leaf-blower from the plastic grass in a nearby pub garden.

I don't have time to do this every week.

I don't have time not to do this every week.

The simple act of reading aloud, passing the book from hand to hand, sharing words, it's a powerful thing.

Letters to the Earth is one of those books you need to keep a small stock of, close by, to give to those who need it, to share with others.

AFTERWORD

My reading began in a library, guided by a librarian. At first I would take books out and look at the pictures. When asked if I had read the book I would say 'yes', but I could never make my way from the start to the end of a book. Reading was just so hard. Too many words on a page, sentences that I had forgotten the start of by the time I reached the end, and the way the words swam on the page ...

But I loved stories, and I learned to pin those words to the page with the edge of a postcard, and to take time and give books time. Now I know how to design books to invite even reluctant readers in, giving space for words and images.

I value the ownership of books, but I value far more the commonwealth that is the public library. For so much of my life libraries were my place of access to knowledge, story. At home, at school, in college. Being able to request any book and for it to eventually arrive in the library – how can that be worth so little that library after library has had its hours reduced, its librarians replaced with volunteers? The librarians were the people who took me through the maze of books to the places I needed to be. Those who are privileged enough to be at ease with books from an early age do not realise how intimidating it can be for those who haven't had that experience, for whom a library is an enchanted wilderness. It has always astonished me to see how the privileged colonise culture in this way. Closing libraries, selling off the books, sacking librarians, shuts the door on access to books and diversity in all practices, not just the arts, for libraries are the places where children can imagine themselves into the roles of doctors, architects, find new futures. They build aspiration in hearts and minds. To roam in a library unguided is a choice you can make, but with a librarian to befriend, who will begin to understand you, to be your guide, that can change a life.

I learned to read because of the access I had to books in libraries. My working life has been shaped by this, though I would say I am still learning to read. The library is the powerhouse of our democracy and the most democratic of institutions. Libraries don't judge you, question whether you have the right to borrow a book. You don't have to have any qualifications to enter through the doors, it doesn't matter how wealthy your parents are, nor the colour of your skin, nor the faith you follow. With a library ticket everyone is equal.

But you do need a trained librarian.

Watching libraries close is heartbreaking, like slamming the door on our children's futures.

Doris Lessing wrote of the library:

> With a library you are free, not confined by temporary political climates. It is the most democratic of institutions because no one – but no one at all – can tell you what to read and when and how.

If you want to give the gift of reading then buy books for friends, from independent bookshops, secondhand if they are out of print.

If you REALLY want to give the gift of reading, then support libraries, fight against closures, work towards making it a statutory requirement for ALL schools to have a library with a trained librarian, and a ring-fenced budget for books. That is a real gift of reading.

© Jackie Morris, 2020

JAN MORRIS

'The "gifts of reading" are of course infinite but the gifts of writing are sundry, too — and one of the best presents I ever had, long, long ago, when I was young, was unexpectedly to change my life forever, and give me pleasure ever since. Here's how it happened! (I have loved exclamation marks ever since!!)'

Celebrated by Rebecca West as the 'greatest descriptive writer of her time', Jan Morris was one of the most lauded British writers of the post-war era. Journalist, writer about places, novelist, diarist, she fashioned a distinctive prose style that is elegant, witty, intimate, and sometimes gloriously gaudy. As James Morris she was the journalist who brought back the story of the conquest of Everest in 1953 and also wrote a highly acclaimed bestselling trilogy about the rise and fall of the British Empire, *Pax Britannica*. She wrote more than forty books in total, travelling the world, delighting and inspiring legions of readers with her memorable stories. Even in her nineties, she continued to write from her home in North Wales, Trefan Morys, which she shared with her civil partner, Elizabeth. She died in November 2020.

'A gift of writing' – An outsider on Everest

JAN MORRIS

This 'gift of writing' was originally a speech, delivered by Jan Morris as the Second Annual Sir Edmund Hillary Memorial Lecture to the Royal Geographical Society on 27 May 2010. It appears in print here for the first time.

Once upon a time a leader-writer on *The Times*, at Printing House Square in London, was required at the daily editorial conference to write a leading article for the next morning's paper about, well, let's say about demands for educational reform in Ruthenia.

He returned to his own room upstairs, with its cosy coal fire, customary in *Times* offices then, he sent his copy-boy off for a bottle of claret – anther custom of the paper – and he settled down to order his thoughts about the condition of Ruthenian education (which was not, to be honest, one of his particular specialities ...).

Well, the hours passed, press-time approached, and the boy was sent upstairs again to see how the piece was coming along. He opened the leader-writer's door, and this is what met his eyes. The fire had burnt down to its embers. The bottle of wine was empty. The leader-writer appeared to be fast asleep. And on his typewriter, as far as he'd got with his Transylvanian conclusions was a single, very *Times*-y word: *Nevertheless*.

Such was the style and the ethos of *The Times* of London, not only in mythical times of yore, but even well into the twentieth century. It was a venerable institution of very pronounced character, generally thought by foreigners to be more or less an organ of the British Government, even a subsidiary of the monarchy, and generally considered by the British themselves to be something distinct from the Press as a whole. 'Send up the gentleman from *The Times*,' duchesses were supposed to say, 'and ask the reporters to wait.' It was a bit snobby, you see, a bit pompous, a bit stuffy. It had no news on its front page, only advertisements, and its staff writers were all anonymous, but still it was the one newspaper whose opinions could influence the nation, and even the world.

The Times had not always been like this, mind you. It had once been as racy and raffish as any tabloid, first with the news, first with the sensations, sometimes first with the scandals too, and it had also traditionally been notable for its reportage of exploration and adventure, especially of course adventure of a properly British and imperial kind. In particular it had subsidised attempts to climb Mount Everest, the highest mountain on earth, which offered in the first half of the twentieth century the last of the supreme terrestrial objectives. The ends of the earth had been reached, but not its roof: and since neither the North Pole nor the South had first been reached by British adventurers, it was all the more desirable that the Union Jack should be the first flag to fly on the world's summit, preferably placed there, as it were, by financial courtesy of *The Times*, and certainly to be proclaimed first in its own columns.

By the 1950s, the protracted sporting event of Everest had long become a matter of national aspiration. There had been eight expeditions to the mountain by then. Almost all of them had been British, if only because for so long the Himalayas had been, as they used to say in the old Empire, a British sphere of influence. And almost all had been supported by *The Times*, in return for dispatches to be sent back from the mountain by the several expedition leaders. This was a civilised arrangement, and the climbing leaders fulfilled their part of the contract with civilised letters from the mountain, generally well written and entertaining, which were later reprinted in civilised and splendidly bound books. Public interest in the expeditions then was warm but generally less than frenzied.

But things had become rather different after the Second World War. By then climbers of other nations were active in the Himalayas too. The British no longer had imperial influence in those parts, and rival nationalisms had set in. Nanga Parbat had become known as 'the German mountain'. Annapurna was climbed by the French. The Americans had adopted K2. And in 1952 a Swiss expedition very nearly got to the top of Everest itself – dear God surely that mountain of all mountains ought to be first climbed by the British!

By then, too, expeditions to the top of the world had become much bigger news to the world at large, tabloid news in fact. When in the following year, 1953, yet another British expedition prepared to go to Everest, partly subsidised yet again by *The Times*, a far more competitive element had been aroused. Even the mandarins at Printing House Square had caught the infection! Another well-known anecdote of the paper concerned its dramatic critic, who was once attending the first performance of a play when the theatre burnt down. He failed to mention this fact in his critique of the performance, and when the editor mildly remonstrated, he replied haughtily: 'You misunderstand the nature of my employment with this journal. I am your dramatic critic, not your *newshawk*.' Well, by 1953, the newspaper had come to realise that when it came to the climbing of Everest, it was a newshawk, not some preoccupied gentlemanly mountaineer, that was needed to report the news. It was going to be hot news now! Brasher competitors, from Fleet Street and from around the world, were sure to try to steal the story – confound the cheek, what? *The Times* could no longer rely only upon climbers' civilised and knowledgeable essays. If it wanted to have the news from Everest to itself, it would have to send with this expedition a reporter of its own, a professional hack – not necessarily a gentleman, as the old duchesses might have preferred, but decidedly a *newshawk*.

But who? That leader-writer wouldn't have been much good, would he? Nor I suspect would the dramatic critic, and most of the other people hanging around the editorial conference were too elderly, too scholarly or too infirm. There was, however, one young foreign correspondent, lately home from an assignment in Egypt, rather at a loose end, fit enough and almost vulgarly ambitious: and so it was that the editor's speculative eye landed upon me, and made me the ultimate Outsider on Everest.

I was no mountaineer. I'd never been very interested in mountaineering. I'd never been on a big mountain in my life. I didn't know much about Everest. When I rang my brother Gareth, from a country call box in Wales, and told him I was going there, he thought there was something wrong with the telephone line. When I was introduced to John Hunt, the dauntingly dedicated and experienced army colonel who was going to lead the expedition, he looked at me I thought in a distinctly dubious manner, and made it clear that if I was to go with them, I would have to look after myself, and rely on them for nothing.

But, as the greybeards of *The Times* had recognised, I did have some useful qualifications. I was extremely keen on my job, and I was also very interested in the technical side of the foreign correspondent's work – how to get news safely and exclusively home to one's newspaper from distant and foreign parts. *The Times* itself had often been no slouch at this. During the Napoleonic Wars, the paper had its own sailing cutter to scud across the English Channel with the news from the continent; if we are to go by old pictures, its master leapt ashore on Dover Beach to hand the day's dispatches to a courier waiting there, his horse champing at the bit, to gallop instantly up the Dover Road to Printing House Square. During the Russo–Japanese War, in 1904, the paper had chartered its own steamship and sent messages from the battle-scene by radio to its own specially built receiving station at Wei Hai Wei on the coast of China! You see what I mean? No slouch! Well, inflamed by such antique examples at the *Times* office, everyone gave me avuncular advice about the best ways of getting the news home from Everest, to be first with the news about the expedition's progress.

The mountain stands bang on the border between Nepal and Tibet, and before the war all the expeditions had travelled through Tibet, to the northern side of the mountain. By 1953, Tibet was closed to mountaineers but Nepal, to the south, was fairly reluctantly open to them, and so Hunt's team were going to make their assault by the southern route. They were going to take with them what they used to call in those days walkie-talkies – short-range radios for communication on the mountain – but the Nepali government forbade the use of long-range radio. This was our problem. Like all news dispatches in those days, my messages would have to go to London by cable, but the nearest cable station to Everest was at Katmandu, the Nepali capital, which was about 180 miles away from the mountain – roadless, wheelless, horseless, telephone-less and largely mapless miles. How should we bridge that gap? That was the thing. No galloping horseman would be awaiting my news. No steamship would get up steam. There was nobody at Wei Hai Wei listening for the tappings of my Morse code. How they racked their brains, at Printing House Square, to solve the problem! What amusement they had from it! There was a river called the Dudh Koshi which ran southwards from the Everest region and eventually into India, and one suggestion was that dispatches might be floated down it, in special containers, into the hands of some associate who would be, I suppose, permanently stationed on the riverbank to catch them. Actually this was an idea long before pursued by one of the pundits, the British intelligence agents, Indians themselves, who had wandered these parts undercover a century before: he had suggested floating sticks down the Tsangpo River with secret messages attached. It seemed fun, but not very practicable to me. Nor did the notion of carrier pigeons, to flutter direct from Everest to the Katmandu cable office, or beacons flaming from peak to snowy peak. Still less convincing was somebody's idea that since Everest was in profoundly Buddhist country, some obliging transcendental holy man might be induced to *think* my messages home.

So no, in the end it was decided I would have to send my messages home by runners, preferably men from the Sherpa community who lived around Everest and were known for their reliable toughness. They would have to be tough, because they would have to run fast over those extremely rough 180 miles, which would include crossing three mountain ranges more than 9,000 feet high. It might also entail keeping my dispatches safe from predatory competitors – for there were sure to be rival reporters or their employees ready to waylay, bribe or cajole my messengers on their way to Katmandu.

In Katmandu, a *Times* colleague would be waiting to take my dispatches to the cable office, but even then the news might not be secure. Dastardly rivals might be hanging about that office, looking surreptitiously over shoulders. All-too-human cable operators might welcome a little something in return for a quick glimpse of a dispatch. So if *The Times* wanted to keep its news to itself, it had to be sent in code. I knocked one up in no time! It was a very simple code, though, in which every vulnerable word had its coded equivalent: Everest itself, for example, was 'Golliwog'. This footling cipher *The Times* people had printed for me on waterproofed cardboard, in the touching belief that I would be constantly pulling it from my anorak pocket in the teeth of stinging blizzards. They also supplied me with padlockable canvas bags to send my dispatches in, and a banker's order for several hundred pounds to be collected in Katmandu in hard coin. No paper money would satisfy my runners, unimpeachable oriental experts assured me, although they might accept barter, they said – strings of beads, perhaps, in return for services performed, like explorers in the Congo. Oh, it was fine cloak-and-dagger stuff – the cleft-stick tradition of journalism. The old boys at Printing House Square loved it, and so did I!

So off I flew to Everest, and it feels but yesterday! So much has happened to me since then that my whole association with the mountain seems like a kind of dream – an outsider's dream. Next time I look back at myself in those days I am far from Printing House Square, but am sitting in a floppy brown hat, looking a bit sort of blistered, drinking something out of a chipped tin mug, eighteen thousand feet up at the head of the Khumbu Glacier, at the Base Camp of the British Mount Everest Expedition, 1953.

I must say I am a bit hazy about how I've got there, but I've evidently made that 180-mile trek from Katmandu, and I've pitched my tent close to, but decidedly separate from, the tents and stacked equipment of the expedition climbers. They have their own corps of Sherpa porters, I have mine, including that team of sinewy runners that we had talked about at Printing House Square. Outside my tent, on the moraine of the Khumbu Glacier, I have erected a small radio aerial, and perhaps you can hear music sounding, very likely the song

'Beyond the Blue Horizon', which is an inescapable signature tune of Radio Ceylon – or if it happens to be a Mozart horn concerto from the BBC, as it once was, a few Sherpas will be listening appreciatively with me, Mozart and the French horn turning out to be very much to their taste.

Inside the tent is my sleeping bag, of course, my typewriter, a few books, some of those padlockable bags and two excruciatingly heavy boxes full of money – a perfect curse to me, and still more to my poor porters, because the advice of those unimpeachable orientalists at *The Times* turns out to have been nonsensical, and my employees are perfectly happy with paper money, and don't in the least want to barter beads, either. There are also, of course, safely underneath my sleeping bag, my papers and copies of my codes – but not, you may notice if you fiddle around there, not only one code, but two. This is because something interesting did happen – I remember now! – in the course of that trek from Katmandu.

About twelve miles south-west of Everest, on the outskirts of a village called Namche Bazaar, it transpired that there was an Indian government police post, with a radio transmitter. Indian soldiers ran it, and its purpose was to keep an eye upon traffic crossing over nearby passes out of Tibet into Nepal, and then potentially into India. It was housed in a shed, and its power was provided by a man turning the wheels of a bicycle, but it was in frequent communication with Katmandu, and I had arranged with its commanding officer that in an emergency of some kind he would send for me a very brief message to the Indian Embassy, who would pass it on to the British Embassy, who would send it by their diplomatic radio link to London. This meant that at a pinch I could be in touch with Printing House Square in a matter of hours, rather than days or weeks. But only at a real pinch.

Well you can imagine what I was thinking! I was thinking that if Everest was actually climbed this time, I might make use of that radio to get the news home really fast, if only in a few words. But I also realised that the message would hardly be secure – the Indian radio people themselves, the people at the Indian Embassy, anyone who happened by or overheard, any subtly enterprising newspapermen might get hold of that news before it reached London, and it could be in newspapers around the world before *The Times* ever heard of it.

So I had devised another, much more Machiavellian code, a code to baffle Bletchley Park itself. In it every word would make sense, but it would be the wrong sense. Since I could only use it once anyway, it really was impenetrable. A copy of this devilish device I had sent home by runner, and now I slept on it every night, waiting for the chance to use it, and thinking that those unimpeachable experts might be proud of me after all.

In the meantime my runners were in action. I paid them, from my bottomless coffers, according to a sliding scale – the faster they ran, the more they got. This worked a treat, for them as for me. Two of them did the journey in five days – a marvellous achievement, 180 miles across that terribly demanding country at an average of nearly 35 miles a day, usually travelling at night and sleeping through the heat of the day. Could that really be right? I think it was. They never quibbled about payment (which was, as a matter of fact, extremely lavish by Nepali standards) and sometimes, when they returned and claimed their money, they gave me small gifts in return – hen's eggs wrapped in leaves, or little pots of raksi, the marvellously potent rice spirit of the country.

I used to love to see them off at the start of their terrific journeys. They generally travelled in pairs, for safety, and I can see them now going on their way. Can you see them? There they go, two odd, tough little figures in high hats, cloaks, pigtails, woollen boots – there they go, scrambling neatly over boulders, weaving a way between ice-pinnacles, already moving at the same steady pace that they will keep up for the next couple of hundred miles. I wait always until they reach the last ridge down there, and then – d'you see? – they pause, they turn, they wave goodbye and they proudly pat their chests, just to say, 'Don't worry, sahib, we've got it all safe here!'

And so they always had. They were often stopped and interrogated on the way, but so far as I know they never let me down. One was actually lured into a Katmandu hotel by a well-known British correspondent and plied with whisky in the hope of extracting my news from him, but he gave nothing away, and returned to base to tell me hilariously all about it. Our rivals, British and foreign, were certainly doing their best to beat us. Every scrap of rumour from the mountain was seized upon, and my own reports, when they appeared in *The Times*, were immediately lifted, rehashed, reinterpreted and distributed to papers around the globe. One or two marvellously dauntless reporters made it all on their own actually to the Everest region, and one of them settled for a time in a house he had rented from a monk at Namche Bazaar. He really deserved to steal my story, I thought, but nevertheless I spread the rumour that if he or anyone else got up to Base Camp with an illicit radio transmitter I would fall upon it with my ice-axe like a wolf on the fold and smash it to smithereens. I meant it, too, I think, although in retrospect, I wonder if I would really have had the heart. One Indian reporter did get there, but he was far too debilitated by the altitude to be any threat to me, and I was terribly kind to him.

On the whole, though, the system seemed to be working well enough, and presently I pooled my supplies with those of the expedition, moved my tent rather nearer theirs, and found myself accepted as a sort of licensed hanger-on. So it was that I found myself in their big main tent when a meeting was convened to hammer out plans for the assault on the summit. I disposed myself unobtrusively in a corner of the tent, and took mental notes of the climbers around me. There was our leader himself, looking epic, the very personification in fact of a Leader. There were two New Zealanders, at least one Welshman, eight assorted Englishmen and one Sherpa, the famously experienced Tenzing Norgay, who had twice climbed Everest before. Two men were surgeons by profession, two were regular soldiers, two were schoolmasters, one was an agricultural statistician, one something to do with the oil industry, one a bee-keeper, one a physiologist, one a professional photographer, one ran a travel agency and one, the Sherpa, was a professional mountaineer.

And there was me. I observed them all carefully, one by one, as they discussed the plans, and suddenly and disturbingly it dawned upon me that within the next few weeks any of them might be dead. This was a dangerous place, after all, and they were doing dangerous things in it. Goodness, that was a thought. Shouldn't I prepare obituaries of them all, just in case? Hadn't I better write them now, and send them back in advance, so to speak. How long should they be? What about pictures? And as I meditated in this way, and looked at those eager bronzed faces in front of me, I vaguely heard Hunt's voice sounding in my direction, as he summed up his intentions.

'What about you, now?' he was asking me. 'How about you? Do you know all about it now?'

'Oh, yes, everything, thank you, John,' I replied, wondering if half a column would be enough for him. But in the event not a soul was killed or injured on his expedition, bless his soldierly heart.

I was a sort of mirror of the expedition itself. As over the weeks the climbers steadily prepared a way to the summit, labouring up and down its lower slopes, working out routes, taking up stores, estimating oxygen rates, so I tagged along to see what was happening and to write my dispatches – which were generally getting home in eight or nine days. The climbers, with their Sherpa porters, patiently let me hang on to ropes with them, and so I went up and down too, returning always to Base Camp to send off my runners with the news of our progress.

Look at me now, on my first excursion into the Khumbu Icefall, the mighty jumble of ice-blocks, crevasses, pillars of ice and snow cliffs which is the beginning of the glacier proper, where it spills out of the mountain mass. It is an awful place, about 19,000 feet up, but there I am, in snow-goggles and crampons, with a big rucksack on my back, clutching an ice-axe, tied to a rope between George Band the oilman and Michael Westmacott the agricultural statistician and making an awful hash of things as we labour into that morass – which reminds me, more than anything, of a gigantic collapsing meringue. This is my introduction to mountaineering. My snow-goggles seem to be steamed up, so that I can't see anything properly, one of my bootlaces trails behind me, my crampons seem to be loose and every few minutes I tangle up the rope, to the amusement of the four Sherpas on the rope behind. Every now and then a rumble, somewhere offstage, marks the passing of an avalanche. Once my automatic watch is scraped from my wrist by an obelisk of ice, and falls irrevocably into a chasm – where I like to think it is still being wound up, year after year, by the movement of the glacier.

Here you see me, looking tense, crawling along a slippery pole over what appears to be a bottomless crevasse; and here you see me, looking decidedly relieved, tumbling into a small tent half-way up the icefall, huddling into my sleeping bag and scribbling the rough draft of a dispatch. Band and Westmacott, doubtless relieved to have me off their hands, are amicably chatting nearby, as if they have returned from an evening stroll. But I am thinking gosh, probably *The Times* never carried a dateline higher than this: Camp 2, Mount Everest. Beat that, I am smugly thinking.

In between such forays, now and then I took time off in search of a secondary story, as it were – namely to see for myself the Abominable Snowman. This is what we used to call, in those days, the elusive and possibly mythical creature called the yeti. Most of my Sherpas claimed to have seen it, at one time or another, and spoke of it almost as if it were a commonplace of the country, but no European had ever encountered more of it than a footprint in the snow. So now and then I wandered off by myself into side valleys from the

Khumbu Glacier and although I never did see the Snowman I did one day have a haunting experience. I was utterly alone in a vast blank snowfield, at about 19,000 feet I suppose, far above all human habitation, when I saw something moving in the distance. My heart leapt, of course! At first I could not make out what it was – only a black swaying speck, indescribably alone in the desolation. As it came closer, though, I could see rather to my disappointment that it was human, so I plunged through the loose slow to meet it, and presently, there near the top of the world, thousands of feet and many miles above the trees, we met face to face. It was the strangest encounter of my life.

He was a holy man, wandering in the mountains, I suppose, for enlightenment's sake. His brown, crinkled, squashed-up face looked back at me expressionless from beneath a yellow hood, and seemed to find nothing strange in my presence there. He wore a long yellow cloak and hide boots, and from his waist there hung a spoon and a cloth satchel. He carried nothing else, and he wore no gloves. I greeted him as best I could, but he did not answer, only smiling at me distantly and without surprise. Perhaps he was in a trance.

I offered him a piece of chocolate but he did not take it, simply standing there before me, slightly smiling. Presently we parted, and without a word he continued on his unfaltering journey, making for Tibet I suppose, without visible means of survival and moving with a proud, gliding and effortless motion that seemed inexorable. He did not appear to move fast, but when I looked around he had almost disappeared, and was no more than that small black speck again, inexplicably moving over the snows.

I have no explanation for that – perhaps I was in a trance myself? – and I never thought of trying to enlist his transcendental powers, as that old boy at *The Times* had suggested. So, it's back to the mountain again, and here's another cameo of the Outsider on Everest. I am at Camp 3 this time, near the top of the icefall, comfortably exhausted as I snuggle into my sleeping bag, to dream perhaps of a softer bed at home, and a better breakfast in the morning. But no. A sort of scuffle at the tent flap, a stamping of boots in the snow, heavy breathing, the flap is thrust aside and there is the large snow-encrusted face of a mountaineer, wearing a striped linen helmet like somebody out of the Foreign Legion.

'Wakey, wakey!' he says in a loud, jolly kind of way. 'Look, there's a nasty bit down there by that last crevasse. I'm going down to cut a few more steps in it. What about coming and belaying me? D'you feel like it?'

I do not feel like it. I remember that nasty bit too well. I do not want to get out of my sleeping bag. I am your newshawk, not your dramatic critic! Nevertheless ... I am ashamed to be lazy, ashamed to be scared, and also, that large smiling face in the tent-flap is the face of Edmund Hillary, whose invitation to join him out there on that damned crevasse I am too weak to decline. Hillary was an inspirational sort of man and I crawl out of that tent slightly proud to have been asked.

I dare say you can imagine us there now, in the half-light of the icefall: me on the lip of the crevasse, with my ice-axe stuck firm in the snow with our rope around it, Hillary over the edge of the chasm, hacking away in the ice to remove some obstacle or other. *He* looks big and bold and burly – like an American freight train I thought wildly at the time.

I look cold and frightened but determined, as though I am praying to the gods of the mountain not to let Hillary slip, and thus require me to save him from oblivion. (Although to be honest, perhaps I am rather hoping he *does* slip, and I *do* save him; it would make a modest sentence or two, wouldn't it, in tomorrow's dispatch ...)

But he didn't slip so I didn't have to save him, and so it comes about that a month or so later I am sitting waiting for him at about 22,000 feet in the gulf in the flank of the mountain that they called the Western Cwm. It was called that because so many British Everesters had first practised their skills in Wales, and Cwm, CWM, is the Welsh for a valley. But they seldom learnt to pronounce it properly, so they generally called it the western *combe*, as in COMBE. It was a mysterious place, at the head of the icefall, but an exact opposite in character to that unlovely feature. It was a couple of miles long, I suppose, perhaps a mile wide, rising fairly gently in altitude towards the face of the mountain Lhotse which stood at the head of it. The Swiss had called it the Valley of Silence, and when I had first looked into it, a month before from the top of the icefall, I didn't like the look of it at all – the weather had been bad then, the sky was overcast, the air was thick with driven snow, like a veil, and the Cwm seemed decidedly ominous.

But now it's some weeks later, the weather has cleared, and I am lazing about in the sunshine outside the expedition's big main tent among eight or nine of the climbers and half a dozen Sherpas. We are at Camp 4, at about 22,000 feet – my datelines, you see, have got higher during the three months I've been on Everest. Now the Valley of Silence seems to sparkle. All around, those terrific snowpeaks seem to look down at me amiably – Lhotse at the head of the Cwm, Nuptse to my right, and to my left the top of Everest itself, flaunting like a banner its plume of driven snow. There's not much wind in the Cwm itself, though. Everything really is silent, except when a boulder screams down somewhere from the heights above with an eerie high-pitched whistle. It's the sort of day when great things happen, and as I bask there in the sun I fondly imagine I might now really see a yeti far away up the cwm, all big and hairy, and with his feet on backwards! Do I have a code word, I wonder, for the Abominable Snowman? But no, actually I am waiting for an even bigger story to break today, because somewhere up there in the vast flank of Everest Ed Hillary and Tenzing may or may not have reached the summit of the world. They were due to make their final assault yesterday, but we don't yet know, have no way of knowing, whether they made it or not. Round and round in my head go my thoughts about how best to deal with the news, how best to get it home, and presently John Hunt wanders over and asks me how soon I think I could get word home to London. It would be good, says he, wouldn't it, if they've made it to the top, and the news gets home in time for the Queen's Coronation. The Coronation! The Coronation of Queen Elizabeth II – I've forgotten all about that, but yes, it's true, she's to be crowned on 2 June, and today is 30 May. Yes, the conjunction would be good, wouldn't it, but only of course if *The Times* has arranged it!

Well the hours pass, the sunshine fades a bit, we fiddle around with this and that, the climbers talk climbers' talk, Hunt looks ever and again through his binoculars, I sort out lyrical phrases in my mind, no yeti turns up, the odd boulder screams off Nuptse, now and then there's a burst of laughter from the Sherpas. A radio receiver is murmuring away there in a corner of the big tent, and at about one o'clock All-India Radio informs us that according to news agent reports the British assault on Everest has failed, and the expedition is withdrawing from the mountain. My competitors have been busy! Mild guffaws all round, and then, suddenly – 'There they are!'

One and all we rush to the door of that tent, and nobody rushes harder than me, metaphorically clutching my notebook in my hand. There they are, just emerging from a gulley, and as we race and skid up the snow-slope to meet them Hillary brandishes his ice-axe in weary triumph, Tenzing flashes us a dazzling smile, and George Lowe the other New Zealander, who'd come down from the heights with them, gives us a conclusive thumbs-up. They've done it!!

They've reached the top of the world! We pump each other's hands. We embrace. We laugh. We almost cry! One veteran Sherpa bows reverently before Tenzing to touch his hand with his forehead. Oh yes, angels fly over the Western Cwm today!

And nobody in the world knows but us ...

Actually, in the context, so to speak, of this essay, nobody knew but me! I had within my grasp what we used to call in those days a scoop – my first, and probably my last. I latched on to Hillary and Tenzing, poor fellows, as they drank their mugs of tea in the big tent, and got them to tell me at some length just what had happened up there on the top of the mountain (incidentally neglecting to ask, newshawk that I was, which one of them had actually stepped on the summit first ...). I took copious notes about it all, and as we talked, as the sun began to go down, I thought about the Indian radio transmitter down below Namche Bazaar. My long dispatch about the climb would have to go by runner, of course, and couldn't be in London in much less than a week: but that one short message – remember? The one with its own code? – if I could get that one down to Namche fast enough, it might just get into *The Times*, and tell the world that Everest had been climbed, in time to give extra excitement to the Queen's Coronation.

Mind you, I am myself a Welsh republican. I stand for an independent Welsh republic within a federal Europe, but I do like a bit of English pomp and circumstance – tradition, trumpets, dukes, guardsmen, archbishops, etc. etc. I respond to the poetical, Shakespearian side of it all, and I was moved then by the thought of the young Queen and her sailor husband trundling across London in their gilded coach to the Coronation ceremony. Also I was conscious that this expedition was a last symbolic exploit of the old British Empire. Just as I was a sort of aesthetic monarchist, so I was a kind of aesthetic retrospective imperialist, too. I didn't approve of the basic principle of empire – how could I, as a Welsh radical separatist? – but I loved the swagger and the colour and scale and the humour of it – trains sweeping across Indian plains, battleships at Malta, all that kind of thing. And I thought to myself, if I could bring together these two fascinating abstractions, on the one side a grand old empire fading, on the other a rejuvenated monarchy to revive the confidence of the nation perhaps and bring pleasure to the world, both subsumed, as it were, within the revelation of a great adventure – well, I thought, if I could do that it would be more than a mere success for *The Times* and for me, wouldn't it? It would be historical allegory.

I had just three days to get that news home! When I'd heard the story of the triumph that afternoon, from Ed and Tenzing, it dawned upon me that I *could* just get it into the paper for the very morning of the Coronation, if I went down the mountain that same evening, and made use of that Indian radio station. I'd only come up the icefall that morning, and I was very tired, but Mike Westmacott volunteered to come with me. He knew the icefall better than anyone else, because he'd spent long perilous weeks keeping a way open among its cliffs and crevasses, so we roped up and set off together into the gathering dusk. Poor Mike, I was even more than usually incompetent. The summer thaw was setting in, and the snow was so greedy that at almost every step I sank deeply into it, often up to my thighs. My boots kept coming undone, my crampons came off, I fell over all the time – of course! – and I banged my big toe so hard on an ice-block that for years afterwards the toe-nail came off every five years. We slithered and we stumbled through the assembling shadows, sometimes glissading down a slope, sometimes hacking our way through an ice-block, with me constantly patting my pockets to make sure my notes were safe, and Mike now and again looking round to make sure I was still on the other end of the rope. Who would have ever have thought, three months before at Printing House Square, that my assignment would end like this, scrambling dizzily and feverishly down through a wilderness of ice in the gathering gloom? Never mind, long after nightfall we made it to Base Camp, and out of the darkness appeared an elderly Sherpa with a lantern to guide us in. 'Anybody arrived at Base Camp?' I urgently if breathlessly asked him, thinking of the competition. 'Nobody, sahib,' he replied. 'Nobody here but us Sherpas. How are things on the mountain, sahib? Is all well up there?' All was well, I told him, shaking his good old hand. All was very well.

My day was not over, though. Before I could go to sleep I had a job to do. I extracted my typewriter from the back of my tent and with two dirty broken-nailed fingers, by the light of a flickering hurricane lamp, I wrote a message for *The Times*. This is what it said: SNOW CONDITIONS BAD STOP ADVANCED BASE ABANDONED YESTERDAY STOP AWAITING IMPROVEMENT – which really meant that Everest had been climbed on 29 May by Hillary and Tenzing. I checked it for accuracy. Everything was right. I checked it again. Everything was still all right. But as I folded the message to put it in its package I remembered that dear old Sherpa who had greeted us with his lantern when we fell out of the icefall. ALL WELL, I added to the end of the message.

First thing next morning, as dawn broke, I gave it to the most reliable of my Sherpa runners, a lanky, sinewy young fellow, and asked him to take it to the Indian sahibs with the radio transmitter, down at Namche, as fast as he could, talking to nobody on the way. I paid him handsomely in advance, I watched him, as always, as he strode away down the glacier, and I waved goodbye to him as usual when he turned to reassure me. I then wrote a much longer, more literary dispatch about the ascent of Everest, and in the afternoon I shook hands with Mike and left the mountain myself. I prayed to all the gods there were that the Indians wouldn't smell a rat in that mendacious message, but would send it to Katmandu and thence safely to London. I didn't want to have to answer awkward questions about it, though, so I hastened with my remaining Sherpas off the glacier moraine, skirting Namche and the Indians, into greener, wooded parts below. The next evening, 1 June, we pitched our tents beside the Dudh Koshi river – the very river that somebody at Printing House Square – do you remember? – had thought I might float my dispatches down! I erected the aerial of my radio receiver and I settled down for the night, wondering what had happened to my message. Was it safely on its way to London? Had it got lost, stolen or misinterpreted somewhere? There was no way of knowing. I was alone in a void. I went to sleep.

When I woke up in the morning I turned on my radio. It was 2 June, Coronation Day, and the BBC bulletin led with the news that Everest had been climbed, and by a British expedition. After thirty years of trying, spanning a generation, the top of the planet had been reached and one of the greatest of all adventures accomplished. There were huge crowds waiting in the streets for the Queen's procession to pass, on its way to Westminster Abbey, and they'd laughed and cheered and danced to hear the news of Everest. And that news had arrived, the announcer said, bless his heart, in a copyright dispatch from the mountain by the anonymous special correspondent of *The Times*. I had my scoop!

But of course the message had really come from all of us on the mountain that day, and in a way I suppose from all the climbers who had ever tried to get up Everest before, and sometimes died in the attempt. We had all of us sent that message to the young Queen, to the crowds in the streets of London, to the British people on their morning of celebration, and it went on, of course, generously to ring the world. Since then many hundreds of people have reached the summit of Everest but the memory of that message, the result of that slithery run of ours down the mountain, is still giving innocent pleasure, far, far away in time as in space. And not least to me!

© Jan Morris, 2020

SISONKE
MSIMANG

'My mother's need for independence and for breathing room was a gift. As she sought her own freedom, she pushed her girls towards books ... By insisting that we read, our mother was gifting us big hearts that have carried us this far.'

Sisonke Msimang is a South African writer whose work is focused on race, gender and democracy. She has written for a range of international publications including the *New York Times*, the *Washington Post* and the *Guardian*, and has received fellowships and residencies from the Aspen Institute, Yale University and the Rockefeller Foundation. Sisonke is the author of two books – *The Resurrection of Winnie Mandela* and *Always Another Country: A memoir of exile and home*.

The solace of Sundays

SISONKE MSIMANG

As a child, I read to escape, to pass the time, to stave off boredom, to learn new words. On Sundays, my mother insisted that my sisters and I read in bed, while she napped. In retrospect, I realise it was her way of finding space, of seeking time away from our demands, from the drudgery of motherhood. On Sunday afternoons she could lie in bed without interruption. No questions, no little faces peering up at her.

Her need for independence and for breathing room was a gift. As she sought her own freedom, my mother pushed her girls towards books.

When I was a teenager, my mother told me always to buy presents for people that I would want for myself. It was a lesson in generosity, but also a reminder of her wise selfishness. The most important gifts she gave us were also gifts to herself. She understood that our freedom was a prerequisite for her own.

On those Sundays, we could read whatever we liked. I read a lot of books about horses, most of them not very good. But I was given a copy of *Black Beauty* by a passing comrade from the UK. That book broke my heart and made me hate adults with a vehemence that my father had to temper with long talks and bedtime tickles. It taught me that books were good not just for reading, but for crying too. I loved *Anne of Green Gables* as well. And because I had once had a good friend named Diana, I thought that the book was really about me – a headstrong girl whom everyone adored. In my house, of course, there were far too many of us for me to be adored quite as much as Anne.

As I hit my teens, I took books off my parents' shelf. I gobbled up *A Dry White Season* by André Brink, often returning to the sexy bits, in part because I couldn't fully understand the other stuff. I was too far removed from South Africa to see the mastery in Brink's depiction of Ben Du Toit's guilt, nor could I fully understand the banality of a young poor black boy's disappearance in a country I had never visited. I wasn't old enough to appreciate how well he had portrayed the quiet malevolence of the apartheid system my parents had escaped.

I cried and cried when I read *Bury My Heart at Wounded Knee*. I haven't read that book in years and I have no idea if it is as good as I believed it was. In many ways I am afraid to reread it. I am not the girl I was back then. Still, it developed my conscience, in much the same way as *Oliver Twist* and *Black Beauty*. And of course, as I think about it now, it is obvious that by insisting that we read, our mother was gifting us these big hearts that have carried us this far.

Years later, when I read *The Fire Next Time* in university, I thought back to Dee Brown's book. James Baldwin wrote, 'You think your pain and your heartbreak are unprecedented in the history of the world, but then you read. It was [books that] taught me that the things that tormented me most were the very things that connected me with all the people who were alive, or who had ever been alive.'

* * *

When I went to college I moved far from home. I left East Africa where I had grown up, where my mother had forced me to lie on the top bunk reading. I travelled to America to study and there I met a woman who taught me how to read aloud. She supplemented the gift of reading my mother had provided. While at home I had learned to read in solitude, in America I learned to read aloud. From my new friend I learned that words are too important not to be spoken aloud, to be shared sensually.

We met on campus during our first week. We were only eighteen so we didn't yet really know who we were, although we thought we knew. There was a notion of who we might become but we were still developing, still becoming the women who would one day mother and write and lecture with ease. My ideas were not yet fully formed but I did not know this and so I spoke with great certainty and conviction. My dear friend was the same.

Had it not been for that first gift of reading from my mother – the love of books, the instinctive need for them when I had nothing else to do – I might have remained insufferably sure of myself. But I was lucky, I loved the kind of books that forced me to be more thoughtful. I was luckier still to find a lover of books who insisted that we think together, that we read aloud. So we read Pearl Cleage's essays in *Deals with the Devil and Other Reasons to Riot*, and for the first time put a frame of analysis around the violence we had both witnessed against women in our communities as we grew up. We sat in silence together after reading *Mad at Miles* – her incredible polemic and love letter to Miles Davis. We sat thinking about why male genius was so often connected to male violence. We sat and we sat. And then, we talked.

She is no longer in my life. Growing up parted us, but the gifts we gave one another endure.

We both loved books and we were both burning with self-righteousness and the anger generated by indignation when one is eighteen. We recognised this fire in one another – and reached out to touch one another's heat. Soon we could not remember how it had been to read alone.

We read together, aloud, in concert. We read to each other and over one another. We scribbled down the sentences we loved and committed them to memory.

We usually took refuge in her room and shared our books there. With her favourite singer, Prince, blaring, we would scream at one another over the music. We would squeal with delight when we came upon a passage in which we recognised something we knew the other would love. We understood what we liked and what we disliked. There was little difference between her heart and mine.

Sometimes she would draw my attention to a detail I had neglected, a comma that had import, or a joke I had missed because I did not fully understand the grammar of American blackness. I would marvel at her brain, amazed that reading had brought me the gift of her.

Sometimes I saw her look at me the same way. We were evenly matched: as smart as one another, as full of shit and bravado.

We began with Ntozake Shange's *For Colored Girls who have Considered Suicide When The Rainbow is Enuf.* We could not afford to buy it because neither of us came from money. Indeed, none of the books we read aloud to one another in those years belonged to either of us. It was a luxury to own books but a necessity to read them, so we lived in the library. We would check out the titles we wanted and needed, then photocopy the pages we loved the most.

It is hard to explain exactly why we loved the books we loved except to say that when life happened to us and we fell for men who were still boys and our hearts broke, we would rifle through our folders and cry on one another's beds, safe in one another's arms.

We would recite Shange in unison and laugh or cry, depending on the moment, depending on the man-child whose foolishness we were lamenting. We would be derisive or heartbroken and always we would stand up tall by the end, because it was impossible not to when these were the words tumbling from our lips:

> *one thing I don't need*
> *is any more apologies*
> *i got sorry greetin me at my front door*
> *you can keep yrs*
> *i don't know what to do wit em*
> *they don't open doors*
> *or bring the sun back*
> *they don't make me happy*
> *or get a mornin paper*
> *didn't nobody stop usin my tears to wash cars*
> *cuz a sorry.*

I didn't know I could tell a lover his apologies weren't good enough until I read that poem. My friend knew how to say things like this because hers had been a different path. Still, she had not yet mustered the courage to mean what she said.

We would use these words again and again over the years. We would reach for the feeling in them. There was a rhythm to telling a man to stop hurting us and this poem taught us how to be the kind of women who stood up for ourselves without losing our identities.

Shange's words were not just a thing of irregular black wisdom and beauty steeped in a language I was still learning to fit around my tongue. No, her words were a call to prayer; a way of beginning to worship ourselves.

Mari Evans was the godmother of the black arts movement and we discovered her shortly after we found Shange. Evans's words practically levitated off the page. She was the pain your aunty hid in her glass, a sweet, sad familiar haint.

Poetry was one of the gifts my friend gave me before life made us too busy to bother trying to make sense of fragments. Now I deal only in what is whole – what presents itself to me without the need for interpretation. The fact that I don't remember the last time I read a poem is a reminder that we don't get to keep all the gifts reading gives us.

Still, reading together made us better readers. It helped us to understand that we were not the most sophisticated analysts of our condition, nor the most witty. To read Nikki Giovanni, who was in a special category of gift – she was a present – was to revel in the sly wit of a woman whose smarts made you jealous.

I remember how we shrieked with laughter when we read 'Nikki-Rosa' which began so unceremoniously and seemed to go nowhere and then ended with that sting in the tail:

> childhood remembrances are always a drag
> if you're Black
> you always remember things like living in Woodlawn
> with no inside toilet
> and if you become famous or something
> they never talk about how happy you were to have
> your mother
> all to yourself and
> how good the water felt when you got your bath
> from one of those
> big tubs that folk in chicago barbecue in
> and somehow when you talk about home
> it never gets across how much you
> understood their feelings
> as the whole family attended meetings about Hollydale
> and even though you remember
> your biographers never understand
> your father's pain as he sells his stock
> and another dream goes
> And though you're poor it isn't poverty that
> concerns you
> and though they fought a lot
> it isn't your father's drinking that makes any difference
> but only that everybody is together and you
> and your sister have happy birthdays and very good
> Christmases

and I really hope no white person ever has cause
to write about me
because they never understand
Black love is Black wealth and they'll
probably talk about my hard childhood
and never understand that
all the while I was quite happy

It took me two decades and two books to properly understand what Nikki meant. This became clear to me only when well-intentioned American reviewers mined my book for trauma and only wanted to talk about my hard childhood, ignoring the fact that 'all the while I was quite happy'.

Another gift from this time was James Baldwin. His sentences were torrents of feeling and intellect and it often felt that his pages were on fire, singeing our fingertips. It seemed as though he was speaking directly to us in our very own voices.

Baldwin's was the voice we chose to mimic when we wrote assignments for the lecturers we wanted to impress. It was those long sentences and that unassailable logic we sought to emulate. But before we had the confidence to even try to turn ourselves into mini Baldwins, we had read him out loud to one another and wept with the realisation of how little the circumstances he described had changed.

We wept, knowing that our lives in the 1990s in the shadow of Rodney King's pummelling and the rage of the streets were not so different from Baldwin's thirty years prior. We stopped, angry and elated and vindicated, whenever we read his best lines.

> To be a Negro in this country and to be relatively conscious is
> to be in a rage almost all the time.

We committed that one to memory.

When it was not enough to read aloud to one another, we gathered a small group of friends. Now there were five. We gave our circle a funny little name – Sisters in Struggle. It is embarrassing to think of it now. We were so young.

We took over stages with no talents of our own save the desire to hear the words we loved spoken out loud. Seething with anger and bursting with love and full to the brim with these precious words we didn't care whether we were good or not, what we knew was that the words were good, which is to say they were important. This was the next gift reading gave me – the gift of recognition.

Reading gave us a platform and let us channel our rage. In Bill Clinton's America, during the era of crack dens and welfare queens and the low-grade war against black communities masquerading as concern, the act of reading out loud, of committing our words first to memory then to the air so others might hear them too, was political.

Sometimes the words we read aloud made others want to tear down walls and pump fists in the air. Often, the poems just made people want to weep.

The moments I remember the most were afterwards, when the silence that always followed the readings took hold. There would be a stillness I can only describe as tenderness, a reaching out and across. Sometimes it was the clasp of warm old ladies' hands on our faces. Often, it was the embrace of brothers who didn't want to sleep with us, who only wanted to touch us in order to say 'thank you'. The moments after our performances were soft and more powerful than rage.

* * *

We are coming to the end of my memory, and it is time I told you a truth I have been withholding. I don't like to give away books. I prefer to keep them. I am aware that this is selfish but my reasons are sound. It niggles a bit that I may be considered ungenerous but I give away many other things – clothes and shoes and all sorts of household items that have their own stories. But books, ah those are far more difficult to lend or gift.

If I do not keep my books, my children will have nothing else of value to remember me by, even if I am no longer convinced that the books will survive the decades to come as sea levels rise and storms gather and plastic strangles everything that grows.

Still, until the apocalypse comes I will keep the books for my children on my shelf, in the hope that their lives are not so very different from the one I lived as a child. I will keep the books for them as a way of staying hopeful. The books I keep are a promise, a whisper to the wind. Let them grow and prosper. Let them have their own children and may they love them as fearsomely as I was loved. Let them gift their own children the solace of Sundays.

Let them read *Alice in Wonderland* and giggle and roll their eyes the way I once did. Let them read *A Grain of Wheat* and *So Long a Letter* and feel in their chests the swell of pride at what Africans have done with the pen. Let them discover Edwidge Danticat and Zadie Smith and Jamaica Kincaid. Let my grandchildren read *The God of Small Things* and let them marvel at the beauty of the planet as it once existed. Let these books be their memory.

In the end, this is why I keep my books. I keep them because words are the most precious gifts I know how to share and I want my children's children who have yet to be born and whom I may never meet, to learn how to pass time, to stave off boredom, to learn new words.

I keep my books – I hold on to them tightly – because my mother pushed her girls towards books and I am hopelessly nostalgic. I keep my books because if there is anything I have learned it is that nostalgia is the mother of posterity.

I keep my books because although the very idea of the future is almost laughable at this point, it is also unimaginable that in the ill-defined distance ahead, my children's children might exist without them.

© Sisonke Msimang, 2020

DINA NAYERI

'In Oklahoma where we were granted asylum, my first and best gift from an American was a library card ... To be set free inside a library, to build a pile of books without having my choices checked – this was my first true taste of freedom.'

Dina Nayeri was born in Iran during the revolution and arrived in America when she was ten years old. She is a graduate of Princeton University and of the Writers' Workshop at the University of Iowa. Dina is the author of two novels – *Refuge* and *A Teaspoon of Earth and Sea* – and her stories and essays have been published in over twenty countries in publications including *Granta*, the *Guardian* and the *New York Times*. Her memoir, *The Ungrateful Refugee*, was published to considerable critical acclaim in 2019, described by Robert Macfarlane as 'a vital book for our times ... written with compassion, tenderness and a burning anger'. Dina is currently a Fellow at the Columbia Institute for Ideas and Imagination in Paris.

A life's work

DINA NAYERI

(دینا نیّری)

My father once gave me a prize, a professionally wrapped and ribboned hardback with my name written in black marker across the bright paper.

دینا نیّری

I tore it open at my wooden desk, my best girlfriends in grey school hijab, gathered around me, whispering and craning their necks. It was a children's illustrated introduction to the universe: stars, planets, constellations. In America, such a book might reflect a parent's hopes ('maybe she'll love science'), but in Iran, it was a reward. In our academic culture, when a child had performed well, her parents were asked to send a book to school, to be presented in front of the class – the more grown-up the subject, the more enviable the distinction. The ritual was designed to make children crave future distinctions, in university and beyond. That night in bed, I cradled that book into the small hours. I read every word and memorised every picture.

My mother was a Christian convert, working with the

underground church. She gave me a Bible and *The Little Black Fish* by Samad Behrangi, a revolutionary children's book about a fish who craves open waters. By eight years old, I knew that I was to be academic, free-thinking, subversive to governments, obedient to God. In my room in Isfahan, I would read books at my desk and pray.

When we escaped Iran without warning in 1988, I left all my books behind. In the years that followed, no one gave books as gifts. They were impractical and scarce, expensive, and who knew what language might be appropriate in an Italian refugee camp full of Middle Eastern asylum seekers headed to America, or England, Germany, or France?

In Oklahoma where we were granted asylum, my first and best gift from an American was a library card, arranged for me by our sponsor Mary-Jean who, at nearly sixty, wore tube tops and drank blue slushies and shopped for hairspray. Mary-Jean told me that I could take home thirty books at a time, and she let me loose with hours to spend among the stacks. The gift, she thought, was time and access to words so that my English would improve. In fact, the English was easy. I was young; I learned it in no time. The real gift was the permission, the trust.

In Iran, we weren't allowed to read just anything. Many books were banned. And my mother monitored everything we read. She was religious and strict. To be set free inside a library, to build a pile of books without having my choices checked – this was my first true taste of freedom. And because I was driven by all that was uncensored, my tastes became eclectic and strange. One week I liked Native American folkore, the kind with tortured ghosts and inexplicable skinnings. The next week, stories of cults and witchcraft, witch trials, burnings. The next week, tales of troublesome puberty. The next, sexually charged kidnappings. All these things I had to hide from my mother. I had dark taste. She covered her own dark patches with treacle and religion and surface good deeds. She cooked for everyone. She only read the Bible and medical books.

I never kept books. Only borrowed them. When I moved to college, I took none with me. I dreamed of soon having access to the legendary Firestone Library.

Over the years, I grew into an eccentric person who worked hard to seem conventional. I hid my strangeness behind achievements, and I prayed. Because I hid my secret world, everyone disappointed me. I became difficult to shop for, emotional, with odd, specific tastes.

At some point, men began to give me books.

Their choices decided things between us. The gift's first mystery was always this: was this book chosen to communicate something about them … or about me?

I married a man I met at Princeton. He was conventional down to his toes. Storybook handsome, kind and good, he wanted to take care of me. He was smart in forgettable ways. If I said something alarming or strange, he informed me that I didn't really mean that and hugged me until it was gone. It was a comfort and so, I married him. He never gave me books. He gave me watches and scarves and holidays. I gave him books he didn't read. I stayed in that draught for twelve years before someone woke me up.

* * *

I fell briefly in love with someone else. Shortly before my divorce, this new man gave me Saul Bellow's *Seize the Day*. It was my first romance in over a decade and I was clumsy with my own heart, a novice. Each time I began to tire of him, he'd find a way to awaken my obsession again. I knew that inside these pages some hidden thing would infuriate me, or break me, or make me run to him, or away from him – depending on what he wanted. I suspected he had found someone new.

I began thumbing through, letting my gaze fall on words from my own life. I stopped at a line that seemed to solve the mystery. It was written there, plain as a letter:

I want to tell you, don't marry suffering. Some people do. They get married to it, and sleep and eat together, just as husband and wife. If they go with joy they think it's adultery.

Was this the message? That I should forgive myself for straying? For leaving? I turned to the first page and started to read.

I devoured the book, hungry for another dose of absolution. I *was Wilhelm* – unmoored, living in a transitory place, an unfinished divorce weighing me down. You're either creating or destroying, Bellow said, nothing in between. I was rotting in my own errancy, unable to create. If I had picked up the book at a library, that first read might have enthralled me. But as a gift from this man that I craved so badly ... I was in turn insulted and angry and (yet, still) riveted. Here was a useless contemptible character, like me, awakened to the freedoms and obligations that come with certain death. Awakened to beauty, to himself, and to what he is meant to do. '*You can spend the entire second half of your life recovering from the mistakes of the first half.'* I didn't want to do that. I wanted to create something lasting. I turned back to the first page and started again. I no longer believed in marriage, in men, or in myself. I was losing faith in my mother's fickle god. But when I reached Wilhelm's desperate prayer, childlike, as I used to pray in my room in Isfahan, I cried a hole through the page.

> 'Oh, God,' Wilhelm prayed, 'let me out of my trouble. Let me out of my thoughts, and let me do something better with myself. For all the time I have wasted I am very sorry. Let me out of this clutch and into a different life. For I am all balled up. Have mercy.'

* * *

In the months between then and my divorce hearing, I read. I was obsessed with errancy and so I read Nabokov's *Lolita*. I took night walks around Iowa City (where I had fled from my marriage to do an MFA in fiction) and listened to Jeremy Irons as the voice of Humbert, beautifying the most despicable life with words – it gave me hope. I was no worse than Humbert. Yes, I had humiliating desires, was self-obsessed, had made no use of my talents. But Humbert took great joy in language, and so he wasn't lost ... right? I didn't want to analyse *Lolita*. I just wanted to hear the sumptuous words, the elegant sentences one after another, and to know something beyond my ugliness was possible. Something beautiful and redeeming and worthy could be made of it.

I needed a tapestry of words. Something extraordinary. So, I went looking for a book by a prose-master. I found it in a secondhand bookstore and the owner said, 'You're in her MFA program, aren't you? This one's on me.' And so, the book I was searching for came to me as a gift. I took home my used copy of Marilynne Robinson's *Housekeeping* and within a day I knew why it had found me. I stared at the passage that would become one of my favourites, and I read it a hundred times, until I had committed it to memory:

> To crave and to have are as like as a thing and its shadow. For when does a berry break upon the tongue as sweetly as when one longs to taste it, and when is the taste refracted into so many hues and savors of ripeness and earth, and when do our senses know anything so utterly as when we lack it? And here again is a foreshadowing – the world will be made whole. For to wish for a hand on one's hair is all but to feel it. So whatever we may lose, very craving gives it back to us again.

The world will be made whole – a promise. I had all that I craved in my mind, in my body. It wasn't so errant or wrong or sinful. It was there, fulfilling itself.

I moved to New York and met a clever Brazilian man, an economist who could have had a career in tennis. He was charming and young and uncurious. His role in my life was hardly a mystery: he was here for sex. He kept dragging it out with dates. 'You're not one of the ones you sleep with on the first date.' *Jesus* ... I didn't want to hurt him by saying that, *yes, I am.* I'm not going to marry you. I don't want more dates or cheesy seductions. I have a book to write, and I'm not sure I've ever felt love, and I'm running out of skirts.

I had to agree to be his girlfriend and let him try to fix me. I enacted dramas to satisfy him. I would leave his apartment while he was in the shower, so that he could come and fetch me. I would disappear for days, then write him sad letters from a rooftop (I was lazy, assuming clichés would be enough). It was a lot of work, and only occasionally awakened my senses.

The book he gave me was Saramago's *Blindness*. I believed at the time that he wanted to show me he was literary – I know now that he was perfectly aware of how I saw him, that I was blind to his value. One night at an Austrian restaurant, he said, 'It's useless to be heartbroken. It never lasts long for me.' When I asked why, he said, 'Because I know that it's never the other person who creates that feeling. They might ignite it ... bring it to life. But the feeling is a thing inside me that I created.'

'My teacher wrote something like that,' I muttered. 'That wanting and having are essentially the same thing. That wanting is self-fulfilling.'

'Exactly. So, every time I fall in love, it's just confirmation that I'm still capable of it, and I can do it again. I just need an object.'

'Ah,' I said, 'so I'm an object.'

'Everyone is,' he said. 'We never really know other people. All you can know is what's inside yourself. And that's another thing ... when you're blind, you look inward.' He pushed the book toward me and took a bite of his schnitzel. 'Read it.'

He savoured food in a way that was refined, yet perfectly wanton, a combination that made you crave whatever was on his plate. And yet the food hadn't suddenly improved, had it? It was altered by him. Once he told me a Brazilian joke: eating and travelling are the best four activities on earth. Because in Portuguese travelling is slang for getting high and eating is slang for sex. 'Fine,' I said. 'I'll read it.'

I thought of buying him a copy of *Housekeeping*. Then chastised myself. Let's not encourage the gift-giving, shall we? Eating and travelling, that's what we're doing here.

I found the book profoundly disturbing, and it woke me from a stupor. It satisfied my dark subconscious by succumbing to the notion of a sordid, feral self, a creature lurking so close below the refined, civilised surface that it only takes the loss of a single simple thing to unleash it. This thing I had already lost. Sight. In New York, I couldn't write, this time because I couldn't see anything good or beautiful to write about. I underlined a sentence and put the book away:

> I don't think we did go blind, I think we are blind, Blind but seeing, Blind people who can see, but do not see.

After that, I tried to look inward. Sometimes I closed my eyes – keeping them closed far longer than comfortable, because I wanted to feel what it was to be blind. I sat at my desk, allowing the stories to materialise, scene by scene.

* * *

Sam and I have built a life based on our shared thirst for books. In 2014, we arrived at the MacDowell Colony and I fell in love with him in a day. He was seeing someone else. But he read voraciously and every morning he shared authors he thought I'd like. Primo Levi, Hannah Arendt, Annie Dillard, Joy Williams, Rachel Cusk, Lydia Davis. Better works by Nabokov. Iranian writers I didn't know. He gave me a copy of *The Reader* by Bernhard Schlink, with a comment about how complicated stories should be written simply, without fanfare, chronological and rooted in the body and the senses.

The first book he gave me was *Stoner*, by John Williams. In 2014, everyone was talking about *Stoner*, which had been plucked out of obscurity after half a century and recognised for its genius. 'It's so richly written, so generous,' Sam told me. 'It's a simple story about an ordinary life, banal but also full of wonder. The prose manages to be both terse and lush. It's like Mr Bridge without the irony ...'

I took the book to my cabin. One page was dog-eared and I went right to it. I wish I hadn't read it first, because when I reached it organically the second time, it was a gong, a revelation, a hot hand to the chest.

> In his extreme youth Stoner had thought of love as an absolute state of being to which, if one were lucky, one might find access; in his maturity he had decided it was the heaven of a false religion, toward which one ought to gaze with an amused disbelief, a gently familiar contempt, and an embarrassed nostalgia. Now in his middle age he began to know that it was neither a state of grace nor an illusion; he saw it as a human act of becoming, a condition that was invented and modified moment by moment and day by day, by the will and the intelligence and the heart.

The book transformed me – it was such a celebration of a life spent thinking and teaching and learning how to love, proof that such a life can brim with purpose. Stoner had accomplished so little in the world's estimation, but he made other lives seem impoverished in comparison. While I didn't crave Stoner's decades of quiet austerity, I knew that my own strivings would never be enough. What's more, the prose was so physical, so sensuous and humble, that it gave me faith in my writing. Elegance lies in simplicity and a connection to the physical. And happiness lies in the physical too. The mind and the body.

'Lust and learning,' Katherine once said. 'That's really all there is, isn't it?'

So, Sam and I read books, our serenity shattered (as Stoner says) by all we didn't know.

We read Annie Dillard in a cabin in the New Hampshire woods, where Thornton Wilder had written and Leonard Bernstein had composed. In an essay called 'Seeing' she wrote:

When I was six or seven years old, growing up in Pittsburgh, I used to take a precious penny of my own and hide it for someone else to find ...

Reading, I thought, is finding pennies someone else has left. And so is the best writing. You have to look. And yet it's so easy to walk around, missing the glint of all those coins.

Years later, I gave myself the gift of Rilke. There was an unconscious moment, sometime in my thirties, when I stopped believing in my mother's god, when I thought I had been duped – by Jesus and the idea of marriage and even love and monogamy. And Rilke's *Letters to a Young Poet* soothed that anger. At about the same time, I had a baby. During my Caesarean section, Sam read Elizabeth Bishop's poem 'The Fish' to me, and he copied it into our daughter's baby book. We spoke at length about our work, about the direction of our gaze (on ourselves or other people), and how to write something generous and true. I turned my attention to the refugee crisis, a crisis I had lived, and in the context of which

I had learned about human nature and politics and history. Sam gave me two books of testimonies: Svetlana Alexievich's *The Unwomanly Face of War,* and Anton Gill's *The Journey Back from Hell.*

These stories had so much more power and empathy than anything I had read before. And yet the authors were invisible, their egos elusive, their personalities unknowable ... all they revealed of themselves was their immersion in the subject, and the craft they had perfected until it had made their own hand invisible, and the enormity of their heart. They had become, as my old teacher says, porous to the world. They weren't looking inward any more, though it was clear that they had done plenty of that, and knew how to retreat there. They had the stamina, it seemed, to spend a long time looking outward, wanting nothing from others, but no longer blind to them either. For these writers, other people weren't objects, as my Brazilian used to say, but the most enthralling of subjects.

This, I thought, will be my worthwhile work. This is the way I'm meant to write.

Fulfilment in love and work and art, I decided, comes in phases. We are born obsessed with ourselves, our oddities ... little black fish in an enormous universe. We think no one sees us and so we embrace our strange fetishes, the villains and the errant stories that make us feel less obscene. Maybe someone gives us a library card and we discover a thousand other lives before we're ready to step out into ours.

Then we become aware of other people, but only in so far as they can redeem us, love us, help and reflect us. We crave their adoration, like a berry breaking on the tongue, and so we write about love and desire and all the endless wanting. We theorise. Is love a false religion? Do I create it inside my heart? Are people just objects? We pray. *I am all balled up.*

Then we lose faith in that too and stop trying to acquire others, or God. We embrace the dark that has travelled with us all along. Then we are alone. We seek out solitude, craft, and self-perfection. We learn to carve beauty out of hideous things. We become artists. That process makes us generous. And so, sooner or later, our blindness is cured, and we see other people as themselves, the pennies they've hidden in the road, points of light without whom our world is desolate. We see their mortality as tragically as our own, and so our gaze turns to children, to mothers, to war. We seek out pain in others, and we ask questions, forgetting ourselves, forgetting our voice, the life that led us here. We become porous and empty, ready to be filled up again. We listen. We pick up our pen and write down all that we hear.

© Dina Nayeri, 2020

CHIGOZIE OBIOMA

'I began reflecting on the complex nature of gifts — on how, though it is chiefly the prerogative of the giver who is willingly accepting to give it — there is something mystifying when it is given sacrificially … the sacrificial gift demands an emotional fee which is often more difficult to pay because it cannot be easily replenished.'

Chigozie Obioma was born in Akure, Nigeria. His first two novels, *The Fishermen* (2015) and *An Orchestra of Minorities* (2019), were both finalists for the Booker Prize; he is one of only two writers in Booker Prize history to achieve this distinction. These novels have been translated into more than thirty languages and received many nominations and awards including the inaugural *FT*/Oppenheimer Award for Fiction, an NAACP Image Award, the *LA Times* Art Seidenbaum Award, and a Nebraska Book Award. Chigozie's work has appeared in *VQR*, the *Guardian*, *Esquire* and *Granta*, amongst other publications. He is a professor of Creative Writing and Literature at the University of Nebraska-Lincoln.

The gift that cost me something

CHIGOZIE OBIOMA

Though it might sound ironic, writers, academics and critics are among those who rarely gift books to others. We all dream of building those giant libraries and of filling the shelves with books, our favourites, the ones that move us. So, we often lend out our books in hopes that they will be returned to us afterwards. Do we ever gift away books? That great book of poetry by Sylvia Plath you've had with you since you were a teenager and is marked up to the point of defacement, and which you consult again and again as you write your own poetry? Have you thought of giving it to someone else, knowing that if you did, it would cost you something?

Macfarlane's essay about gifting books awoke in me a reflection of my own history of receiving books, but also, of the pain of giving the treasured ones away. It was the gift of a book that changed my life and made me a writer. That book, Amos Tutuola's *The Palm-Wine Drinkard*, was given to me by my parents when I was about eight years old. Up until then, I had been in awe of both of them, especially of my father who told me most of the stories, dramatising them with movements of his mouth, gesticulations, mimicry and all the appendages that could make a story entertaining to a child. I'd often thought they were the most impressive people on earth because of their miraculous ability to create stories, these new worlds filled and animated with fictional and historical characters. Of all the things I saw in my parents, the one thing I most wanted to emulate had been the ability to tell stories. Then one day, longing to be transported into that sublime world, I'd asked that my father tell me a story. But tired, having just returned from his day job, he'd simply thrust a book into my hand and said, 'You are grown now, go read them yourself.' I'd sat down and, upon reading, found that the most fascinating of the stories he'd told had come from that book. That was how I became a writer.

I'd often thought then that I could do the same for others and bless them with something that could spark in them a life-changing flame. To do this, though, I recommend books or buy those books for people. Then, one day, while in college in Nigeria, I met a girl I liked and with whom I shared a lot in common. This was 2005, and at the time it was still somewhat rare to find people who wanted to be writers like me in my circles in Nigeria. She wanted to be one and was writing a novel. One Sunday, on a date, I brought with me a copy of one of the books I loved and had owned since I was about ten years old – Rider Haggard's *King Solomon's Mines*. The copy had been almost defaced from frequent rereadings, and the cover image could barely be made out. Though it was not my favourite book, something about this quest, this great journey into the forest and the innocence and fragility of the animals involved, elephants mostly, had often held for me a quiet fascination.

At the sight of it, Ebere seemed to become excited. Her eyes widened. 'What is this book?' she said.

'It is the one I have been telling you about,' I said.

'Oho, *King Solomon's Mines*?'

'Yes.'

With a resurrected sense of purpose, I put the book in her hand, having reached an earlier state of impasse during the date, unable to come up with anything to speak about.

She looked the book over and I watched her face change drama – eyebrows raised on this page, eyes widened at that page, and, in the end, the book between her painted fingers as she read the back page, she said to me, 'Chigoo, I want to read it too. Will you give it to me?'

I was glad at first, glad to have sparked some interest in this woman for whom I was withering away with admiration. 'Yes, it's a must-read, I tell you.'

'I like how you are writing inside the book. Look at all these, here' – she was thumping between the pages filled with pencilled notes, and the end pages on which I'd written favourite lines, new words, ideas of my own bracketed so I could identify them as mine, and even random things like what I wanted to eat on a certain evening so I didn't forget to cook it.

'I like it, you are brilliant, Chigoo.'

I thanked her.

'OK, so, will you *dash* me the book?'

'Ah, *dash* you?'

'Yes, please *jor*. Please *dash* me *naw*, please.'

I recall almost saying no and instead planting my eyes out the window of the empty classroom where we'd stayed behind to meet, to let my eyes fall on students walking along the sidewalks. Then, because I could not resist her charm, I said, yes, that she could have it as a gift.

* * *

I mourned the loss of that book. For some reason, it had not occurred to me to photocopy my annotations or my notes at the back of the book, perhaps I could have felt better knowing I could buy the book and re-insert those. That copy of the book had seemed to me as something that was intricately connected to all that I had added to it, and was therefore not only a book, but an artefact. And in turn the book was wired into me because of all it had added to me. So complete was its loss that I did not replace it and in fact, the loss of that copy relegated *King Solomon's Mines* to the back of my mind so much that even years later, after I published my own first book and began doing interviews, I never once mentioned it as one of my favourite books.

That experience made it difficult for me to lend people copies of my beloved books, even after I became more sophisticated in my reading and my annotations were now scribbled more on stick-notes than as in-text footnotes and margin scribblings. My thoughts and ideas were now recorded in separate books and papers; I still had anxieties for fear of what such a gift would cost me. In the spring of 2013, I registered to take a course on John Milton at the University of Michigan, and after it was over I spoke highly of it to a friend of mine who had not herself taken the course. Then when she wanted to borrow my own copy of Milton's complete works, which contained *Paradise Lost*, I panicked.

Like that copy of *King Solomon's Mines*, the book had become more than a book to me: mostly because of how I had come to own it.

When I was leaving North Cyprus, where I had completed college in 2012, I went to visit the pastor of the church I had attended throughout my time there. He and his wife were British expatriates from Cornwall who had moved to Cyprus as missionaries in the 80s. This man and his wife had been very helpful to the foreign students in the small beleaguered country of North Cyprus – especially to African students and people from poorer countries. He'd helped me even in times of financial difficulties, and I had many memories of spending the Christmas and New Year celebrations, when I would be treated to feasts in their house.

After this particularly rich dinner, Pastor Andrew brought out a book, a hardcover that looked very much like a Bible. It was his father's 1957 copy of John Milton's *Complete Poems and Major Prose* edited by Merritt Hughes. The book, which is a little more than a thousand pages in length, contains, amongst other notable work, Milton's magnum opus *Paradise Lost*. When, early in my time in the country, he'd found out that I was a writer and was working on a novel, he'd recommended Milton's epic poem to me as one of the few works of literature he read and reread. I'd then gone to the university library, read the book and loved it and spoken with him about it many times. With the book in his hand, he told me he'd felt a nudge in him to gift it to me for a long time, but had resisted. But once he learned that I was leaving the country and moving back to Nigeria, then to the United States, he felt it necessary to give me the book. He cherished it and had been reluctant all along because of how much it meant to him and because it was also an inheritance from his father.

Later, after I had put the book into my bag and left his house, I began reflecting on the complex nature of gifts – on how, though it is chiefly the prerogative of the giver who is willingly accepting to give it, there is something mystifying when it is given sacrificially as Pastor Andrew had done. I was reminded of the wisdom compass in King David's theological declaration that he would never gift anything that 'cost me nothing'. Perhaps the difference between the convenient gifts – those birthday or Christmas presents – and the sacrificial gifts is that, though both may cost us something, a few naira or dollars, the sacrificial gift demands an emotional fee which is often more difficult to pay because it cannot be easily replenished.

* * *

I left his house – then Cyprus – with the book in my hand. So big was it that I had to carry it in my hand through the long flights back to Nigeria, as I had already fully packed my things before the visit to Andrew's house. I had known that it would be a demanding experience since the flight was to be routed through Istanbul airport where the African-bound flights were usually deep into the night. In the long hours of waiting, I reread *Paradise Lost* closely, making annotations, pausing here, pausing there, the way I read when I am trying to get more than pleasure from a book.

That reading opened up in me a door that I had been trying to prise open for a very long time. I had been incubating a novel in my head for two years, a story about a lowly poultry farmer who comes to Cyprus and is ruined by his quest to return to the woman he loves. Milton's sublime narrator's quest to make known 'the ways of God to man' would light in me a desire to tell the story through the voice of a chi, a veritable and eccentric spirit that would become the narrator of my second novel, *An Orchestra of Minorities*. Thus, in hindsight, it is safe to say that my novel would not have been possible had I not received that copy of the 1957 edition of John Milton's complete works from my friend, Pastor Andrew.

I did not relent in lending my friend a copy of the book that summer in 2013. Over the course of two days before which I would lend her the book, I made careful arrangements to prepare for the worst, in case I did not get the book back. First, I took out all the stick-notes, arranged them inside a notebook and then made a note of most of the scribblings I had made in the book. Then I took the book to her. A few months later, she returned it, joyful that she had read the epic poem. I was also joyful but I realised I wouldn't have been wounded if she had not returned the book to me. Something had shifted in me, and perhaps I had come to understand that I would not have lost too much if the book had gone or because the humility of Pastor Andrew's sacrificial giving had inspired in me an unconscious zeal for replication. I do not exactly know. What I know is that whenever I recall the day he gifted me the book, what strikes me most of all is the trace of pain I had seen on his face as he gave it to me: the mark of a person whose gift had cost him something, but had given me everything.

MICHAEL
ONDAATJE

'Sometimes we find our true ancestors in other countries and become enlarged because we know their essays, their novels, those paragraphs that becalm us or devastate us, and so we no longer remain solitary in the distance.'

Michael Ondaatje was born in Sri Lanka, went to school in England, and lives in Toronto, Canada. His novels include *In the Skin of a Lion*, *The English Patient*, and *Coming through Slaughter*. *The Cinnamon Peeler* and *Handwriting* are two of his books of poetry. He has written a memoir about his family in Sri Lanka called *Running in the Family*, and a non-fiction book on film editing called *The Conversations* that focuses on the work of Walter Murch. *Anil's Ghost* received the *Irish Times* International Fiction Prize, and the Prix Médicis. *The English Patient* received the Booker Prize and was made into a film. His most recent novel is *Warlight*.

The voice and craft of
Toni Morrison

MICHAEL ONDAATJE

Michael Ondaatje delivered this tribute at a memorial for Toni Morrison held at the Cathedral of St John the Divine in New York in November 2019. It was subsequently published in the New York Review of Books *and also the spring issue of* Brick *in Canada.*

When has a voice been this intimate and versatile? Affectionate, far-reaching, self-aware, and also severe, dismissive of fools? There's that *range* in the manner of Toni Morrison's voice. She is always full of swerves – from humour, to anger, to music. We see all that in the narrator of *Jazz*, who holds this remarkable novel together.

'I like the feeling of a *told* story,' Morrison has said, 'where you hear a voice but you can't identify it .... It's a comfortable voice, and it's a guiding voice, and it's alarmed by the same things that the reader is alarmed by, and it doesn't know what's going to happen next either.' Elsewhere, she writes, 'To have the reader work *with* the author in the construction of the book – is what's important.'

We are always participating when we read Toni Morrison. During a quiet lull, the narrator will remember: 'And another damn thing!' Or in the middle of a flashback, she will parse a gesture: "That is what makes me worry about him. How he thinks first of his clothes, and not the woman .... But then he scrapes the mud from his Baltimore soles before he enters a cabin with a dirt floor and I don't hate him much anymore.' It's those 'Baltimore soles', and the precision of '*much* anymore'. And besides, who else but Toni Morrison can interrupt a flashback? Her stories enact this constant switching of the formal and colloquial, of perspective and vocabulary, so that they feel gathered from everywhere. Where does this voice, this language, come from? Is it American Homeric?

There's a documentary on Charlie Parker that has a famous moment when he is asked what he thought set him apart from all the other saxophone players. His reply was simply, 'The octave, man, just the octave.'

'Do you have your audience in mind when you sit down to write?' Toni Morrison was once asked.

'Only me,' she replied.

I love the faith she has in her own craft. This is her talking to students in Mississippi:

As I write I don't imagine a reader or listener, ever. I am the reader and the listener myself, and I think I am an excellent reader. I read very well. I mean I really know what's going on .... I have to assume that I am also this very critical,

very fastidious, and not-easily-taken-in reader who is smart
enough to participate in the text a lot.

And she speaks often of loving the rewrite: 'The best part of it
all, the absolutely most delicious part ... I try to make it look
like I never touched it.' This care for the gradually discovered
story makes us fully trust her. It is how we are intimately altered
by her books, and it was why *Beloved* would change everything.

I did get to meet and know Toni Morrison now and then, over
the years, and what I remember most is her great humour.
But I am really an intimate of hers *as a reader*. So I speak
today as one of many writers – some of whom grew up in
Pakistan, in Nigeria, Trinidad, Bogotá, or Tripoli – who love
the skill of her craft, her moral voice. She is much more than
'an American Writer'. She is universal. Sometimes we find
our true ancestors in other countries and become enlarged
because we know their essays, their novels, those paragraphs
that becalm us or devastate us, and so we no longer remain
solitary in the distance.

I read *Jazz* for the first time in June of 1992, dazzled by its
choreography: how she drew us with ease from 1926 Harlem
back into the history of her characters; how she constructed
and then reconsidered the story, until there was this fully lit
diorama where we could witness the past while we remained
in the intimacy of the present. All that done by the guiding
voice of a narrator, who is, in a way, the most essential
character in the book.

But here is the long-range octave, or what Morrison would
call 'the kick'.

Towards the end of *Jazz*, the narrator realises that what is happening in the novel is not what she claimed so confidently would happen in the opening pages. She discovers, in fact, that there is more complexity in her invented characters than she imagined. And there is this moment when Morrison, in the voice of the narrator, allows her to confess to misinterpretation of those in the story:

I missed the people altogether.

... Now it's clear why they contradicted me at every turn: ... they knew how little I could be counted on; how poorly, how shabbily my know-it-all self covered helplessness. That when I invented stories about them – and doing it seemed to me so fine – I was completely in their hands....

So I missed it altogether. I was sure one would kill the other. I waited for it so I could describe it. I was so sure it would happen. That the past was an abused record with no choice but to repeat itself at the crack and no power on earth could lift the arm that held the needle.... I was the predictable one, confused in my solitude into arrogance....

... It never occurred to me that they were thinking other thoughts, feeling other feelings, putting their lives together in ways I never dreamed of.

It is this confession, made with craft and voice, that reveals the vast democracy of vision and humanity in Toni Morrison herself.

© Michael Ondaatje, 2019

DAVID
PILLING

'Can you tell what kind of a man I was, and what kind of a man I was not? Can you catch my shadow in these books?

'No. I thought not.

'Still, keep them. Read them. They are my gift to you. From this dark place.'

෴

David Pilling has been a prize-winning reporter and editor with the *Financial Times* for twenty-five years. Currently the Africa Editor, he was previously the Asia Editor and also Tokyo Bureau Chief. His column ranges over business, investment, politics and economics. He has conducted dozens of interviews with world leaders, business executives, economists, artists and novelists from around the world. David has published two books: *Bending Adversity: Japan and the Art of Survival* and *The Growth Delusion: The Wealth and Well-Being of Nations*.

The man I was

DAVID PILLING

If you are reading this, it means you are alive. I am happy to hear that. Are there many of you left? Are there many of us left?

I assembled this box in a moment of some despair. I am weak with the illness. Provisions are running low. My dear wife Lizzie passed on two days ago. 'Passed on' sounds so literary. Like something from a novel. I mean to say she died. My dear Lizzie. I can't believe she's gone.

I am not sure I have the strength to struggle on. My children left for help. What help? I doubt they are ever coming back.

The internet packed up days ago. I can barely remember what we used to do without it. Now I tap the keys of my laptop out of habit, but nothing stirs to life on the dead-eyed screen. Long before Lizzie got sick, the power had given up the ghost. It hasn't blinked back since.

I write this in the last few hours of daylight. I haven't written at such length with pen and paper for years. Nothing more than a shopping list. My handwriting is not what it was. It was never all that much to begin with. Doing it this way, in my spidery longhand, rather concentrates the mind. No cut and paste. Right first time. Each word weighed. Each one measured. Like writers of old, I suppose. Except that I'm no writer.

Soon it will be dark. I will be in darkness. Lizzie is still upstairs. I'll sleep down here. I may get a knife from the kitchen.

I gathered these books from my shelf. The one on the top floor of the house in what used to be my office. I don't know why I chose five. There are plenty more. Help yourself, if they're still there.

There's a near-complete set of Shakespeare. There's Chaucer too and lots of Dickens. All those characters, all those creations. Dickens could people the world with his imagination. Sumptuous feasts by the hearth and wretched children in the street. I can't look at the Thames without imagining a boatman dredging the silt for coins, or bodies.

Why just five? Some sort of symbolism I suppose. Desert Island books. Do they tell you who I am? Who I was? Do they define me? It's possible. But I doubt it.

If you are alive, read them. I don't suppose you'll read them if you are dead.

I'll tell you what each book meant. What each one meant to me I mean. Before I knew how all this would end. Let's call them 'the hopeful years'.

I'll number them. In some attempt at drama. My last act of bravado. I'll wrap each one in this scruffy brown paper. It was all I could find. Either that or Christmas wrapping, which didn't seem appropriate. Though maybe it would have been better. For a gift. A kind of gift from the past. From me to you, whoever you are.

Start with number one. Stupid thing to say. As if you'd start with number five.

Go on. Open it.

That's it. I hope you didn't tear the cover. It's an old book. A flimsy paperback from my childhood. For some reason, I always liked paperbacks, even though hardbacks are meant to be more classy, the type of books you'd give as gifts. These, wrapped in brown paper, are flimsy and light. Bendy. Easier to carry on the tube. I wonder if the tube will ever run again.

The pages are yellowed. Did that happen in my lifetime? In sixty years. Six short decades. Some of the sheets are loose. Perhaps you can stick them back in. To keep the order.

The book is a wondrous thing. The book in general, but this book I mean. Simple words, strung together in just the right order – just so – make a little world. A perfect little world miracled to life by letters from a dead man's hand. How is that possible? How has the writer coaxed this world to life?

I'm rereading the first page now. Can you read it without a lump in your throat? I'm a sentimental old fool. I cried even when I was a child, when it was read to me by my mother, perhaps even my father, when he was around. And I cried when I read it later, as a teenager, and then to my own children, to my precious wife Lizzie in bed, once to a lover, also in bed. What a fool.

But isn't it beautiful? And aren't the illustrations so ... so transporting? Those thin pencil lines conjuring up a world, nudging it into being with a few strokes of lead.

For me it is nostalgic, though I never knew that world. That's an odd thought. Nostalgia for something you never knew. Perhaps I miss the times when I too was a child, with a bear of my own.

It must seem like another planet to you. The England of the 1920s. The little boy in his checked shirt and short trousers. Coming down the stairs. His hand on the banister. Just in case. He's a big boy. That's what he thinks. Still, a hand on the banister is reassuring. He's dragging his bear behind him, backwards. The little stuffed animal's head is bouncing on the step.

Am I allowed to quote from it? Do you have copyright where you are? What do I care. I am long gone. Sue me. I'm chortling. You've brought a smile to my old face. Despite everything. Laughter through the tears. How hackneyed. How stupid. In another time, I might have thought it sweet.

> Here is Edward Bear, coming downstairs now, bump, bump, bump on the back of his head. It is, as far as he knows, the only way of coming downstairs, but sometimes he feels there really is another way, if only he could stop bumping for a moment and think of it.

Isn't that perfect? Isn't every word just where it ought to be? The poor bear can't concentrate. But he's trying, between bounces. How has the author put himself into the mind of a bear, into the mind of a child in the mind of a bear? How can a stuffed toy love Christopher Robin so unquestioningly, more even than he loves honey?

I seem to remember his penchant for that sticky substance got him into sticky situations. Stung on more than one occasion. Didn't he float up to a beehive once on a balloon? Until it burst. And didn't he end up getting his head stuck in a tree stump, someone's home, perhaps Rabbit's? The details are a little hazy and there's no time to reread it now. Besides, I've already wrapped it.

The boy doesn't quite grasp the depth of the bear's love, which makes it all the more poignant. So much more lovely. Will Pooh and Piglet and Eeyore and Owl one day lie abandoned in a box in the attic? Like my old books. Like Lizzie upstairs. Like me, I suppose. Not long now.

How on earth did the author know what it feels like to be a stuffed bear bouncing down the stairs? Have you heard about Keats's negative capability? I bet they don't teach that in school any more, assuming there are still schools I mean. Negative capability. The worst word I ever heard for such a beautiful concept: empathy. But Keats's idea stuck too, like a bear's head stuck in a tree stump.

I seem to recall he wrote about knowing what it was like to be a flower with a drop of water running down its stem. I may be misremembering. But it was something like that. Words that somehow fumble for the unknowable, so that we might grasp how it feels to be somebody else. A tramp or a sailor or an abandoned lover. A man on the last day of his life. Or a bear bouncing down the stairs. To walk a mile in your shoes. And you in mine.

There might be some of Keats's poetry in the office. I can't say I've read much of it myself, if I'm honest. I was never really one for poetry, though when I made the effort I never regretted it. Anyway, if there are some of his poems upstairs, give them a go. Perhaps I was missing out.

Back to the book in your hands, the most charming I have ever read. The open-mouthed wonder of childhood at the huge, mysterious world, the one that goes on for miles and miles, the one you couldn't get to the end of in a whole day, even if you ran and ran and ran.

Read it. You may need some loveliness right now if times are as hard as I suspect. Read it, even if it makes you sad, even if it makes you cry.

This book was written in a kinder age. Come to think of it that's not true. Men freshly slaughtered in the Somme. Vengeance stirring. Hobsbawm called it the bloodiest of centuries. Killing on an industrial scale. He didn't know what was coming. In our particular age of progress and disruption.

Nothing bad ever happens in The Hundred Acre Wood. Not really. Tragedy is a popped balloon. Bother an empty honey pot. Sadness is a lost baby kangaroo, soon reunited with his mother. Rivalry is a game of Poohsticks.

I won't tell you the stories. You must discover them for yourself. If there are children around, read them out loud and watch their faces.

When you do, please forgive Piglet his excitement and Owl his pomposity. Forgive Pooh his laziness and gluttony. Forgive Eeyore his melancholy. And most of all forgive Christopher Robin. If he grows up. And leaves.

Shall we open the next one? Number two.

Maybe you should open one each day. To keep up the excitement. The suspense. Or one each week. Or even one a year. I don't know how much time you have left. I don't suppose any of us do.

When you're ready, tear off the paper. This book is completely different from the last. It's from my teenage years. Can you guess?

It was written in Russian, though of course I read it in English. Russian is a beautiful language. I even learnt some myself, and slogged my way through Pushkin and Turgenev.

Go on, open it. That's it. Not such a big surprise then. You probably read it yourself, though I bet it's worth rereading, now that you have changed, now that things have changed.

When I was young, it was a rite of passage, dark and sinewy and violent. Not what it's like to be a flower. But what it's like to be a killer. What it's like to be a young man so full of idealistic rage that he kills an old woman with an axe to test his theories. Bolshevism in a single act. Revenge and revolution and putting things to rights, with the edge of a blade on a human skull.

The early chapters are unbearable. As the young man musters up the courage to put his ideas into motion, his terrible ideas into motion. The reader is willing him on. At least I was. As a teenager. Complicit. Pick up the axe and strike.

I wouldn't today. That is the mystery of words. You can never read them twice the same way. What do they say? Never step into the same ink pot twice. For me, back then, Raskolnikov was a revolutionary. Deluded, but motivated by an impulse to change the world.

The woman he killed was a moneylender. Didn't she deserve it? Of course she didn't. In his righteous indignation, Raskolnikov stepped across a line, stepped in blood. Did we learn our lessons? Did we hell.

I hope I haven't given too much away. I think most people know that much. Anyway, that's just the start. Like Macbeth killing Duncan, the psychological drama unfolds thereafter. Or unravels, more like. Out damned spot. The cat and mouse detective. Malcolm and his damnable forest. What to do with the axe? What to do with your conscience?

At least with Dostoevsky there is a possibility of redemption. I don't remember Macbeth having that. Raskolnikov has a sliver of a chance, a gift given by an angel in the darkness. I remember rolling my eyes. The religious connotations. Salvation. Bah. Humbug. I'd like to read it again. I might think differently now. With the light fading.

Are you ready for another one? Number three.

This reminds me of the ghosts in *A Christmas Carol* who visit Scrooge each night. Three in all. One after another. Past, present and future – the last the most terrifying of all.

Go on, open it.

Yes, it's non-fiction. Are you disappointed? Don't be put off. It's very readable. I wanted to include something like this. A different way of grappling with reality. I used to enjoy learning from clever people who thought they might have figured out our world. Our fathomless planet. Our full stop in the universe.

It was fun to read books like *The Selfish Gene*, which turned our human-centric ideas on their head. Shocking really. A cold intellectual shower. Genes our masters. Our bodies mere receptacles. They killed us when we had done their bidding.

Years later I read that the agricultural revolution was a trick played on us by wheat. While we toiled, bent double over the hard earth, the wheat gene spread like a forest fire. Did wheat survive, without its human slaves?

I digress. I'm sorry. My mind is wandering. Let's get back to the task at hand, while there's still time. I could have put any one of Jared Diamond's books in this box. *The World Until*

Yesterday. *Why Is Sex Fun*?. That made me smirk. The title, not the book. *Collapse*. Now wouldn't that have been appropriate? The last Easter Islander chopping down the last tree. But I liked this one, the classic I suppose: *Guns, Germs, and Steel*.

I loved the premise most of all, as well as the sheer intellectual showmanship, the daring to construct a theory cobbled from bits of human knowledge: linguistics, bird evolution, archaeology, genomics, chaos theory, bits of string. As I recall it went like this. Why did a few hundred Spaniards in the army of Hernán Cortés defeat the great empire of the Aztecs? Why was it not the other way around? Why didn't Moctezuma come riding into Madrid and sack the Spanish empire?

There's one explanation. The one based on racial or cultural prejudice: that Europeans were somehow better, their civilisation destined to rule, with God on their side. I love the way Diamond simply rejects that argument in a sentence or two. We're adults here. We can do better than that. So what's the real reason? How do we explain the accidents of history? Why did some have the guns, germs and steel and why were others powerless to resist?

I won't spoil the argument. Not that I can remember it all. Moctezuma didn't ride to Europe on horseback for the simple reason that there were no horses to ride. Was he going to invade Madrid on a llama? Societies developed in the context of their physical realities. The Inuits didn't grow roses on their icebergs. Not like Lizzie in her postage stamp of a garden, with a mirror on the back wall, to make it look bigger. But then Lizzie didn't know fifty words for snow.

Let's press on. There are five ghosts to get through.

I realise now there are no women authors here. Forgive me, though it's unforgivable. I grabbed the first books that came to mind, almost the first that came to hand. Was it an unconscious bias? Have I lived but half a life?

I should put this right. I must put this right. But I am so weak and the steps are so many. And I can't face Lizzie up there. Not now.

If I could, I'd fetch *Wuthering Heights*. Do you remember that line? It's one of the few in prose I've committed to memory. I hope I've got it right.

> My love for Linton is like the foliage in the woods: time will change it … as winter changes the trees. My love for Heathcliff resembles the eternal rocks beneath: a source of little visible delight, but necessary.

You don't need me to parse that for you. The lines speak for themselves. I always smiled when interviewers asked Bob Dylan to explain his lyrics. His answer was always a variation of the same. If he had meant something different, that's what he would have written.

A love that resembles the eternal rocks. Another like the leaves that crinkle, flutter and die. Can you have them both? Do we need to choose?

I could have picked Marilynne Robinson, a writer whose every word is mysteriously transformed by the alchemy of placement. Each word's neighbour pulses against the next, so that each is charged with the electricity of proximity.

I remember her describing a water fountain. Somehow she zooms in and slows down so that the movement of the water becomes all there is, all that matters. Gerard Manley Hopkins found God in the flight of a windhover or in the spark of a plough gashing open a black stone.

Instead you have this. Number four. A book by another man. A Nigerian man. A dead Nigerian man.

Don't be deceived by how slim it is. Achebe should have won the Nobel Prize, not that it matters. Bob Dylan won it, and he didn't even show up to collect the praise.

Ah, there's a bonus. I see now. On the very first page. A stanza from a poem by W.B. Yeats, to set things rolling, to set things unravelling.

> *Turning and turning in the widening gyre*
> *The falcon cannot hear the falconer;*
> *Things fall apart; the centre cannot hold;*
> *Mere anarchy is loosed upon the world …*

Did Yeats know what was coming? Or is that just the human condition he was referring to? The illusion of permanence.

Achebe's book has always left me with a feeling of imminent doom. When one thing intrudes upon another, collides with another, unknowingly, uncaringly, unthinkingly.

Okonkwo is a wrestler and a strong man, arrogant and foolish. His life is defined by his shame for his do-nothing father, who died with too much debt and too few wives. All that he took to his grave was his mastery of the flute. Okonkwo strains to be different. Would that he had strained to be the same. Isn't that the stuff of our lives? Our pointless rebellions, our reactions and counteractions, our seething resentments and the settling of scores, driving us on – over a cliff.

Okonkwo thinks the world is in his hand. In the end, the world crushes him like a kola nut. He misreads the changing times. Didn't we do the same? Shouldn't we have known all those years ago? It's not like we were never warned. All those little warning signs; the ice melt and the silent pathogens.

I was amazed to learn, years after first reading it, that this was Achebe's first novel, written when he was just twenty-eight. It reads like the work of a sage. A wise man. Maybe it's not a question of years. Of lives lived and lessons spurned. I am more than sixty, and little sager for that.

As a teenager, I read the book as a simple story of white aggression. The white man comes with his religion and his guns and things fall apart. There is truth in that interpretation. That is there. But there is much else besides. The village also carries the seed of its own destruction. Okonkwo, violent and proud, carries the seed of his own destruction. That's Shakespeare, no? King Lear and Macbeth. Othello and his jealousy.

In Okonkwo's village, proverbs were 'the palm oil with which words were eaten'.

Fearful of snakes, at night villagers referred to their slithery foe as 'string'.

How charming. Less charming when a boy from a neighbouring village is sacrificed to appease the gods, or some drugged-up priest. Okonkwo loves the boy. But he carries out the act himself so as not to appear weak, or feminine. Was that the seed, the seed that led to this? This that we have done on an industrial scale.

Still, the village has its charms. I underlined some of the proverbs, all those years ago. (My father's books were dense with notes and underlining, since books were to be used not revered, he told me.)

Okonkwo takes these old superstitions too much to heart, more's the shame. Those codes of manliness, those false prophets of what it is to be strong. Life blesses those who get ahead, who push ahead.

I wish it blessed the weak, the unassuming flute-players.

I like this one. I just found it now, flicking through these old pages.

If men's arrows unerringly strike, then birds must learn to fly without perching, it says.

And so it goes on. This dialectic of progress, this nuclear war of evolution. This perpetual game of catch-up, this art of humiliating and crushing the Joneses, lest they humiliate and pulverise you.

Okonkwo had Joneses of his own. The other villagers who snickered at his father's flute and tutted at his father's debts.

Okonkwo would have done well to have ignored them and to have taken up the flute himself. And to have remembered his mother. That is strength. That might have tempered his arrogance and saved him. And saved us all.

All right, shall we open the last one. The smallest. It doesn't look like much, does it?

That's where you're wrong. Open it, carefully.

That's it. It fits in your top pocket. You can carry it wherever you go. I would if I were you.

Walt Whitman's *Song of Myself*. I read it for the first time not so long ago, actually. I must have been fifty. I felt fifteen again, those words coursing through my veins.

It read like a revelation. The intoxicating meaning of all of this captured in words, captured in cadence. The ecstasy of living. Remember that.

High on coffee I read with increasing excitement. Each word drilled into my flesh. Each word a flash of understanding as though I had cracked some code.

It was blazing hot outside. The hottest summer in years. I read the whole thing in one go. One giddy morning, bleeding into afternoon. A fifty-year-old going on fifteen. Going on sixty. Going on to this.

Listen to the wonder, and to the conviction.

> *A child said* What is the grass? *fetching it to me with full hands;*
> *How could I answer the child? I do not know what it is any*
>   *more than he.*

And the defiance.

> *I wear my hat as I please indoors or out.*

I love that. I even put it on my Twitter handle. A bold statement, though I never wore a hat.

The Japanese worship in the mirror, when it comes down to it, at those Spartan temples dedicated to themselves. With a clap and a bow.

> *I celebrate myself, and sing myself,*
> *And what I assume, you shall assume,*
> *For every atom belonging to me as good as belongs to you.*

That belief in flesh and bone, in the stuff of life.

> *I lean and loaf at my ease observing a spear of summer grass.*

What is grass? And what is this life we lead? This life we led.

How does it end? Spoiler alert. Snorting now, chortling, through this old nose.

I bequeath myself to the dirt to grow from the grass I love,
If you want me again look for me under your boot-soles.

Do you see me there, under your boot-soles? Do you sense me in these words?

Can you tell what kind of a man I was, and what kind of a man I was not? Can you catch my shadow in these books?

No. I thought not.

Still, keep them. Read them. They are my gift to you. From this dark place. From me. And from Lizzie.

© David Pilling, 2020

MAX PORTER

'I believe in the gift economy, especially if what you are giving is words and images, ideas and stories. Let us give and give and give.'

Max Porter is the author of two highly acclaimed novels, *Grief is the Thing with Feathers* and *Lanny*. He has been the recipient of numerous awards and, in addition to his novels, has written and published poetry, essays and short stories. He is also a dazzling speaker. Prior to his writing career, Porter managed the Chelsea branch of Daunt Books, winning the Bookseller of the Year Award in 2009. He was Editorial Director at Granta and Portobello Books until 2019. In addition to writing fiction, he engages with literacy initiatives. 'I want to commit myself to closing the gap between literacy and the literary, because I think that gap is widening in a worrying way, and I don't think there's any point in us publishing or writing books if we're not growing new readers.'

It could be any book

MAX PORTER

I have been a dedicated giver of books for as long as I have been able. Because it is beneficial to the cultural ecosystem, because books are extraordinarily good value, because part of being evangelical about literature and literacy should be putting your money where your mouth is. It is a political gesture now to borrow books from a library, to buy books from a bookshop, to pay for an album, to go to a museum. These gestures keep culture alive, and we know beyond any doubt that culture is our lifeblood, is civilisation's impulse towards betterment, complexity, nurture and growth.

I take a book to meet a friend. I take a book to meet an enemy. My mind is made of books. My marriage is made of books. My children fall asleep every night clutching books. In this world of entrenched opinions and partisan politics, the book as thoughtfully crafted, slowly imbibed vehicle for nuance, for diversity of opinion, becomes ever more important and ever more radical.

I believe in the gift economy, especially if what you are

giving is words and images, ideas and stories. Let us give and give and give.

There is a book I have recently been giving as a gift.

This particular book only costs a pound, which helps. Given what a coffee costs, or a pair of shoes, or a disposable whatnot from the whatever-we-have-to-keep-upgrading-to-next shop, this book is a miraculous bargain. The bookshop I worked in years ago still gives me a staff discount, so actually this book cost me *sixty pence.* The price of a chocolate bar.

And so when this short book impacted me as much as it did, I felt compelled to share it, so I bought fifty copies. I carried copies of the book around with me. I gave it to my friends and family, to colleagues, fellow writers, and audience members at events. I also gave it to some strangers. I gave it to a woman who was protesting Donald Trump's state visit to London, and she was extremely grateful. She knew of the author. I offered it to a man who asked me for a cigarette and he said No, he didn't fancy it. I told him what it was about, and he said, No, definitely, that sounded boring, he would rather have a cigarette. But most people did accept the book, and the fifty copies didn't last long.

The book is printed on Forest Stewardship Certified paper, which is important. It fits inside a standard pocket or adult human hand. It weighs about as much as ten acorns.

The book moved me greatly, because it is by a wise and kind man who loves language and the planet. The short essays it comprises were originally written some years ago, before the full extent of human damage to the environment and to other species was fully evident. Before the normalisation (linguistic, political and practical) of our complicity in that damage was so entrenched. What I mean is, it's prophetic.

This book does a thing which is very unusual in these hot-headed days of extremist social media opinion; it gently suggests some ideas on a subject. Then it shares the criticisms that were levelled at those ideas when the ideas were first published. Then it calmly responds to those criticisms, accepting some, cleverly rebuffing others. Its main characteristics are warmth, receptiveness, courage of conviction and wit. The wit is the best bit. The wit's the thing I drank most thirstily, in these humourless times, when I first read this book.

I met this book during a local political crisis overshadowed by the planetary ecological crisis and I realised that the earth-facing, generative, cautiously romantic, considered, poetry-enriched, ethical, crafted and worked-hard wisdom of this book was exactly what was missing from the behavioural vocabulary of the present. And I know ... it was ever thus. We read things by wise and brilliant people and fantasise that the author could be running whatever shit-show we are currently observing. We wished for more John Berger and less Margaret Thatcher. We wished for more Thomas Browne and less Charles I, more Virginia Woolf and less Neville Chamberlain.

I knew I could not travel to the author's farm in Kentucky and bring him back here, to heal our local wounds, touring him like a guru to speak truth to assembled fans, deniers or hecklers. I would not do that to him.

So buying the book and giving it as a gift was a decent place to start.

Beyond that, beyond the physical book, I resolved to weave this man's spirit into the work I make, into the conversations

I have, into my ideas and behaviour. From the intimate workings of my domestic life (how did I speak to my son, when he angered me, this morning?) to the ways in which I treat other humans, and non-humans, in this time of ecological disaster.

This book sent me off into other books. It sent me to my apple tree. It sent me to my best friend to apologise. It sent me to a website about recycled keyboards. It sent me to the charity shop to see if they had a vase for the flowers I was given (to thank me for the book), because the idea of buying a new vase seemed preposterous after reading this book.

I've had a couple of good conversations with people to whom I gave this book, but for the majority of recipients I have no idea what they thought. I don't know if they enjoyed it, or binned it, or had a profound intellectual reckoning with it. It's important not to need to know. We don't plant trees to know with any certainty how long they will survive, who will stand beneath their branches, or what they will live to see. As Lewis Hyde says, 'the passage into mystery always refreshes.'

I felt refreshed by this little book, and refreshed again every time I gifted it.

I will list some of the book's gifts to its reader:

- A gorgeous non-doctrinaire feminism.

- A chirpy, melodic, rambunctious intellect.

- A visionary understanding that rampant capitalism's end-game would be planet death.

- A self-deprecating honesty.

- A taking of umbrage to meanness.

- A conservationist political impulse, in the content and the style.

- A profound love of language, and attention to its details.

- A celebration of craft.

- A refusal to flinch from the philosophically unanswerable.

You see? Sixty pence incredibly well spent.

I think the point I'd like to make about giving books is this: do you need to know the title and author of the book I've been describing? I hope you do not. You will have given or been given books like this. As well as books which offended, revolted or bored you. Each of us wanders along our reading maps nudged and steered by the gifts of others, dragged hither and thither, distracted, sometimes lost, sometimes charging forward with great purpose. It could be any book. Any book given with good reason from one person to another.

It is one of the most wonderful things about this short strange life, to give these little paper packets of set-down thought to other people, and to receive them in turn.

But I'm keen for you to share in my joy, and maybe spread it further. The little book is called *Why I Am Not Going to Buy a Computer*, by Wendell Berry.

© Max Porter, 2020

PHILIP PULLMAN

'There are books that every household containing children ought to possess. . . . It's worth pointing out that a really good book for children is one that parents don't mind reading aloud several hundred times.'

Philip Pullman was born in Norwich and educated in England, Zimbabwe, Australia and Wales. He studied English at Exeter College, Oxford. To date, he has published over thirty-five books, read by children and adults alike. His most famous work is the *His Dark Materials* trilogy. These books have been honoured by several prizes, including the Carnegie Medal, the Carnegie of Carnegies and (for *The Amber Spyglass*) the Whitbread Book of the Year Award. The first volume of *The Book of Dust – La Belle Sauvage* – was published in 2017 to great acclaim, securing Philip Pullman Author of the Year at both the British Book Awards and the Specsavers National Book Awards. He has received numerous other awards, including the Eleanor Farjeon Award and the Astrid Lindgren Award. He was knighted for services to literature in the New Year's Honours List 2019.

Giving books

PHILIP PULLMAN

It ought to be so easy. You go into the bookshop, which covers several floors and sells books on every conceivable subject, find the perfect one for your giftee, pay for it, go home and wrap it up. One of those activities takes a great deal longer than the others, though, and keeps being interrupted by the thought 'Oh, but I'll get this one for myself – and that – and X's biography of Z – and I see there's a new Mick Herron just out – and while I'm here I'll just look at the maps – and I've got a couple of 3 for 2 books so I must look for a third ...' and by the time you have to leave you still haven't found the perfect book to give someone else.

There's no such thing as the perfect book, really. You have to take a chance.

My stepfather's parents were very good at taking chances with books. One Christmas they gave me Leslie Charteris's *The Second Saint Omnibus*. I don't know why they started with the second, and I've never seen the first from that day to this, but I thought it was terrific. It filled the gap between Biggles and James Bond as if it had been made to fit, and gave me food for thought for a long time. Simon Templar had a style and wit and zest quite different from the harder, cooler, cold-eyed hero of Ian Fleming's books, though not so far off the Bond of the films. There was a TV series starring Roger Moore, but I don't think it got the Saint quite right, and in fact I don't think he's ever worked successfully on the screen.

The following Christmas, I remember, my step-grandparents gave me the first Jeeves I'd ever encountered. No preparation – that's the way to do it. If you tell someone that there's this marvellous book, oh it's so funny, you'll laugh all day, I can't tell you how amusing it is, there's this story where … You'll hate it before you start. It hasn't got a chance. Don't say a word: just hand it over, and hold your tongue. So, with no helpful advice, never having heard of Jeeves or Bertie Wooster or P.G. Wodehouse, I unwrapped the modest-looking Penguin paperback called *Very Good, Jeeves*, and started to read. That was fifty-nine years ago, and I'm still reading Wodehouse, still laughing, still entranced by the fountain-like brilliance of the style, and increasingly, now, marvelling not so much at the cleverness of Jeeves as at the miracle of a hero who is faultlessly good and yet such delightful company. Bertie's only flaw is the most forgivable and harmless one of vanity: we know we can rely on him to be seduced by this pair of Old Etonian spats, or that white mess-jacket, or that Tyrolean hat, and that Jeeves will reliably deal with the situation (he persuades Bertie to relinquish the hat by telling him that the police are looking for a burglar known as Alpine Joe). Good characters are much harder to write than villains, as every storyteller knows, and Wodehouse pulled off a double miracle by making us believe that the 'mentally negligible' Bertie is a master of the most sparkling style in English literature.

I don't remember my step-grandparents as being great readers themselves; their house had a lot of books on the shelves, but they were mainly of the Reader's Digest Collection of Great Books sort, bound in luxurious Skivertex. They must have taken a chance on Charteris and Wodehouse, and they came up trumps.

Other book-givers were less lucky, or I was. I remember some relative giving me a copy of Walter Scott's *Quentin Durward* when I was about ten: unreadable then and now. And Henry Seton Merriman's *Barlasch of the Guard*, ditto with knobs on. I thought Kenneth Grahame's *The Wind in the Willows* was all right, though the chapter about the Piper at the Gates of Dawn was pretty rum, and I was at first bemused and then repelled by his *Dream Days* and *The Golden Age*, which seemed to me not fit for children. I have mercifully forgotten who gave them to me.

But Uncle Tony and Auntie Poppy struck gold when they gave me *Emil and the Detectives*. Erich Kästner's masterpiece was included in a volume together with its sequel, *Emil and the Three Twins*, and a non-Emil story of comic nonsense called *Thirty-Fifth of May*. They were all illustrated by Walter Trier in a swift, flexible pen line just the right side of caricature. I didn't know then what enchanted me about *Emil*, but I fell for it at once. It just seemed *real*. The first story was published in Germany in 1930, and it tells the story of young Emil going to visit his relatives in Berlin and being robbed of some money his widowed mother has given him to take to his grandmother. It's only a small sum, but this family isn't rich, and Emil is appalled at his own carelessness, as he sees it, and stricken with guilt.

But he meets a group of boys (and one girl) who rally round and help find the thief and run him to ground, and Emil and the detectives become famous. There is nothing in the least magical or even unlikely in the plot or the characters; we are firmly in the real world, where poor families do run short of money, where thieves and robbers do prey on the innocent, where big cities can seem frightening places to those who are new to them, and where human friendships and cheerfulness and decency are all we can rely on – but are enough.

The second story, *Emil and the Three Twins*, affected me deeply, and it astonishes me now that I didn't understand why at the time. Emil and his mother love each other very much, and want nothing more than to go on living together for ever; but Emil is growing older, and one day his mother receives a proposal of marriage from the local police inspector, Herr Jeschke. Emil was once afraid of Herr Jeschke, but the policeman turns out to be surprisingly friendly, and actually asks Emil for his agreement to the marriage, which Emil gives. Then he goes away for a seaside holiday with his new friends from Berlin, and there's a scene where he's alone with his grandmother, and they talk about his mother and Herr Jeschke. He confesses that he's intensely unhappy: really he'd much rather she didn't marry, but stayed alone with him; and his grandmother shows him a letter from his mother, in which she tells the old lady that she, too, would rather remain alone with Emil, but Emil's growing up, and before very long he'll leave home, and what's more her hairdressing business isn't going very well; and Herr Jeschke is a decent man. So Emil and his mother are each sacrificing what they really want for the sake of the other.

A full account of the emotional depths and turns in this conversation between the boy and his grandmother would be enough to fill an entire essay. I found it then, and still find it now, intensely moving. By the end of the chapter, Emil has resolved that he must never tell his mother what he feels, but accept the situation and be cheerful about it, and his grandmother gently approves.

The strange thing is that when I read the book then, in my childhood, I never consciously made the connection between Emil's situation and my own. I had to wait till I was middle-aged before I realised why I loved the book so much. My mother was widowed when I was seven, and she married again, and my stepfather, like Herr Jeschke, was a good and decent man, but as every stepchild knows, that isn't quite the point. In any case I wasn't an only child, like Emil: I had a younger brother. But I understood Emil's turmoil completely, and I read the book again and again.

I have no idea whether the relatives who gave me the book had that scene, and my situation, in mind. I don't suppose for a moment that they actually read it before they gave it to me; they were probably relying on its reputation. And I never spoke about it to anyone.

I think it illustrates an important point about giving books to children: we never know what will resonate with the reader, or why. Reading is so private, the things that move us or frighten us are so secret, that the best we can do is guess, and hope that no deeply suppressed trauma has given the child a horror of bears, or doorknobs, or steam trains, or whatever else features in the story we've just handed over. For years I was terrified of the word 'Paris', because I associated it with a penny-in-the-slot machine I'd seen on Brighton Pier, which showed someone being guillotined. When someone gave me a book called *Adventure in Paris* I had to hide it away on the grown-up bookshelves, back to front so I couldn't see the title, and never look at it. No one noticed. But since that's the sort of thing that we can't know about, we have to take a chance.

When it comes to picture books and stories for very young children, though, things are much easier. There are books that every household containing children ought to possess, and there's a new generation of five-year-olds (four-year-olds, six-year-olds, etc.) every year, who've never seen *The Gruffalo* or *We're Going on a Bear Hunt* or *Dogger*, and welcome them with wonder. Anything by Janet and Allan Ahlberg is bound to work, and so is the loving family life depicted by Shirley Hughes. It's worth pointing out that a really good book for children is one that parents don't mind reading aloud several hundred times.

Books for adult friends are a different matter. Knowing what they're interested in helps a bit, but then they might already have read everything there is on the subject, damn them. A good place to look used to be a second-hand bookshop. That's not so easy any more, when the combined effects of rent, council tax, internet bookselling, and (I'm sorry to say) charity bookshops nearby that don't have to pay for their stock, have swept so many of these precious places into the dustbin, to the impoverishment of civilisation. Looking for a book on the internet is (a) easy, but (b) empty of pleasure. Shelves and shelves overflowing with old books, that's what we need; books in piles on the floor, books on trestle tables on the pavement and a proprietor who's grumpily reluctant to sell anything. A sleeping cat, a certain amount of dust, windows that haven't been cleaned since 1960 and pencilled prices in pounds, shillings and pence make it perfect.

We need to be able to browse, because we never know what we'll find. If you already know exactly what you want, and you don't want anything else, you never encounter the true and serendipitous pleasure of discovery. It does help to know a *little* about what you want, mind you. For years I enjoyed looking (not urgently, but purposefully) for books by the American novelist MacDonald Harris, because they were quite rare and unusually good. When I found one, the pleasure was intense, but I've got them all now, and I'm not giving them away.

As for birthday presents for friends, I used to like finding books that were first published (and actually printed and sold) in the year of the giftee's birth. The literary quality of the book and the renown of the author were quite immaterial, as long as it was in good condition; all I needed was to be able to point out that the book had lasted better than the friend had. Many of my friends were born during the heyday (1941–75) of *The Saturday Book*, that annual miscellany of stories and essays and articles on literary and artistic matters by celebrated authors of the day, illustrated with drawings and photographs: all rather Festival-of-Britainish, decoratively speaking, and as middle as a brow can get. Ideal for gifts of that sort, though if the friend is under forty-five, you'd have to find something else.

But that's not so easy now the second-hand bookshops have mostly disappeared. The grumpy owners, the sleeping cats, the dusty windows, the treasure-filled shelves have all been swept away into the iniquity of oblivion. We shall all join them soon enough.

ALICE PUNG

'Reading and writing changed my life, and took me to unimaginable places — literally. This is why Room to Read is so important. Having come from a refugee family that survived war, I personally understand the transformative power of literacy to build better lives.'

Alice Pung is an award-winning writer, editor, teacher and lawyer born in Australia to ethnically Chinese refugees from Pol Pot's Cambodia. She is the bestselling author of two highly acclaimed memoirs, *Unpolished Gem* and *Her Father's Daughter*, and the editor of the anthologies *Growing Up Asian in Australia* and *My First Lesson*. Her first novel, *Laurinda*, won the Ethel Turner Prize at the 2016 NSW Premier's Literary Awards. She was also named one of the *Sydney Morning Herald*'s Young Novelists of the Year. She lives with her husband and her young family at Janet Clarke Hall at the University of Melbourne where she is Artist in Residence.

Reading between the lines

ALICE PUNG

Having survived starvation and been spared execution, my father arrived in this new country, vassal-eyed and sunken-cheeked. I was born less than a month later and he named me Alice because he thought Australia was a Wonderland. Maybe he had vague literary aspirations for me, like most parents have vague infinite dreams for their babies, so small, so bewildered, so egoless. I arrived safe after so many babies had died under the regime created by a man who named himself deliberately after ruthless ambition – Political Potential, or Pol Pot for short.

'There was a tree,' my father told me when I was a teenager, 'and this tree was where Pol Pot's army, the Khmer Rouge, killed babies and toddlers. They would grab the infant by their ankles and swing them against the trunk and smash them again and again until they were dead.' When I was an adult, I found out that there was not just the one tree. There were many such trees from which no cradle hung.

But as a child, growing up in Australia, the oldest of four, I knew the words to comfort crying babies. They'd been taught to me by my schoolteachers, with rhyme but without reason: *When the bough breaks the cradle will fall and down will come baby, cradle and all.* A gentle song to rock my sisters to sleep. If my mother understood the words I was singing, she'd yell at me.

My mother was always hollering at me about one thing or another. After the age of eight, I was never left in peace. She repeatedly told me that babies had really soft skulls, that there was even a hole in their heads that hadn't yet closed. When I looked at my baby sister, I could see something pulsing on the top of her scalp, beneath the skin. Never drop a baby, they warned me, or your life will be over. They spoke in warnings and commands, like Old Testament sages. They'd seen babies dropped dead. Their language was literal, not literary, but it did the trick.

We could not complain that we were dying of boredom because they'd seen death close-up, and it was definitely not caused by a lack of Lego. We could not say that we were starving because at one malarial point in his life, my father thought that if he breathed inwards he could feel his backbone through his stomach. We could never be hungry or bored in our concrete house in Braybrook, behind a carpet factory that spewed out noxious methane smells that sent us to school reeking like whoopee-cushions.

But in this scatalogical suburb, I was indeed often bored shitless. Imagine this – you go outside and hoons in cobbled-together Holdens wind down their windows and tell you to *Go Back Home, Chinks.* So you walk home and inside, it's supposed to be like home. But it's not a home you know. It's a home your parents know, where the older siblings look after the younger ones and your mum works in an airless dark shed at the back making jewellery, and you think it's called outworking because although she's at home she's always out working. Just like her mum in Phnom Penh and her mum's mum in Phnom Penh and every other poor mum in the history of your family lineage. 'What are you doing here? Stop bothering me,' your mum would tell you. Or when she was desperate, she'd be cajoling: 'Take your siblings out. Go for a walk. If you give me just one more hour, I'll be done.' Her face would be blackened, her fingers cut. She'd have her helmet on, with the visor. She looked like a coal miner.

Back in Cambodia, the eldest siblings looked after the bevy of little ones, all the children roaming around the Central Market, en masse. Here, in these Melbourne suburbs they'd call it a marauding Asian gang, I bet. I preferred to stay at home. I had plenty to keep me occupied there. Our school library let me borrow books, but I can't even remember the names of the librarians now. They didn't like some of the kids because sometimes we stole books. My best friend Linda read a book about Helen Keller that so moved her, so expanded her ten-year-old sense of the world that she nicked it and stroked the one-line sample of Braille print on the last page until all the raised dots were flat. I nicked books too, books on needlecraft and making soft toys. Sometimes one of my aunts would come by and give us a garbage bag filled with fleecy fabric offcuts from her job sewing tracksuits in her own back shed. Being a practical kid who bugged her parents at every opportunity possible for new toys, I wanted to have reference manuals on how to make them. I didn't nick story books or novels because to me, those were like films I often only wanted to experience once.

One day, my baby sister rolled herself off the bed when I was supposed to be watching her. She was three months old. I had just turned nine. My mother ran into the house and railed at me like a dybbuk, 'You're dead! You're dead!' She scooped my sister out of my hands. 'What were you doing? You were meant to watch her!'

'She was asleep,' I sobbed, 'I was reading a book.'

While my mother was working to support us in the dark back shed, I had been in the sunlit bedroom, staring for hours and hours on end at little rectangles, only stopping occasionally to make myself some Nescafé coffee with sweetened condensed milk. If this wasn't the high life, then what was? Those books were not making me any smarter, she might have thought. Or even said, because it was something she was always telling me, because she couldn't read or write herself. The government had closed down her Chinese school when she was in grade one, as the very first step of ethnic cleansing in Cambodia.

My mother called up my father and roared over the phone for him to come home immediately because I'd let my sister roll off the bed and she might be brain-damaged. 'If she's brain-damaged, you're going to be dead,' my father said to me, before they both left for the hospital with my sister.

I hated my parents at that moment, but I hated myself more. I also hated the Baby-Sitters Club, all of those twelve-year-old girls for whom looking after small children was just an endless series of sleepovers and car-washes and ice-cream parties and they even always got praised and paid for it. The only people I did not hate were my siblings. They were blameless.

This fucking reading, I thought, because this is how I thought back then, punctuated by profanity, because this is how I wrote back then in diaries I made at school of folded paper stapled together with colourful cardboard covers that I'd then take home and fill in with pages and pages of familial injustice. Sometimes the pen dug in so aggressively underlining a word of rage that I'd make a cut through the paper five pages deep. And this is how the kids talked at school, and also some of their parents who picked them up from school. But then I also realised, *reading's the only fucking good thing I have going for me.*

It showed me parents who were not only reasonable, but indulgent. They were meant to be friends with their kids. They were meant to foster their creativity and enterprise. They hosted parties and baked cupcakes and laughed when their children messed up the house, and sat them down and explained things to them carefully with great verbal displays of affection. *But only if* the kids were like Kristy or Stacey or Dawn in the Baby-Sitters Club. If they were anything like me, then they didn't talk very much. We were refugees in school textbooks, there for edification, to induce guilt and gratitude. The presence of third-world people like us in a book immediately stripped that book of any reading-for-pleasure aspirations. We were hard work. We were Objects not Subjects. Or if subjects, subjects of charity and not agents of charity. Always takers, never givers. No wonder people resented us.

Hell, even *I* resented us! 'Girls are more responsible,' my mother always told me. When my aunties dumped their children, my little cousins, with me, they'd always say, 'Alice is so good. We trust her.' What's one or two or three more when you already have so many in the house? they reasoned.

A few years ago, a friend moved into a flat by herself. Her next-door neighbour was a single dad living with his son. The duo seemed good mates, and the dad was taking the boy to school. But then the school break rolled around, and dad was at work all day in a factory. My friend had been watching the boy for a few days. He was home alone most of the time. She was worried about him. *So she called the cops on his dad.* I was livid when she told me. It was school holidays, he was safe at home in his flat, playing with his computer game. *If you were so worried about him, do the neighbourly thing and have him over some afternoons in your flat,* I thought. 'What happened to the dad?' I asked, concerned. 'I don't know,' she replied, 'but they moved out shortly afterwards.'

I imagined if some prying interloper had called the cops on my parents when I was young, seeing our makeshift crèche with no adult supervision around. 'If you tell the government what I do,' my mother always warned me when I was a child, 'they'll take me away and lock me up and your brother and sisters will be distributed to your aunts and uncles or be put in foster homes.' What she did – her fourteen-hour days in the back shed, working with potassium cyanide and other noxious chemicals to produce the jewellery for stores that would then pay her only a couple of dollars per ring or pendant – she thought was a crime. She got paid cash in hand, so she never paid any taxes. She just didn't understand that she wasn't the criminal; she was the one being exploited.

My mother began work at thirteen in a plastic-bag factory, after her school was closed down. When all the men were at war, the factories were filled with women and children. One afternoon, she told me, she accidentally sliced open a chunk of her leg with the plastic-bag-cutting machine. She had to stay home for the next two weeks. She spent those two weeks worrying whether she'd be replaced by another little girl. In her whole working life, spanning over half a century, my mother has never signed an employment contract because she can't write or read.

'People can rip me off so easily,' she would often lament, 'that's why I have to have my wits about me at all times.' She'd always count out the exact change when she went grocery shopping even though it mortified me as a kid, and drove those behind her in line nuts. 'If they overcharge me and you're not here, how can I explain anything to them?' she'd ask, 'I don't speak English.' She'd memorise landmarks when driving, because she couldn't read street signs. During elections, she would put a '1' next to the candidate who looked the most attractive in their photo. And she'd ask me to read the label on her prescription medicines. 'Tell me carefully,' she'd instruct, 'too much or too little and you could kill me.' The power over life and death, I thought, not really a responsibility I wanted at eight. But power over life and death is supposed to be what great works of art are about. Sometimes, there's not a huge chasm between being literate and being literary. They are not opposite ends of a continuum.

Sure, I enjoyed the classics, especially that line in *Great Expectations* when Pip determines that he will return a gentleman and deliver 'gallons of condescension'. But the depictions of working children, children treated as economic units of labour, as instruments for ulterior adult ends – this was nothing new to me.

Looking after children is hard work. No one cares when things go right, it is the natural course of the universe. But everyone swarms in when things go wrong. A whole swat team, sometimes consisting of your own extended family members, ready to whack at you like a revolting bug if harm should befall your minor charges. The sad reality is that when you slap a monetary value onto these services, people sit up. They pay attention. They first splutter about how outrageous it is. Then slowly they accept it. You hope that one day no children will be left at home, minding other children while their parents work, because all working parents will be able to access good, affordable childcare. Often when people rail, *think of the children!* they are not really thinking of the children. Otherwise, they would listen to the children, not condemn the parents for situations beyond their control – illiteracy, minimum wages, poverty.

Jeanette Winterson wrote about art's ability to coax us away from the mechanical and towards the miraculous. It involves just seeing the extraordinary in the ordinary. To understand that an eight-year-old can and will take responsibility and care of themselves when left to their own devices requires imaginative empathy, not judgement.

Reading showed me what the world could be. My life told me what the world was. It was not Jane Eyre or Lizzie Bennet or even Nancy Drew that opened my life to the possibility of a better existence. It was Ann M. Martin and her Baby-Sitters Club. That children should get paid was a crazy idea, that they should get paid for babysitting even more audacious. That a handful of pre-teen girls could start a small business from Claudia's home – beautiful artistic *Asian* Claudia Kishi with her own fixed phone line – and that they could muster all the neighbourhood children under their care and largesse was revolutionary to me.

In my life, the miraculous does not involve magic. There is nothing that makes the state of childhood particularly magical. There is a lot that is frightening, brutal and cruel about every stage of life. After all, I know that a single tree can harbour a cradle or a grave. But to be able to do what my hardworking, wonderful mother never could – time-travel, mind-read, even never to mistake dish detergent for shampoo because the pictures of fruit on the bottle are similar – this is a gift I will never take for granted.

JANCIS
ROBINSON

'One of the things that attracted me to Room to Read back in 2003 was John Wood's proactive plan to recycle books, sending them to a remote but needy Himalayan village on a yak.'

ॐ

Jancis Robinson OBE MW is one of the world's top international wine authorities – and she loves and lives for wine in all its glorious diversity. She writes daily for JancisRobinson.com and weekly for the *Financial Times*. She is founder-editor of *The Oxford Companion to Wine*, co-author with Hugh Johnson of *The World Atlas of Wine* and co-author of *Wine Grapes*, each of these books recognised as a standard reference worldwide. Jancis has been a committed and generous Room to Read ambassador for almost two decades, appearing at gala wine events all over the world. Wine has played a significant part in generating many millions.

Vintage reading

JANCIS ROBINSON

B ooks, books, books. We drown in books.

We moved three years ago from our large family home to a brand-new three-bedroom flat whose initial design included no bookshelves whatsoever (although there were four television screens). We insisted that nearly fifty metres of bookshelves were incorporated into the plans and today the first thing you see when you walk into our flat is a wall of books, illuminated by the skylight above or the light on the sole painting we have hung in a nook in the bookshelves.

It took us a year's worth of weekends to sort through our books and decide which ones would go with us to the new place and which we would take to the local charity shops. Where I live, charity shops play a massively important part in spreading literacy and knowledge. One of the things that attracted me to Room to Read back in 2003 was John Wood's proactive plan to recycle books, sending them to a remote but needy Himalayan village on a yak. Part of the way.

But once we'd unpacked our boxes of books in the new flat there remained worryingly little empty space on those shelves;

already books are piling up horizontally on top of the neat ranks of vertically stored ones. Reading is my husband Nick Lander's chief activity. I reckon he buys three or four books a week. As authors ourselves, keen to sustain those who write and sell books, we feel supportive rather than guilty about this.

The unfortunate thing in some ways is that our tastes in books vary quite substantially. Nick likes admirably heavy reading about history, biography and crime. My days are spent writing about and tasting wine and reading is what I do, chiefly and often all too briefly, before falling asleep. The last thing I want to read about is wine and I'm generally looking for uplifting, resonant or entertaining fiction. The setting of the stories I most treasure tends to be domestic, with authors such as Anne Tyler, Tessa Hadley, Lorrie Moore and Richard Yates being tried and tested examples of those who can be relied upon to provide nourishment. But some of Nick's books are irresistible to me. The only problem is that he likes to put them in the bookshelves as soon as he has finished them and there is never any rhyme or reason as to where they go.

My bedside table meanwhile groans under the weight of books that I have either managed to save from his out-tray or that are in my in-tray, awaiting a holiday, when I read voraciously and fast. I know many people who swear by Kindles for their holiday reading but, although we have twice been given them, we have never transferred our loyalties from the printed word, the thrill of scouring a good bookshop wherever in the English-speaking world it might be, and the enjoyment of a fine typeface and book design.

Much of my reading is done in the summer afternoons of the days we spend in our house in the Languedoc. One year

I went there not direct from London as usual but via a fact-finding tour of smart Bordeaux châteaux with my colleagues on the Royal Household Wine Committee. I was teased mercilessly about the extent to which my luggage rivalled a small bookshop. It was so heavy that several times I left it in the entrance halls of the châteaux rather than having to carry it up to the bedroom floor.

Our house guests during these summer weeks are invariably family and the friends we have who similarly enjoy lying by the pool reading. Some summers there are books that are so widely popular that they are passed from hand to hand as soon as one reader finishes them. The one that springs most readily to mind is *Bad Blood* by John Carreyrou, the almost incredible true tale of how a young woman who worshipped Steve Jobs managed to convince the likes of George Schultz and Henry Kissinger to invest millions in her blood test start-up without the merest shred of evidence about how or even whether it worked. Another was the true story of how the equally charismatic leader of Britain's Liberal party, Jeremy Thorpe, covered up his involvement in a plot to murder his young gay lover, *A Very English Scandal* by John Preston.

I am equivocal about sharing books. Or perhaps I should say I am regretful about it. My instinct as soon as I finish a book I have enjoyed is to want others to experience similar enjoyment, which means that I tend to give away the books I enjoy most so that it is the second-rank books that swell our shelves. As Robert Macfarlane notes in his essay, Lewis Hyde argues in his book *The Gift* that the gift economy contrasts magnificently with the market economy of property that one hoards rather than passes on. Value is supposed to accrue 'between individuals by means of giving and receiving'.

It's a fine idea but I am so neurotic about things that people lend me that I put myself, and probably them, through terrible hoops in my insistence on returning them, something that I don't think is generally reciprocated. Though I have to say that my elder daughter, with whom I share an intense love of reading and taste in books, has inherited my propensity to return. We regularly share both books and impressions of books – usually fiction such as *Florida* by Lauren Groff, Meg Wolitzer's *The Wife* and *The Interestings*, Rose Tremain's *The Gustav Sonata*, *Crow Lake* by Mary Lawson and Gary Shteyngart's *Lake Success* and *Absurdistan* (ridiculous but very funny). But we like some non-fiction too such as *Airhead*, the behind-the-scenes professional memoir of BBC news reporter Emily Maitlis, and historical recreations such as Kate Summerscale's *The Suspicions of Mr Whicher.*

The most touching example of giving books I experienced recently was when London's most famous restaurant reviewer Fay Maschler lost her beloved husband Reg Gadney. A prolific author, artist and much else besides, Reg had a collector's instinct as far as books were concerned. They shared a large house in central London and Reg's extensive study-studio was littered with books, many of them unread.

Exactly a year after he died, on the publication day for his posthumously published *Albert Einstein Speaking*, Fay gave a party to which she invited perhaps 100 friends. She described it in the emailed invitation as 'an opportunity for friends to take away some of the millions (it seems like) of books that Reg owned. Please bring a bag to take books away. A big one if you are a fan of contemporary Japanese fiction ...'

This occasion was a wonderful way to keep Reg's spirit and influence alive, and for us all to remember some of the many things that distinguished him. A great idea that deserves emulation. I was thrilled to snag a clutch of travel books by Lawrence Osborne, and another copy of Tom Rachman's first novel, *The Imperfectionists*, a book I have recommended to many a fellow journalist.

I don't mind in the least if donated or returned books are obviously read and battered. I take it as a great compliment to the book if it is reader-worn – particularly if it's one of mine, of course. At a book signing in Toronto, I was presented with a paperback copy of my professional memoir *Confessions of a Wine Lover* to sign by a young man who complained that it was all he had had to read while backpacking around Australia, as though it were my fault. There's obviously a shortage of charity shops in the outback.

I know that Room to Read's Founder John Wood and his wife Amy are great annotators of books, not least because they left three or four favourites after their stay with us in the Languedoc in summer 2019 (which I returned, natch, bearing a rather unseemly carrier bag to the subsequent London fundraising wine gala). I'm sure that annotated books will have great value in the long term, but have never felt confident that my own thoughts are worth recording. Besides, I'm probably too impatient a reader to want to slow down to write before turning the page. I should add here, however, that I absolutely love the fact that John publishes an annual list of his favourite recent reads.

So how do we decide which books to read? Recommendations from friends are surely the surest source. They know our tastes and we know theirs. I read book reviews and lists of books of the year avidly but always feel that book reviewers talk, or at least write, a little over my head. On the other hand, if I see a novel chosen by one of the populist book clubs we have in Britain, it rather puts me off, snob that I clearly am, despite the fact that they have included books that I have enjoyed.

We have some good French friends who share our love of wine, food and books (a phrase that reminds me of the interests I have listed in *Who's Who*: wine, food and words), and are much better able to read books in English than we are to savour books in French. Every time we meet – which is quite often since their children and grandchildren live in London – we swap not just recommendations but books themselves. I deeply admire their grasp of English. Marc is more a fan of thrillers than I am, but we share an appreciation of the novels of Jonathan Coe, whose work seems to reflect the current social climate in the UK as accurately and provocatively as the talented John Lanchester, whose novel *Capital* was almost as prescient as Zadie Smith's *White Teeth*.

I love the way fiction such as *White Teeth* can take the reader inside completely different cultures. Rohinton Mistry's *A Fine Balance* is a particularly compelling example and I am also really enjoying the novels of various immigrant communities in the US, such as Jhumpa Lahiri's *The Namesake* and Kathy Wang's *Family Trust*.

Another very successful source of recommendations, and the books themselves, has been Hazel Broadfoot, owner of an excellent local bookshop, Village Books of Dulwich, a prosperous area of south London. I have twice performed at the sort of events that good bookshops organise nowadays designed to sell books and provide an entertaining evening for their customers. Each time Hazel has sent me three or four books afterwards, expressly chosen to suit my tastes. Spot on. It was she who introduced me to Elizabeth Strout's unusual but intensely believable *Olive Kitteridge*, and followed up by kindly sharing with me her pre-publication copy of the equally powerful *Olive, Again* (which was also included in my children's Christmas present to me, coincidentally).

The number of good booksellers in my old stamping ground in north London shrank during my time there, jeopardised by the growing power of online bookstores. But the small Daunt Books chain, with two branches in NW3, seems to prosper, as it deserves to. Their warm, friendly shops (I'm convinced lighting is very important, as well of course as stock and staff) are open almost incredibly long hours. The one that used to be closest to our home was next to an independent cinema and was a welcome refuge before screenings. I also have fond memories of the close ties between Waterstones bookshops when they were still independent and the Oddbins chain of inventive and rather offbeat wine shops. Oddbins always supplied the wine for their author events and the ethos of the two companies, emphasising staff recommendations, was remarkably similar.

I have long seen strong parallels between a good bookshop and a good wine retailer, each of them preferably independent and able to express their own preferences and tastes. The art of selection is surely a major attribute in both cases – and in the wine world, so much more admirable and valuable than simply offering bottles that third-party palates have scored highly.

Casual but enthusiastic wine drinkers often ask me how they can learn more about wine. I should of course direct them to my website (where there is a wealth of free information) or to my books. But what I always recommend instead is that they develop a relationship with their local wine retailer. Like good bookshops, they are usually staffed by enthusiasts who like nothing more than discussing what they sell. Tell them which wines you have enjoyed, I say, and ask them to recommend other wines that they think you will like, perhaps ones that are a little out of the ordinary or better value. It is in their interest to make useful recommendations. If they don't, then move on to another shop.

This is exactly the same process as should operate in good bookshops with their well-informed staff and little handwritten notes about favourite books. Bless them for fanning the flames of literacy so much harder than Amazon could ever do.

I love the fact that so many bookshops now actively welcome young children. There are few rewards greater for a grandparent than to learn that a particular grandchild has reached the stage of devouring books, whatever they are. Our six-year-old second grandson is completely enthralled by the Dogman series. And I have lost count of the number of copies of the Ahlbergs' clever and always satisfying *Each Peach Pear Plum* I have bought in my time.

I have a particular reason to love books, of course. For over forty of the forty-four years I have been writing about wine, I have been dependent on book sales for a varying but significant proportion of my income. My first book, imaginatively called *The Wine Book*, was published in 1979.

It was followed in 1981 by *The Great Wine Book*, a wonderful excuse to visit most of the finest wine producers in the world. Since then I have written so many books that I truly have lost count. But what I am most grateful for is not the money they have earned but the global network of like-minded people they have introduced me to.

Because I am the author, editor or co-author of two, arguably three, of the most popular wine reference books, and because wine has become such a popular subject for students all over the world, I have met countless strangers who feel they have a warm relationship with me. Much of what is in these books is available only in them, so that those who read them in preparation for the wine exams that are increasingly popular around the globe are often flatteringly grateful to me for having helped them in their studies.

The London-based Wine & Spirit Education Trust is the global leader in wine education; by 2019 there were educators in seventy countries and over 100,000 students. They have almost as many students in China as in the UK, so popular has wine become among the urban Chinese. The most memorable book signing I ever did (and I have done many) was in Shanghai. My extremely efficient young Chinese business manager Young Shi, currently studying to become a Master of Wine herself, arranged things so that I sat at a table with an empty chair beside me. Each of those who lined up patiently to have a book signed was asked to hand over their smartphone to a colleague of Young's before sitting next to me. The colleague would then take a picture of the two of us as I signed a book and return the phone to the purchaser of the book. So efficacious. So Chinese.

But with one of these young women I was aware of some agitation. The minute she sat down, she flung her arms round me, gave me a smackeroo and declared breathily, 'I *love* you.' Perhaps her English was less than perfect.

I am always puzzled that people act as though it might be an imposition to ask me to sign one of my books. It is a huge honour – so much more than being asked for a selfie by someone who then walks away without comment.

Through books we really do forge human contact.

© Jancis Robinson, 2020

SF SAID

'This is what children's literature is all about. It can express the biggest ideas in forms so beautifully simple that anyone can not only grasp them, but come to live by them, because they take up residence at your very core. What an extraordinary set of gifts to give a person.'

SF Said is the award-winning author of *Varjak Paw, The Outlaw Varjak Paw* and *Phoenix*. Described by *The Sunday Times* as 'the cat's whiskers', *Varjak Paw* has been translated into fourteen languages, with worldwide sales of more than half a million copies. It has also been adapted as a stage play and an opera, and a film version is in development. SF Said was born in Lebanon but has lived in London for most of his life. In addition to writing children's books, he is also active in the wider world of literature and the arts. He is a popular speaker and has written extensively on children's and young adult literature for the *Guardian* and the *Daily Telegraph*.

The best gifts you can give

SF SAID

Children's books are the gifts I give. I give them to adults as well as children. You're never too old to read them, because children's books are really books for an audience that includes children, but excludes no one. They are books for everyone.

I give children's books for the same reason that I write them: because I think they're the most important books of all. They're the ones that make us readers in the first place. And because they come first, they shape us most profoundly, giving us ways to think about the world and our experiences of it, opening windows to other worlds, other experiences. The books we love when we're young are the ones that change our lives and stay with us forever. So I think they're the best gifts you can possibly give.

When I was a child, books were the gifts I always wanted. They showed me that the giver had thought about who I was, and what I might like. (Clothes were the gifts I hated; they seemed to be gifts for my mother, not for me.)

My very first memory is a memory of someone sharing

a book with me. I was three years old. The person was my uncle, and he was reading me *The Cat in the Hat* by Dr Seuss. I was electrified. I wanted the cat to come to my house and smash everything up! I think I knew at that moment that I would always love books and stories, because it seemed like anything was possible in them.

My uncle didn't read me *The Cat in the Hat* to teach me anything. He did it because it was fun, a kind of play that we shared together. It was a gift he gave to me freely, because he loved it as much as I did. He was an anarchic teenager at the time, so I suspect he wanted the cat to come and smash everything up as well.

But of course, *The Cat in the Hat* did teach me all sorts of things, because that is the nature of stories. It taught me that anything might be possible, but that everything had consequences, too. It taught me, in the cat's words, that 'it is fun to have fun, but you have to know how'.

I believe all stories encode values, ethics, politics, however simple they may seem, and whether their writers and readers are aware of them or not. All stories embody ideas about who we are and what it means to be alive in the world; about how we should live in it, and behave towards others; ideas about what matters, and what doesn't.

Even *The Cat in the Hat*. It didn't surprise me to learn, years later, that Dr Seuss was also a political cartoonist. He was an anti-authoritarian and anti-Fascist who really did believe in a radical idea of freedom, in which existing power structures must always be questioned; in which we must always discover who we are and how we should live anew.

'I'm subversive as hell,' Dr Seuss once told Jonathan Cott in an interview. '*The Cat in the Hat* is a revolt against authority, but it's ameliorated by the fact that the cat cleans up everything in the end. It's revolutionary in that it goes as far as Kerensky. It doesn't quite go as far as Lenin.'

Similar ideas informed another book that changed my life: *The Little Prince* by Antoine de Saint-Exupéry, translated from French into English by Katherine Woods. This was my mother's favourite book, and we read it together so many times, every night, it felt totally natural when I realised I knew what those marks on the page meant. I knew the sounds they represented, the meanings they encoded, and I could now decode them on my own.

My mum never said: 'Now I'm going to teach you how to read.' She just shared her favourite book with me, a gift she never tired of giving. And as if by osmosis, I learned the book, and through it, I learned to read, and to think.

Because like *The Cat in the Hat*, *The Little Prince* urges its readers to take nothing for granted, be open to anything, and question everything – right from its opening image, which appears to be a hat, but is in fact a boa constrictor swallowing an elephant.

Question everything. Many years later, studying politics, I came across that idea again in John Stuart Mill's classic text *On Liberty*. Mill believed that questioning everything was the essential foundation upon which liberty was built. But I already knew this. Saint-Exupéry had given me the idea in a way that I could grasp, even as a very young child, and never forget.

This is what children's literature is all about. It can express the biggest ideas in forms so beautifully simple that anyone can not only grasp them, but come to live by them, because they take up residence at your very core.

What an extraordinary set of gifts to give a person. An entertainment that empowers you, teaches you how to think, and to find out anything else you might wish to know; a skill that unlocks so many other skills.

I believe this is not just what children's literature can do, but what it is for. The great stories that human beings have handed down from generation to generation – the great myths and tales and legends whose roots might be as old as humanity itself – these stories all embody ideas about what it means to be human and alive in the world. I sometimes feel as if there is a great chain of stories that links us all through the ages. And each link in that chain is a gift received and passed on in turn.

Books can come to us as physical gifts. They can also come as gifts of time and energy, as when adults read books with children; or through the gift of recommendation, which can also change lives, as every librarian and bookseller knows.

And then there is another way of passing on the gifts of reading: by moving from reading books to writing them. All writers are really readers who take one more step, and pass on what they've received, adding something of their own along the way.

The book that began my journey from reader to writer was *Watership Down* by Richard Adams. I was now eight years old. My mother gave me a 500-page book with a picture of a rabbit on the cover. I'd never read a book that long, and growing up in London, I don't think I'd ever seen a rabbit in real life, either.

'I've just read this,' my mum told me as she handed over the enormous book. 'I think it's the best book ever. You have to read it!' She must have seen the look of panic on my face, because she immediately said, 'Don't worry, if you don't like it, you don't have to read the whole thing! But give it a go. Try page one. See what happens.'

I opened it up, started to read – and from that very first page, I really could not stop. And as I read the adventures of those rabbits, trying to survive in a dark and dangerous world, with only their wits and courage and friendship to sustain them, I thought to myself, 'My mum was right: this really is the best book ever!' And I remember thinking that one day, I wanted to write something that was even half as good. That moment – the first moment I can remember in which I imagined myself as a writer – has defined everything else that's followed.

I still have that same copy of the book. I've kept it through all the changes of my life. As one of only a few objects to survive from my childhood, it's a priceless treasure to me, though the battered back cover tells me it was originally priced at 50p.

One thing I especially loved about *Watership Down* was the fact that the rabbits' legendary ancestor, the hero of all their myths, was named El-ahrairah. The greatest rabbit of all time had an Arabic-sounding name? It's difficult to explain how deep a chord this struck for me.

My family is originally from the Muslim world. My ancestors are Iraqi, Egyptian, Kurdish, Circassian. I was born in Lebanon, lived briefly in Jordan, and then came to Britain with my mother when I was two years old, and have lived here ever since.

Back then, in the 1970s, there weren't many other Muslim kids around. My Arabic names were totally unpronounceable to English-speakers and brought me so much trouble, I eventually decided to use initials instead. There was such a gap between the world at home and the world outside. In Britain, I was seen as a foreigner, while on holiday in the Middle East, I was seen as British. I felt like I belonged nowhere.

Well, that's not quite true. There was one place where I felt at home, and that was in books. Books were always there for me. And to find a hero with an Arabic-sounding name in what was clearly the best book ever – this was astonishing. It gave me a sense that my background might not be a burden; that difference could even be something to celebrate. Surely that is one of the greatest gifts one human being can give another.

It's worth pointing out that *Watership Down* wasn't a book I encountered at school. But I engaged with it more deeply than with anything we were doing at school. To be honest, I wasn't the most attentive student. I was frankly suspicious of anything that smacked of work. And in my school, back then, schoolwork largely meant taking notes while a teacher dictated them, and then regurgitating them in a test.

But I remember one teacher who did things differently. On Friday afternoons, before we went home, a certain Mr Evans would stop everything, and just read to us. He read us ancient Greek and Roman myths. Stories of gods and goddesses, heroes and heroines, terrifying monsters. I was absolutely spellbound, and so was everyone else.

We didn't have to take notes. Mr Evans never tested us on the myths. But precisely because we weren't asked to do anything but listen, those lessons were the ones I most looked forward to, and they're the ones I will always remember. It's true that they had no measurable outcome, no quantifiable value. But not everything that has value can be quantified, and not everything that can be quantified has value. That teacher gave me a foundation course in the mythic that underlies everything I write – a gift beyond all measure.

Around the age of eleven, I decided I no longer wanted to read children's books. I didn't see myself as a child any more, and wanted to get on with being a grown-up. That meant reading grown-up literature, and trying to write it myself. This was a shame, because it meant I missed out on some of the very greatest children's authors, who I was just about ready to read: Susan Cooper, Alan Garner, Ursula Le Guin.

I was fortunate enough to find all of them and more at university. At Cambridge in the late 1980s, my friends and I had something of a second childhood. We rediscovered children's books, sharing our favourites with each other: a great torrent of gifts, treasures that we discovered in the second-hand bookshops of the town.

This was a time when children's literature was deeply unfashionable. But we began to feel it was richer, deeper and more rewarding than any grown-up literature we could find, including the kind of thing that won the Booker Prize.

Cooper's *The Dark Is Rising*, Garner's *The Owl Service* and Le Guin's *A Wizard of Earthsea* all came to me as gifts at that time. I loved them all, though *Earthsea* had perhaps the deepest impact. For in that book, I found an astonishing inversion of every fantasy story I'd ever read. The great wizards, the good guys, the point-of-view characters – their skins were all brown, or copper-red, or black. This was something I'd never seen before: a perspective shift after which everything looked different.

But all these books proved to me that children's literature could be great literature. They were stories of stunning ambition, full of unforgettable characters and worlds, powered by huge ideas and beautiful prose. They were profound and yet page-turning, making connections between ancient myth and contemporary reality, using fantastical elements to communicate deeply resonant thoughts about the real world. They contained everything I wanted a book to contain.

This, I remembered, was what I really wanted to write. Books that could be read and loved at any age. Books that would be exciting and pleasurable, but that would also have other levels, and resonate in other ways. Books for everyone.

I never thought it would be easy, but I was unprepared for just how hard it would be. My first attempt to write a book for everyone was rejected by every publisher I sent it to. Forty of them, in fact. The same thing happened with my second attempt. Another forty rejections. I was up to eighty in total now, and I will admit there were times I wanted to give up, and thought it would never happen. Far from writing books for everyone, it seemed I was writing books for no one.

I remember receiving a rejection letter in the early 1990s telling me that there was 'no longer any market for children's fantasy'. But this was my dream, the one thing I'd always wanted to do, ever since reading *Watership Down* as a child. And my belief in the form was vindicated by the new wave of children's literature that emerged as the 1990s went on.

I returned to Cambridge later in that decade, ostensibly to do a PhD, though I secretly spent most my time reading and writing children's fiction. It was here that I was given Philip Pullman's *The Subtle Knife* as a birthday present.

It was exhilarating to see a writer putting into practice all the things I believed. Pullman's books confirmed that there really were no limits to what the form could do. My excitement grew as it became apparent that his project was political, philosophical and scientific as well as literary; that it embraced everything from climate change to dark matter to the nature of consciousness; and that it had room for shamans, quantum physicists and armoured bears alike.

Pullman has done so much to validate children's literature as literature. It may be the cornerstone of our civilisation, the basis on which all adult reading is built, but you would never know this from the media. British national newspapers still give child-ren's books just 3 per cent of their book review space, though children's publishing accounts for over 30 per cent of the market.

Yet Pullman brought children's books into the cultural mainstream, making it possible for adults to take them seriously. As I read the books that followed the path he opened – books like J.K. Rowling's *Harry Potter*, Malorie Blackman's *Noughts & Crosses*, David Almond's *Skellig*, and many more that were read by adults as well as children – it became clear to me that this was where the best new writing was taking place. And that I had to keep going, whatever it took.

I tried to imagine books that combined all the qualities of the books I'd loved, right back to *The Cat in the Hat*. Books that might give other readers something of what had inspired, moved and thrilled me.

I began to write a new book, putting years and years of

work into it, draft after draft, making it as exciting and page-turning as I possibly could, but also filling it with the biggest ideas and questions that I had. And finally, after a career total of ninety rejections, the ninety-first time I sent a book out, it found a publisher.

That book was *Varjak Paw*: a story about a cat going out into the world for the first time in his life. I watched the book itself go out into the world in many ways, through bookshops and libraries, families and friends, schools and literacy organisations.

I began to be invited into schools where they were reading *Varjak Paw*, and saw the magic that happens when teachers share whole books with their classes. I met kids who'd never liked reading before, but who somehow got it with *Varjak Paw*, and now couldn't stop. Something genuinely life-changing was going on in these schools, and my book seemed to be part of it, having the kind of impact that my own favourite books had on me, an astonishing thing to see.

And visiting schools, I learned more about the gifts of reading. It turns out that the benefits of literacy go far beyond books. Research shows that kids who read for pleasure do better in almost every way than kids who don't. Indeed, reading for pleasure has the greatest impact of any factor on life chances and educational attainment, outweighing even socioeconomic background. So the gift of reading really is the best gift you can possibly give.

It's incredibly moving to hear from people who were given your book as a child and kept it, as I kept *Watership Down*, and now, as adults, are passing it on in turn. This is perhaps the most meaningful gift of all, for a writer: to see your book become a part of other people's lives, a link in that great chain.

I was lucky enough to meet Richard Adams once, and to thank him for all the gifts he'd given me. I'd just finished writing *Varjak Paw*, but was working as a journalist, and doing an article on *Watership Down*. So I reread his book, for the first time since I was eight, and was even more amazed. It seemed an even greater achievement, now I had some idea of what it must have taken. And it was stunning to see how deeply that story had shaped my imagination; how much *Varjak* owed to it.

At the end of the interview, I told him how important his work had been to me, and how I'd now written a book of my own. He said he wanted to read it, so I gave him a proof copy of *Varjak Paw*, thinking he was just being polite. But then he wrote me a letter telling me how much he'd enjoyed it; he actually used the word 'brilliant' about my book. That was the most unexpected gift I have ever received.

I always tell kids about *Watership Down* when I visit schools. And I always ask them what their favourite books are. Some of their recommendations have joined the classics I've mentioned here, taking their place in the repertoire of books I give as gifts: twenty-first-century classics like Michelle Paver's *Wolf Brother*, Andy Stanton's *Mr Gum*, Maria Turtschaninoff's *Maresi*, Alex Wheatle's *Crongton Knights*, Julie Bertagna's *Exodus*, Louise Erdrich's *The Birchbark House*, Jonathan Stroud's Bartimaeus Trilogy, Frances Hardinge's *A Skinful of Shadows* and Jacqueline Woodson's *Brown Girl Dreaming*.

I also give non-fiction books like *The Lost Words* by Robert Macfarlane and Jackie Morris, a book so many people wanted to give, it inspired a wave of crowd-funding campaigns to buy copies for schools around the country. I give picture books like Polly Dunbar's *Penguin*, and poetry like *Long Way Down* by Jason Reynolds and Chris Priestley, which I left as a gift in a family home, thinking it might appeal to a seventeen-year-old boy, only to discover it had been devoured instead by a thirteen-year-old girl.

That's the thing about gifts. Whenever and however you give them, you can never know where they'll end up. You can only give them in the hope that they will find their way to whoever needs them. You can only put back into the world what the world put into you, keeping that great chain going, and passing on the flame.

© SF Said, 2020

MADELEINE THIEN

'The reader paces back and forth between many rooms, away and back; and in so doing, perhaps we encounter a room unknown within ourselves.'

Madeleine Thien is the author of four books, including *Dogs at the Perimeter*, and a story collection, *Simple Recipes*. Her most recent novel, *Do Not Say We Have Nothing*, was shortlisted for the 2016 Booker Prize, the Women's Prize for Fiction, and The Folio Prize; and won the 2016 Scotiabank Giller Prize and the Governor-General's Literary Award for Fiction. Madeleine's books have been translated into twenty-five languages and her essays and stories have appeared in the *New York Times*, the *Guardian*, *Brick*, *frieze*, *Granta*, and elsewhere. She lives in Montreal and is a Professor of English at Brooklyn College.

Spinoza's rooms

MADELEINE THIEN

1. SPINOZA'S ROOMS

For three years, I have been sitting in Spinoza's rooms. He had several: some in Amsterdam, one in Rijnsberg, two in The Hague. The year is 1656 or 1661 or some parcel of time before his death, at the age of forty-four, in 1677. All of Spinoza's rooms are small, and only a few have a window.

He lives in one more room, too, which is only real in my imagination. This is a small room located far in the future, a century from now.

Actually I've come to think that many fictional works, especially those existing in the historical past, are set in the future, and that we writers are trying to see around the curve of time. What comes into being after we're gone? Perhaps multiple universes of our own past; or shadows cast forward from our present.

In my imagination, Spinoza lives next door. I drop by to see him nearly every morning. I pretend I'm pulling time behind me, like a long garment, until the year 2020 squeezes through the doorway of the year 1660, and even manages to escape

upstairs to the year 2300. I take a seat beside him. Spinoza, or
Bento as his neighbours call him, is meticulous and patient,
'eerily self-sufficient', and barely registers my arrival, which
suits my purposes all the better. I don't need to tell him, *Keep
doing what you're doing, Bento!* Or, *Pretend I'm not even here!*

Bento is awake early. He is a lens-grinder and the work
cannot be done by candlelight; the rising and setting sun
determine his hours.

Lens-grinding is a physical job, a mathematical job,
and also an ear-splitting job. *Bang, clank, whirr.* That's the
machine, the lathe, that was in former times called the mother
of all machines. It explodes into life the moment Bento nods
his foot against the treadle, which activates the crankshaft,
drives the flywheel and sets the spindle turning. Despite
appearances, Bento's work is highly delicate. Out of rounds
of glass he is making lenses for eyeglasses, microscopes and
telescopes. To do so, he must polish out, by lathe or by hand,
the sagittal arc which is a measure of the exactitude of glass to
be ground out in order to create an optical curve. (We know
the sagittal most intimately as the line or curve that runs over
the top of our heads, the little groove in which we can feel,
with our fingertips, the two halves of our skull.)

2. FICTIONAL TELESCOPES

Spinoza's field is geometric optics, the branch of physics
concerned with properties of light as understood through the
laws of reflection and refraction. Spinoza made lenses for both
microscopes and telescopes; he had many clients, including
Christiaan Huygens, the Dutch mathematician who was the
first to identify, in 1656, a moon of Saturn (it was a moon, and

not what Galileo called 'Saturn's ears').

A telescope is a point of view. It brings objects nearer by first using a lens to gather light, and then bringing that light, which is the image, into focus. A second lens, the eyepiece, magnifies that image across the viewer's retina. Just like that, two lenses carry Saturn's moon – nearly one billion kilometres away – right up to the eye. One billion kilometres collapsed in space and time, so that Saturn feels as near as the cup of coffee on your desk.

The greater the distance of magnification, the further we see into the past; light takes time to reach us. Our most powerful telescopes, like the Hubble, receive images of things as they were 13.2 billion years ago.

In Spinoza's time, the cellular universe came within view, increasingly fine-grained, radically complex. Meanwhile, looking up through the first telescopes – the so-called *starry tubus* – men hoped to glimpse God's patterns. The further they saw, the smaller we became. Philosophy begins with wonder and, just as powerfully, ends with wonder. Wonder is forgiving. I need not cast aside my bewilderment, or believe only one truth, or have an answer at the end, in order to sustain my wonder.

To the question, *what are we within the scope of the universe*, Spinoza's contemporaries intuited an answer that was cataclysmic for faith, religion, philosophy, politics, science, art, selfhood. 'For in the end,' writes Blaise Pascal in *Pensées* in 1670, 'what is a man as regards nature? Nothing compared to the infinite, everything compared to nothingness, a medium between nothing and the all, infinitely distant from understanding the extremes.'

Through the telescope – that series of glass lenses – we arrived at another point of view. The world changed its meaning, or to put it another way, we wondered if we might interpret it differently.

3. GOSSIP

I know a lot of things about Spinoza which he does not tell me and which come to us, thankfully, by way of gossip. Gossip: a word derived from the Old English *godsibb*, godparents.

To his friends, Spinoza was a great soul, a brilliant and generous teacher; to his detractors, he was total evil, a monstrosity, Satan himself.

Baruch Spinoza, or Espinosa, was born in Amsterdam in 1632. He is known by a trinity of names: Baruch, Bento and Benedictus, all of which mean blessed. His Portuguese Jewish family had fled the Inquisition and he grew up in the Vlooienberg, the Jewish quarter, where the painter Rembrandt van Rijn made his living. By the time Spinoza was twenty-one, he had lost his mother, brother, sister, stepmother and father to illness and he was the guardian of two surviving siblings. The following year, 1654, when he was twenty-two, the plague returned to the Netherlands, killing 17,000 in Amsterdam alone.

Bento was reading Descartes and Euclid, and studying Latin; he was running a business importing olive oil, figs, wine and sugar. When he was twenty-three, a notice appeared up and down his neighbourhood:

By decree of the angels and by the command of the holy men, we excommunicate, expel, curse and damn Baruch de

Espinoza, with the consent of God, blessed be He, and with the consent of the entire holy congregation ...

Community elders accused Bento of 'wicked ways', 'monstrous deeds' and 'abominable heresies' – without ever naming the exact crime itself. The Edict continues:

Cursed be he by day and cursed be he by night; cursed be he when he lies down and cursed be he when he rises up. Cursed be he when he goes out and cursed be he when he comes in. The Lord will not spare him, but then the anger of the Lord and his jealousy shall smite against that man, and all the curses that are written in this book shall lie upon him, and the Lord shall blot out his name from under heaven ... But you that cleave unto the Lord your God are alive every one of you this day.

If anyone came within 'four cubits' of him – about two metres – or if they read his writings, they would, like Bento, be cast out of their place 'in this world and the next'. Bento had not yet published a single word.

The elders also castigated him for being an ungrateful student. Spinoza is said to have thanked them for their teachings, and to have replied, In return, I am unexpectedly teaching you something. I am teaching you how to excommunicate someone like me, and how to remove all dissenters and freethinkers from your midst.

Biographical accounts claim that Spinoza was unbothered by these events, but I really doubt that. I think he had a poker face. Throughout his life, in all the letters that he wrote to cherished friends, and in his own later philosophical works, he never referred to this time. Not once. My personal belief is that the most painful things never meet the page.

Spinoza packed his belongings and moved into what would be the first of many transient rooms. First, he lived in the house of his Latin teacher. This was a busy place, with scores of students young and old running up and down the stairs. A high school, basically. Spinoza began teaching Latin. They say that he watered down his ale. Beer was the drink of choice, cleaner than water. And that he had three sets of clothes, no more. (Clothing was prohibitively expensive back then; an ordinary Amsterdam worker could afford to replace his coat only once every ten years.)

Perhaps teaching Latin did not suit him. He began to work, in his small room, as a lens-grinder. This involved, as we have seen, pressing a lump of glass – about the size of one's palm – against a metal dish, called a lap. The glass was ground down, first with the lathe, and then by hand, according to ever finer calculations, using ever finer abrasives. Describing this process, Christiaan Huygens wrote, 'It is best to be alone.'

All of Bento's rooms, we can imagine, are alive with dust. Glass particles that soak into his hair and garments, and scintillate in the air.

My Bento, my fictional Bento, has a cat named Brother Orange who is his stalwart companion. It is likely Spinoza never had a cat; he probably did not love animals. But one takes liberties in fiction.

4. EMPTY ROOMS

A room is the concentration of a life and perhaps, for a brief time, life's afterlife.

When my father passed away in 2017, I emptied his apartment, which consisted of two small rooms. I cleaned the apartment to make it ready for future lives. I had done something similar for my mother, nearly twenty years earlier.

At the time, there was no one to help me, and in hindsight I'm grateful. Alone, I could tell myself that my father might return at any moment. His things were here after all. His favourite chair looked so well worn. In the last week of his life, I rarely left his side. When he could still speak, and knew he was dying, he asked me to do one last thing for him – which I could not fulfil. Let me go home, he said. I want to go home.

In my father's rooms, I took comfort seeing the light wash in, wash out; hearing the shouts of the boys shooting hoops across the street; hearing the elevated train hurtling by. Sound, like light, takes a little while to reach us, and so scientists say we are 'always hearing back in time'. The mountains hovered, now blue, now purple. I heard the neighbours' doors opening and slamming. Everything continues though nothing returns.

Over many decades, living in poverty, my father became by necessity a frugal man. Later, when life was kinder, frugality became a habit. There wasn't a lot for me to pack, discard or give away – but almost everything felt valuable. My father had kept the same telephone, clock and dishes for more than forty years.

Chinese artist Sòng Dōng describes the idea of *wùjìn qíyòng* (waste not, or let all things serve their proper purpose). Here,

Sòng's mother describes the life of a piece of paper: 'You can write or draw on it. After that, you can fold it and make toys for children. Or use it as wrapping. You can use it as a tablecloth, or to clean the table. Clean the floor after you clean the table. When it gets too dirty, you can still burn it in winter. And it finally becomes ashes. And that's the end of the life of a piece of paper.' Scraps of fabric, utensils, magazines, bottles, string – they are all wù (物), which can be translated as *things*, *substance*, *creature* or *creation*. Sòng's mother told him, 'Don't waste anything. The future will not forgive you.'

In my father's rooms, surrounded by his belongings, his life seemed to continue and even to be magnified. For here I was in the private world, the one we all have, where we sit alone some nights and listen to the growing dark. Does light have a sound? I felt that it did, in those moments.

The end of our existence is the essence of our being. That was Martin Heidegger and his thinking on being-towards-death. Hannah Arendt answered him a few decades later. The essence of our being, she said, is the beginning. Men and women, Arendt writes, 'although they must die, are not born in order to die but in order to begin'.

We are sequential beings. Actions cannot be undone; life, as we experience it, cannot be reversed. The irreversibility of human life is the source of our pain and also our wonder.

5. UNDER THE ASPECT OF ETERNITY

Bento likes Euclid. He loves geometry. His magnum opus, *The Ethics*, is written in a geometrical style, constructed through definitions, propositions, and scholia. He's interested in the stuff of truth, or what he calls 'adequate facts' – a term of lovely understatement because for Bento an adequate fact is one that exists 'under the aspect of eternity', *sub specie aeternitatis*, and brings us closer to knowledge that transcends time.

But you, me and him, we all exist under the aspect of, not eternity, but time. Bento believes that we recognise ourselves as finite, as creatures who die, only because we have an intuition of timelessness. Reason aspires to something lasting but, Spinoza writes, 'sensuous existence [binds] us to the temporal and partial'. We are, he says, our desires, our *conatus*, our will. Desire is our being, and the only reason that desire can exist in us at all is because we are mortal.

One assumes that someone like Bento – grinding lenses all day, thinking over his metaphysics at supper – would crave some peace and quiet. But no. As he moved from place to place, he was consistently a renter in the homes of large families. The house where he stayed the longest, writing his ethical philosophy, contained seven small children – clattering, shouting, clomping, screaming. Roger Scruton gives a succinct summary of *The Ethics* in five questions. Five questions, he says, which felt crucial in the seventeenth century but which we, in the twenty-first, have largely evaded:

1. Why does anything exist?
2. How is the world composed?
3. What are we in the scheme of things?
4. Are we free?

Spinoza denied that we have free will, and this led to his last question:

5. How should we live?

Only to the degree in which we see ourselves and the human condition clearly, he writes, can we approach freedom by degrees.

In the background, the landlord's children are circling Spinoza's room. Three are shouting, three are crying, and one is about to throw a rock at a bird.

What is this freedom, Bento wonders. Elasticity of thought, freedom of thought without illusions.

Bento imagines beyond his small room, embracing the notion that the greater part of life exists beyond our seeing. Yet he loves this minuscule room, the temporality which gives him refuge, in which human life necessarily unfolds. It can be no other way. This world is, to borrow a phrase from Walter Benjamin, the 'theatre of all our struggles and all our ideas', no matter how fleeting we are in the billion-year tides of the universe.

Mothers, fathers, loved ones, consciousness: everything dies, Bento observes, but we feel and know that existence is eternal – and to this eternity, which stands outside of time and thus beyond our reach, he addresses his deepest and most human thinking.

6. THE NOVELIST AS ERRAND GIRL

There is no such thing, the physicists tell us, as absolute time. Time is the measure of change. If this rock existed for a million years, then three hundred years is the blink of an eye. To this rock, the years 1660 and 2020 might as well be the same moment. But only fiction allows the writer to live out this fantastical yet truthful truth. And what is this truth? Just an observation about proximity. How do we really see anyone – someone in a different century, or our own mother, father, lover or foe? What is the essential gap, the uncrossable breach, between you and me? Is it culture, language, ethnicity, faith, geography, race, experience, time?

Time is bottled up inside us, turning over and crashing like the sea.

If, as Einstein taught us, time is space and space is time, then the past exists in the next room.

Spinoza's room is not the only one I have been visiting. There are others, separated by proximity and walls, which are the thresholds we writers try to cross. The characters and I live in a building which we, together, have named the Sea. It's a massive building and it used to exist in Hong Kong. This building was demolished a decade ago.

In this no-longer existing building, nobody pays attention to my coming and going. The residents, all very busy, have no time for me, the author, the burglar of their stories. I try to move obstacles out of their way, bring tea or coffee, small sandwiches or instant noodles. I find lost keys, deliver mail. I am what I would call the errand girl or page boy or sometimes the Super of the building. I have tasked myself with carrying an idea from one time to another, from one room to the next – ideas which I hope will not dissolve or vanish.

I hang around, wondering: will I understand anything of what they do? Am I misrepresenting them at this very moment? Are they irritated by my not-getting-it? Do they trust me? How is it that I have come to love them, that they are, in strange ways, my flawed and mysterious family, my companions, my world? In the work of writing, I do not wish to let them down.

7. THE NOTARY

Spinoza died at the age of forty-four, without a family or children, loved by a small circle of friends. To pay any last rent owing, his belongings were sold at auction. A notary provides a thorough list: a bed, a small oak table, a three-legged corner table, lens-grinding equipment. One portrait in a black frame. A chessboard. A hundred and fifty books in a bookcase. A complete inventory of these books still survives.

When I visit Bento's room, I'm surrounded by these things. The bed that belonged to his parents. The glass blanks, polishing cloths, and metal laps of his trade. The volumes of Descartes and Hobbes; his books of Spanish literature. In his time, many readers purchased unbound books. Binding or gluing was often more costly than the volume itself, so many of Bento's books are loose pages that have been tied together with string.

In 1940, Nazis entered Spinoza's former room in Rijnsberg, now a museum, and seized his library. His 150 volumes were sent to Frankfurt to join three million other books plundered from across Europe. Did the man in charge of hoarding cultural treasures, Alfred Rosenberg, know that the nineteen crates of books from Rijnsberg were in fact *not* Spinoza's own? They were what we might call a simulacrum, a replica, a re-enactment. 'Spinoza's Library' consisted of the proper editions, according to the 1677 auction list, collected from across Europe.

In 1944, to protect the books from falling bombs, the Nazis moved the collection to a salt mine in the south of Germany. After the war, they were rediscovered. Imagine walking into a mine coloured by salt striations to see thousands upon thousands of crates. You break open these sacred casks. Inside are treasures beyond your wildest dreams. They are books. In the Dunhuang caves in China, also known as the Library Caves, up to 50,000 manuscripts were sealed, in darkness, for a thousand years. There were Buddhist teachings and Hebrew prayers, and all manner of literary and historical treasures. But on the reverse side, the verso of these pages, were more mundane things: receipts, accounts, recipes and letters, including one from a man apologising for getting too drunk the night before; and a letter from a woman to her husband, saying: 'I would rather be a dog's or a pig's wife than yours.' That letter was dated AD 313.

Spinoza's library travelled up to Frankfurt and finally by ship to Rijnsberg, where the books were given shelter, once more, by his small room.

8. LOYALTY

Is fiction a testimonial realm in which we stand as witnesses to our own lives? Is it the act of imagination in which we enter the lives of others? Of course literature answers these and many other callings, but for me – to enter the lives of others has been the salvation. A novelist is loyal to many rooms. Fiction is the act of imagination, and through imagination I give testimony to the complexity of living.

Or as Spinoza thought: Only to the extent to which I see myself and the human condition clearly can I approach freedom by degrees.

Spinoza's ideas made people extremely angry. He said there was no God as we had characterised him. He said there was no free will, no afterlife. Throughout Europe, his ideas elicited horror.

Spinoza answered that we are part of the fabric of time. He said there was joy, freedom and belonging – but only if we gave up our illusions, not only about God but about our egos. People thought he was mad.

He believed such truths could liberate us, not just as individuals but as communities. The end of illusions, he said, is fundamental to democracy. He argued that the main purpose of the State is to protect the freedom to love knowledge, the freedom to philosophise. He argued that only thoughts freely examined can rein in our destructive impulses and build peace. People wanted him dead.

Spinoza was a political radical, but not the kind of radical who wants to take a sledgehammer to the smallness of our rooms. He was a radical who built his philosophy on an assertion that seemed contradictory: our insignificance is the ground of our undeniable belonging.

Rebecca Goldstein says that Bento lived out secularism in a time when the idea was 'all but unthinkable', and that he 'sought to demonstrate that the truths of ethics have their source in the human condition and nowhere else ... The world has been transformed (though not enough),' she writes, 'by … Spinoza's lonely choice to think out the world for himself.'

Bento knew he could never publish *The Ethics*, his most important work, in his lifetime. To the bewilderment of many, then and now, he was moved, deeply, by equanimity. He did not want to impose laws on his fellow citizens, just allow them space to think.

9. THE END

Where are we when we think? asks Hannah Arendt. In what kind of place?

One of the oldest games in the world is called Go in Japanese and Weiqi in Chinese, which means 'the game of surrounding'. Go is a game of unlimited strategy and expression inside a limited board, much like a novel.

The complexity of the game is such that the number of possible moves exceeds the number of atoms in the observable universe. In essence, all pieces (black and white stones) are equal; they acquire strength when joined, and die when completely surrounded or, to use a Go term, when they have lost their last 'liberty'. A move made early in a game can decisively shape a conflict a hundred moves later.

Go is considered a non-chance, combinatorial game, in which all moves are visible – again like a novel, and also like our universe, which as Einstein famously said, does not play dice. Einstein also said, 'I believe in Spinoza's god.' Spinoza's god, nature, has a great deal in common with what Chinese existentialism terms 自然 (tzu-jan) or the cause of itself.

The reader paces back and forth between many rooms, away and back; and in so doing, perhaps we encounter a room unknown within ourselves. Proust imagines it as the place arrived at when *one has knocked at all the doors which lead nowhere,* [and] *stumbles without knowing it on the only door through which one can enter – which one might have sought in vain for a hundred years – and it opens.* Edith Wharton called it the holy of holies, that innermost chamber in which we are necessarily in solitude. In between these rooms we all can meet; a small room of existence where, under the aspect of time, you and I live.

© Madeleine Thien, 2020

SALLEY VICKERS

'As I reread The Blue Flower, *it reminds me again and again (I am a committed rereader) of the potent magic of reading and the privilege of writing for readers who are partners in creating these brave new realities. It is the book that I would most wish to have written myself and the one I would give as a gift to any would-be writer.'*

Salley Vickers worked as a teacher of children with special needs, a university teacher of literature and a Jungian analyst before becoming a full-time writer. Her novels include the word-of-mouth bestseller, *Miss Garnet's Angel*, and more recently the *Sunday Times* bestseller, *The Librarian*, which celebrates the vital importance of books for children and the shaping power of reading. Michael Dirda wrote in the *Washington Post*: 'Vickers is a novelist in the great English tradition of moral seriousness. Her characters suffer, they struggle to be true to both themselves and the promptings of the human heart. If you enjoy reading the work of Marilynne Robinson, Penelope Fitzgerald and James Salter, you should be reading Vickers.'

The allure of the dark

SALLEY VICKERS

Like, I imagine, many writers, I didn't really notice the process of learning to read. But I'm pretty certain what promoted this momentous event in my – in anyone's – life. Without doubt, it was being read to and read to so regularly, and with the child's need for repetition of the chosen subjects for reading, that by the time I was four I had learned whole books by heart. From this achievement it was merely a matter of matching the black squiggles on the page to the words in my ear (to this day I still *hear* what I write or read) and bingo! without any need for dreary 'Janet and John' (the plodding couple of uninspiring children who were the protagonists of the then fashionable learners' readers) I had become my own reader, with the gates to a vast never-ending kingdom open to me for all time.*

---

* I am a truly abysmal speller and for what it is worth I long ago worked out that I see the shape of a word and not the individual letters which make up its composite, which is why I still hover over the endings of certain words, for example irresistible – is it an 'i' or an 'a'? Only through the blessings of a spell-checker do I now know it is the former. This method of reading is surely not uncommon, which is why it is so monstrous to penalise children

Of the books I learned by heart, by far the best beloved, and are to this day, were Beatrix Potter's with their enchanting illustrations. When asked nowadays who my writing influences were, she tops the list for style. Her opening to *The Tale of the Flopsy Bunnies* is renowned for its patrician use of 'soporific' – an alleged effect of eating lettuce – but there are many other examples of a rich and sophisticated vocabulary, and phraseology, offered to her readers without reservation or qualm. It was that thanks to her I squirrelled away for future use 'peevish', 'improvident', 'disconsolately', 'ponderous', 'stricken', 'frugal'; these and other such delicious words were absorbed and grasped through her supremely tactful way of bedding them into a context that illuminated their meaning (a trick that I learned from her and apply myself when I find I want to use an unusual word). Perhaps even more important to my later reading and writing was the cadence of Beatrix Potter's prose. Cadence remains for me one of the hallmarks of a good writer. The part of the brain that responds to music is in a different sphere to the part that responds to language. It is an older, more fundamental part (my Alzheimer's-suffering mother continued to know the words of songs long after she could no longer coherently talk) and the musical structure of a string of words will thus have a deeper heft, be more able to resonate and chime with our physical receptors. It is of course essential that sentences should ring in the mind if one is hearing rather than reading a book (hence the crucial play of rhythm in Homer) but with reading, too, it makes for an

---

who cannot spell. Had I had the bad luck to be a schoolchild under the bad governance of Michael Gove, I would have ditched English long ago and probably never got to university to study it, or become a writer.

added aid to understanding. One of the reasons that, unlike for many, for me Henry James's complicated syntax rings clear as a bell, is that I can inwardly hear the rhythms of his finely balanced clauses.

Most – though by no means all – passionate readers begin their reading life in childhood, so of the books that I would want to give, the first would be by Beatrix Potter. While I am not a children's writer, it is children as readers who interest me most, for that is where the seed is planted. But which of her clever and subversive tales? *The Tale of Mr Tod*, her own *Emma*, for, as she puts it, she has 'made' many books about likeable characters but this is a book about two most unlikeable ones: the sly, rogue badger, Tommy Brock, and his arch enemy, the viciously combative Mr Tod (who in *The Tale of Jemima Puddleduck* appears as the seductively affable 'foxy-whiskered gentleman'); or *The Tale of Jeremy Fisher*, the frog whose fishing expedition ends in a narrow squeak with a hungry trout and who later dines on roasted grasshopper with the Alderman Ptolemy Tortoise and the nattily dressed newt, Sir Isaac Newton (another hallmark of great writers is a talent for names); or *The Tale of Samuel Whiskers*, in which naughty Tom Kitten, on the run from the washtub and a fretful mother, is captured by Samuel Whiskers, the stout and terrifying rat with chattering yellow teeth, and his lean, equally fearsome wife, Anna Maria, and swiftly smothered in pastry to make a roly-poly pudding?

Beloved as these remain to me still, my vote must go to *The Tale of Squirrel Nutkin*. The eponymous squirrel dices with death with his insouciant plaguing of Old Brown, the taciturn but dangerous tawny owl, into whose territory the squirrels come respectfully to gather their store of winter nuts. Beatrix Potter liked rebels. She was herself a rebel who evaded the stuffy female upbringing of her age by developing a scholar's fascination with the natural world through close observation and painstaking illustration. In *The Tale of Squirrel Nutkin*, while the other squirrels bring conciliatory tribute to fend off any potential aggro from Mr Brown, Nutkin taunts him with rhymes and riddles, old as the hills, and it is these ancient riddles, the answers subtly indicated with the use of an italic font in the body of the text, that gave for me the book's specially enticing flavour. There are characteristic Potter features in this tale. Many of her characters risk or have suffered death: Peter Rabbit's father, we are told, was put in a pie, *The Tale of Mr Tod* hinges on the kidnap of a litter of baby rabbits destined for Tommy Brock's cooking pot, as are the Flopsy Bunny babies for Mr McGregor's supper. The simpleton Jemima Puddleduck is similarly groomed for dinner by the foxy-whiskered gentleman. These are the common hazards of animal existence and Beatrix Potter, who late in life became a famous sheep farmer, was utterly unsentimental about the natural world. (I was fond of Alison Uttley's Little Grey Rabbit books too but even as a child I recognised that the world of Little Grey Rabbit was a milk-and-water one, while Beatrix Potter's had teeth.) Nutkin's madcap risk-taking is self-instigated: he temperamentally favours high jinks and dares, rhymes and riddles, over the more pedestrian matter of finding food. As such, he is a kind of artist, one of those liberating characters who years later I encountered in the likes of Huckleberry Finn and Holden Caulfield (two later heroes – *The Catcher in the Rye* is a book I have given in the past to angry adolescents). But for me the impudent, anti-authority Nutkin was the first of that type and therefore the most influential. So much did I identify with him that for years my father's affectionate nickname for me was 'Nutkin'.

Nutkin finally goads old Mr Brown to the point where he is snatched up in the owl's sharp talons and we see him laid out ready to be skinned alive. It looks like the end of the story, but it isn't. Nutkin escapes by losing his tail, which brings the story stylishly around because, we have been told, this is a tale about a tail. Beatrix Potter's often grim humour was another source of delight for me. More than ever today, when regulations rule and the old freedoms of childhood are increasingly trammelled and risk is so widely feared, I would want a child to lark about with Nutkin and relish, without the menace of SATs or the gloom of learning fronted adverbials, her vital, generative prose.

I was blessed as a child with a weak chest, in the days when London was still overhung with a Dickensian smog, with the happy result that large stretches of my childhood were spent off school, alone at home in bed, while my parents were at work and my only companions were the figures I met in books. And how grateful I am now that the weakness produced by chronic bronchitis, and the time that this bestowed on me, freed me from the pressures of school and afforded me a largesse and a receptivity which I miss still. (Looking back, I see that at least six of my own novels were conceived when I was laid low with chest infections.) My novel *The Librarian* arose out of a grateful recollection, in a period of post-novel depression, of a remarkable children's librarian and the many authors she introduced me to, who, in turn, I introduced to my own children and now read to my grandchildren – and this we know is how stories shape our cultural DNA. *The Librarian* celebrates the value of children's fiction, and of the many debts I owe, the debt to the authors that nourished my childhood might be the most significant. And of all the authors the marvellous Miss Blackwell introduced me to, the most important was Philippa Pearce.*

In fact, having read and loved, thanks to Miss Blackwell, Philippa Pearce's *Minnow on the Say*, I bought *Tom's Midnight Garden* for myself with a book token given to me for my tenth birthday. By this time I had become a compulsive reader, and I read it through the night under the bedclothes with my ever-handy torch. (I have wondered about that torch since, for I don't believe my parents would have much minded my reading late and I now think that there is some measure of privacy that goes hand in hand with secrecy that compulsive readers instinctively require.) I can still almost physically recollect the thrill of reading this book for the first time. It sparked my lifelong interest in the conundrum of time, and I am sure was the catalyst for my own exploration of the subject in my novels (it features as the book that lies at the heart of *The Librarian*). Many writers for both children and adults have played with time but none to my mind so successfully as Philippa Pearce.

Tom is a ten-year-old boy, sent away from home because his brother has measles. The book was written and is set in the fifties, when measles could kill or permanently maim so that quarantine was not unusual. Tom and his brother have

---

* Both my sons loved *Tom's Midnight Garden* and Tom's friend Hatty, which gives the lie to the notion that it is a 'girls' book'.

planned to make a tree house over the summer holidays, and it is this loss which makes Tom especially resentful of his banishment. He is sent to stay with a kindly but childless uncle and aunt, who are somewhat heavy handed in their nurture and sympathy. They live in a poky flat in a large Edwardian house and it is a house, they assure him regretfully, without a garden. One night, awake and suffering indigestion from the rich food his aunt has attempted to spoil him with, Tom hears the grandfather clock which stands in the downstairs hallway strike thirteen. He creeps down to investigate and seeing light coming through the backdoor opens it to find himself in a huge and wondrous garden. He is at first furious, convinced his uncle and aunt have conspired to dupe him and are wantonly concealing the garden from him, but further investigation proves that by daylight the midnight garden is only a scrappy yard. The story unfolds as he escapes nightly to the garden where he meets and befriends a girl called Hatty, who almost alone among the other occupants of the household can see him; the only other is the gardener, who views him as the Devil's work. And he has reason for this, as Tom has no corporeal substance in this world: Hatty can pass her hands through him, more easily as time lapses, and there are odd variations in her age. Time is clearly not linear in this garden and indeed reading the face of the grandfather clock Tom finds a speaking text from the Book of Revelation: 'There shall be time no longer.'

Dreams are our natural escape out of linear time and in this story Philippa Pearce does something so clever with this idea that following it still foxes my rational brain. Tom has been cautioned to be wary of the old lady who owns the house and is especially possessive of the grandfather clock, which she ritually winds each evening. She is, it is intimated, difficult and cranky. At the very end of the book, we discover that the seemingly fearsome old lady is his dear friend Hatty, who has been dreaming of her childhood; and Tom, it seems, has entered her past via the portal of her dreams so that the boy who was not yet born remains a vital and treasured part of her childhood history as she will in turn become his. (It is relevant that once she moves into adulthood he begins to fade until he no longer appears to her in time past but can only meet her in time present.) There are material proofs of his presence in her past – a time before he was even conceived – in the form of a pair of ice skates that he asks Hatty to hide under the floorboards of her nursery, which in 'real' time – or I should say current time – is now the room in which Tom is sleeping and where he indeed finds the hidden skates.

This is a story about time and how consciousness can move about within it, connecting us to a past that isn't rationally ours. It has an effect that I am tempted to call mystical because it suggests that we are not limited by the peculiar timeline on which we are born but can move through some trick of consciousness into other timelines (which is what imagination in a weaker sense also does for us). Reading this as, like Tom, a ten-year-old child it rolled back my sense of not just what we are but, in Ophelia's lovely words, 'what we may be'. Philippa Pearce doesn't explain (thank goodness) what it is that has enabled this Möbius strip which connects not only two ages but two distinct and individual consciousnesses – but it is surely relevant that the text that lies at the heart of the story comes from the Book of Revelation. A dream is a form of revelation. It reveals what has been hidden, but what must in some sense remain hidden because its proper home will always be in the dark. (In Orwell's *1984* Winston Smith dreams that O'Brien, who will torture and break him, tells him that they will meet finally in the place where there is no darkness.)

As an adult reader, I encounter dreams in novels with a sinking heart. (I exempt much of poetry and drama from this prejudice, which has something to do with their very different forms.) A dream in a novel is almost always a sign that the writer has given up or is merely taking an idle break and using a load of symbolism to do the hard work. Dreams in fiction very rarely trigger in me the necessary suspension of disbelief perhaps because that needful shroud of darkness has been torn away and the supposed dream moved into some supposedly analytic light. But for reasons I don't fully understand this prejudice of mine doesn't extend to children's fiction, certainly not this book. Perhaps it is because a child's conscious self is closer to the place we call the unconscious – which the ancients called the underworld and the Romantics sometimes liked to locate as heaven ('*But trailing clouds of glory do we come/ From God, who is our home: Heaven lies about us in our infancy!*') – that dreams seem more at home in children's stories. Not only was this book probably the source of my first novel, *Miss Garnet's Angel*, which moves back and forth in time, but I am sure it was the prompt that led to my becoming a Jungian analyst, a form of psychoanalysis which pays special respect to dreams and allows them a wisdom more generous than the Freudian view that they are a kind of emotional detritus. It is a book I would give to any ten-year-old child.

Although I have never grown out of *Tom's Midnight Garden* inevitably I grew up and found other kinds of nourishment in many other books. I must have been eleven when Jane Austen first began to show me how the seemingly parochial could be elevated by a means I have never quite fathomed, into something universal and lasting; the Brontës fed my inchoate feeling for the demonic and the powerful irrational forces that inexorably shape and disrupt our lives. George Eliot, augustly, and Trollope, with less solemnity, developed and extended my sense of the value of kindness, which is to say a felt experience of kinship with those who on the face of it seem 'other' – unattractive, alien or even downright loathsome. *Middlemarch* is one of my 'Desert Island Discs' books. Henry James, possibly my favourite of all English-speaking writers, offered a psychological acuity without any shadow of censoring judgement that was worth all the years of formal psychoanalytic training. As I write this, I am rereading for what must be the fifth time, another Desert Island book, *The Ambassadors.* Dostoevsky made me feel what it might be to have murdered, and gave me the horrors. And Anna Karenina's dreadful dream of the huddled peasant working at a piece of metal, which presages her suicide, is one of literature's few really successful dreams. But of all the 'classic' authors it is Conrad who I would probably want to give because – and this may be for political reasons – Conrad is not today as valued as he should be.

He is not only one of the finest stylists in the English language (and it was his third language after Polish and French); he is a superb psychologist and his *Lord Jim* is the great novel, along with Orwell's 1984, about betrayal. If Conrad nowadays is censored for his lapses of political correctness, he should surely be pardoned for what he does with Jim. A fine upstanding, fair-haired, blue-eyed Aryan sailor lad, Jim's slow-falling arc from grace, because of a fatal inner self-protective cowardice – hidden by his whiter than white public-school persona but hidden most disastrously from himself – is painfully charted for us by Marlow, Conrad's trusty narrator. Like, we guess, his author, Marlow loves Jim and strives to help and indeed forgive him, when, as a senior naval officer, he abandons a ship full of pilgrims to save his own skin, convinced that the ship is going down. We have had intimations which amount to warnings of this flaw in Jim's character from a minor earlier episode in his life, but this later evidence proves defining. The ship doesn't sink and Jim is called to account in a naval court of law. Still Marlow strives to help him redeem himself by finding him another role, this time in a far-flung country, where he becomes Tu'an (Lord) Jim. But the fatal weakness reasserts itself and finally destroys him and, worse, the woman with whom he has at last found love.

Girls aren't supposed to like Conrad. I was indignant when at fifteen I heard that, having just discovered and been smitten by *Lord Jim*. I went on to read his other books with equal appetite and almost equal appreciation. But *Lord Jim* is the pearl and I would give this to any girl or woman convinced that Conrad is a male writer writing for men. Like all great books, it is a book for human beings; it recognises the flickering shadow sides of our nature, mirroring them back to us so that we are no longer alone with our weakness and failings but find them reflected in the characters who are their author's sacrificial victims, acting out our follies for us, for, let us hope, our greater understanding.

There are two authors, both women, to whom I owe special debts. The first, Sylvia Townsend Warner, I was introduced to by my godmother, who also introduced me to Jane Austen. My godmother gave me Townsend Warner's first novel, *Lolly Willowes*, about a spinster who eschews a respectable middle-class town life and moves to the country to become a witch. Not a spooky witch casting malicious spells but a devotee of an unpeopled nature, a disciple of Satan, who appears as a benignly amoral country gentleman. I knew at once that this was one of 'my books'. Everyone has this category: books which may not necessarily be great literature (though in fact I believe *Lolly Willowes* comes close) but which speak to you in a language which they may often have a hand in helping you perceive is your own. I was lucky enough to meet Sylvia Townsend Warner in person when she came to interview my father for her biography of T.H. White, who had taught my father English. I told her that I had read *Lolly Willowes* and that it had inspired in me an ambition to become a witch myself. She looked at me sideways and opined that I showed promise in that direction. I was an introverted child and like Lolly Willowes, mostly preferred my own company, and the book and this tribute from its author bolstered my confidence that it was all right to be a solitary, or to go against a prevailing norm. It is a book I would give to any introvert, male or female.

My other hero is Penelope Fitzgerald. As with Beatrix Potter, it is hard to say which of her books I would pick out as a special gift, but perhaps her last great novel, *The Blue Flower*, is the strangest and most mysterious. It concerns the man who became known as 'Novalis' and the short story, 'The Blue Flower', which he began but never completed. This example of art reflecting life, but not quite – half reflecting a half-completed life, and a half-completed work, the shadow of a reflection – is what Penelope Fitzgerald might, if driven (though her diffidence and modesty concealed a personality it was hard to 'drive'), have hinted at her notion of 'reality' – a notion which has resonances with the ideas about reality of 'Novalis' himself, the man named Hardenberg in the novel of which he is the principal. Penelope Fitzgerald is a writer for whom the nature of 'real' persists as one of the most important subjects in her work. Her own style – allusive and elusive, fragmentary, drily humorous, ironic – gives the best possible clue to her shadowy apprehension of reality; or, to put it another way, her apprehension of reality's shadowy nature is reflected in her form. What does it mean to take a 'real' life and the 'real-life' story which emerged from that 'real' life – whose relation to the 'reality' of that life also poses questions – and weave all these threads into a fiction? What relation to 'reality' does that bear? And what does it tell us about the relationship between the fictional, the illusory, and the real. (I can't help, whenever I think of *The Blue Flower*, thinking alongside it of Wallace Stevens's poem 'The Man with the Blue Guitar', in which 'things as they are' are 'changed' as they are played.)

As with the man with the blue guitar, there are all manner of ways in which Fitzgerald 'plays' with the 'real'. She plays with the life of Hardenberg ('Novalis') and with his story of the Blue Flower – stealing the title and, in a sense, finishing his unfinished story without, in fact, in a masterstroke, finishing either the story of his life or his own fictional creation. She also plays with her reader, tantalising us with her echoing prose, its cessations, jokes and sudden blanks. I read her first while still working as an analyst and to my mind, of all writers, far more than, say, Virginia Woolf, Fitzgerald's writing comes closest to replicating unconscious processes – the work has the ethereal authority of a dream.

She has Hardenberg relate an odd story about a character called the Stranger. We are never told by Fitzgerald, any more than Hardenberg tells us, who this Stranger is. He arrives out of the dark and poses a question about the elusive flower both to the young man and to the listeners to the story, and also to us, the readers. Karoline, the young woman who is in love with Novalis, is the first to hear the fragment, and when asked its meaning struggles to find it and fails, remaining in the dark. In fact we are all in the dark about the meaning of the story and this, I think, is part of the point of Penelope Fitzgerald's own story – to suggest how we are all of us, much of the time, in the dark.

I love the way Fitzgerald works always in particulars (an analyst's way, which also makes me think of Blake's great aphorism, *He who would do good to another must do it in Minute Particulars*), the small telling details of life in eighteenth-century Germany, like a myriad of tiny brush strokes adding up to a vision of existence as lucid and truthful as a Rembrandt painting: a boy's red cap; a cabbage stump; a brass button; a pig's nostril. Each of these seeming insignificances has its unobtrusive emotional and psychological counterpart: the red cap – radical rebelliousness of the recalcitrant young brother of Hardenberg 'the Bernhard'; the cabbage stump – the blighted and fundamentally unnourishing nature of Fritz's bizarre love choice, the apparently dim and foolish Sophie; the brass buttons – the bright ordinary sexual curiosity of George, Sophie's brother, who climbs a ladder hoping to catch in bed with a maid a flummoxed portrait painter, who, in despair at catching a likeness of his subject has withdrawn to his room; the pig's nose – the life of lonely spinsterhood for Karoline, the woman whose empathy and intelligence by rights should have drawn Hardenberg's heart in place of the vacuous, yet weirdly compelling, Sophie. But there are no 'by rights' in a Penelope Fitzgerald novel – of all contemporary novelists she best understood the unpredictable, wayward creativeness of the human heart.

There's a funny and poignant example of this in *The Blue Flower* which is a central feature of the relationship between Karoline and Hardenberg. As we the readers know, she is in love with him – and he, manifesting one of the many blanks that the book adumbrates, is obdurately insensitive to this, and when he comes to advise her of his engagement to the young girl, Sophie, suggests that she doesn't grasp the nature of desire between a man and a woman. Stung into a kind of semi-revelation, Karoline retorts that not everyone is lucky enough to be able to show their feelings but that some are obliged to suffer their love in silence. The remark of course refers to her own feelings for Hardenberg – which incidentally are never actually named; how then are we so sure of them? is another interesting question – but he radically, comically, misconstrues with an immediate belief in an alternative lover for Karoline, whom he then celebrates in a poem.

SALLEY VICKERS

We are specifically told that it is Karoline's wounded love for Hardenberg that has brought forth the mythical lover – and what is both funny and painful is that this defensive creation, Karoline's 'lover', has now become a treble fixture – he exists in the mind of Hardenberg but also in his verse – and out of this misconception he becomes a genuine prop for Karoline's pride. The unreal has been bodied forth by the future Novalis's energetic and protean imagination and then given objectivity in his art. So one has to ask what kind of reality has it become? Is it so different, the novel implicitly asks, from his passion for the childlike Sophie? Does love, in fact, require an object at all – worthy or otherwise? Or is the fact of love in itself enough?

Indeed, it is Sophie's very blankness, her almost non-identity, which summons forth the extraordinary love which Hardenberg feels for her, though in human terms Karoline is clearly much more a match for him – an equal, a companion. She covers her face with her hands and cries, when Hardenberg's brother comes to see her to discuss what they both feel must be a foolish infatuation. 'How could he? How could he?' But it is precisely Sophie's nothingness, her mind empty as a new jug, which is the existential allure.

At one point Hardenberg suggests that what is astonishing is not that miracles make people believe – it is the belief that is the miracle; and this is a novel that, with the very lightest of touches, illumines the extraordinary power of belief, which is the cousin of faith (Fitzgerald remained a believer, if a discreet one, throughout her life and her works have about them a delicate veil of the numinous). The story, or fragment, 'The Blue Flower', is told twice over, and this in itself is suggestive. The original tale is reflected in the narrative of the novel, which itself twice redacts the partial tale. Just as 'A rose is a rose is a rose' alters the nature of 'rose-ness', so the blue flower evolves and grows in our minds through repeated tellings. At one point, Hardenberg tells Karoline that what he has written will not truly exist till she has heard it. This observation has numerous psychological as well as philosophical resonances: it suggests the child whose existence, at some deep level, is not validated until the parental beam of affection brings it to life. The blue flower blooms only at the place of communion, requiring always the delicate conjunction of two to bring forth a third entity. A creation has no meaning until it is perceived, in the way that often a person's self has no meaning for them until they feel they have been perceived. It is the theme of 'The Ancient Mariner': the mariner's experience demands that the Wedding Guest bear witness to it before it becomes in some sense real. I think the importance of this strange book for me has become its infinitely subtle understanding of how writer and reader, writer and listener together may join in creating a third reality; and I am sure it was in the hinterland of my mind as I wrote *The Other Side of You*, a novel in which I explore this theme. As I reread *The Blue Flower*, it reminds me again and again (I am a committed rereader) of the potent magic of reading and the privilege of writing for readers who are partners in creating these brave new realities. It is the book that I would most wish to have written myself and the one I would give as a gift to any would-be writer.

© Salley Vickers, 2020

JOHN WOOD

'The only thing I can think of that is better than giving a book to a friend is to give millions of them — all brightly-coloured and in their mother tongue — to kids who would otherwise not have the opportunity to learn the joy of reading.'

John Wood is the Founder of Room to Read, one of the fastest-growing social enterprises in world history that has brought the lifelong gift of education to nearly twenty million children in sixteen countries across the developing world. John has published five books, including the bestselling *Leaving Microsoft to Change the World*, which was chosen by Amazon as one of the Top Ten Business Books of 2006. Goldman Sachs named him one of the World's 100 Most Intriguing Entrepreneurs and he was awarded Microsoft's Alumnus of the Year by Bill and Melinda Gates. He is a Henry Crown Fellow at the Aspen Institute and was named a Young Global Leader by the World Economic Forum. John is a frequent contributor to the BBC and CNBC.

A challenge, and an invitation

JOHN WOOD

It was a new tradition between old friends, made necessary by the second straight day of cold rain and fog in Amsterdam. Twenty-five years later it still continues.

This was not just any friend, but my best mate from university years. Eric and I had met the first week of our freshman year in Boulder and bonded over the usual student activities – partying, skiing, frisbee, and only if necessary an occasional joint visit to the library. By sophomore year we were planning our class schedules together; by junior year we were roommates, co-parenting a not-very-bright golden retriever named Jake. It was a symbiotic friendship where I pushed us towards academic excellence while he plotted the extracurricular strategy that would help us make a success of our careers. His theory was that we needed to think 'beyond university' to learn the adult skills that would propel us into a future in which we became respected business leaders.

'Like classical music. That's what sophisticated people listen to,' he opined over the roar of the Ramones. Soon Johnny, Joey and Dee Dee were replaced by Handel's Water Music and

Beethoven's 5th. 'And Scotch. We need to learn how to drink Scotch so that if a job interview dinner leads to a nightcap invitation, we can drink something more urbane than beer.' It all sounded good to me – if drinking Scotch would prepare me for success in life, then the next round would be on me. And to continue our jointly mandated self-improvement project, we of course subscribed to *The Economist*.

Eric also decided that we needed to explore beyond our business school textbooks and dive into world history, politics, biography and memoir. We'd ask professors for recommendations and be told, 'If you want to understand the First World War, start with Barbara Tuchman's *The Guns of August*, and 'If you read Frances FitzGerald's *Fire in the Lake*, you can learn why the American war in Vietnam was doomed from the beginning.' I'm certain that during our post-graduation summer of train journeys across Europe, we must have looked quite pretentious reading these tomes, but our intentions were pure. We simply wanted to know how the world worked, in the hope that this knowledge would help us to find our way in it.

We were never again to live in the same city. Graduate school and his consulting career took Eric to Paris and New York, while I was in Chicago and later Seattle. We'd constantly compare our travel calendars in search of potential overlap, resulting in long chatty dinners in cities ranging from Osaka to Seoul to London. It was during a weekend meet-up in Amsterdam that the new tradition was born. The American Book Center – independent, opinionated and cavernous – seemed a great place to wait out the afternoon rain. As we entered, I proposed a novel idea.

'Rather than both of us spending the next hour searching for books for ourselves, let's instead take a small risk and shop for each other. Your mission is to leave here with two or three books you think I should read. I will do the same for you. The only rules are that we can't watch each other, talk or give editorial feedback ("Hey, that book's way too long and complex for me"). And we can't choose books that are "obvious" or that are well-known bestsellers, because what would be the point in that? How about we meet in an hour at the coffee shop across the street and exchange our new treasures?'

With an effusive nod, he responded, 'See you in an hour, pal.'

Eric is already seated when I enter. The smell of coffee is strong and of clove cigarettes stronger. He's arranged the spines of my new books so as to disguise the titles, then suggested that he do the first 'reveal'. I had loved *Bonfire of the Vanities* but had not yet read Tom Wolfe's *The Right Stuff*, which he effusively called one of the best works of non-fiction he'd ever read ('These guys are total stud cowboys!'). Next up was *City of Joy*, written by a formidable writing team – Dominique Lapierre and Larry Collins – he admired and I had never heard of. 'This takes place in the slums of Calcutta, and while you expect it to be depressing, there is so much more to it than that.'

Eric was running late for the train back to Paris. As I walked with him to Amsterdam Central, we agreed: 'Next city, wherever it is, we do this again.'

* * *

One of those opportunities arrived sooner than expected. He'd recently married and proposed to visit me in Seattle with his bride. Over calamari, pasta and Chianti on their first night, Carol, Eric and I talked about their lives as graduate students in Paris, my career developments within Microsoft as the company went through explosive growth, and all the travel adventures we were plotting. Towards the end of the meal, while Carol was in the bathroom, I floated a trial balloon: 'So, what do you think, do we let her into the club?'

The next morning, once again ducking the rain, we walked into Elliott Bay Book Company – Seattle's inspiring Mecca to the written word. Carol had eagerly accepted our invitation and we became the old curmudgeons explaining the rules of our club: 'Nothing obvious please, and avoid the bestseller tables. We each have one hour to buy a book for the other two.'

Afterwards we reconvened in Elliott Bay's busy coffee shop, competing for a table against over-water-logged bookworms. Because Carol had recently finished her MBA and was embarking on her business career, I had chosen Katharine Graham's *Personal History*. What better example could you have of a woman who would not accept yesterday's limits on what women could achieve in business?

Now it was Carol's turn. She excitedly presented me with *China Wakes: The Struggle for the Soul of a Rising Power*. Written by two *New York Times* journalists – Nick Kristof and Sheryl WuDunn – the book chronicled the five years they'd spent living and travelling in China. They were the first husband–wife team to jointly win the Pulitzer Prize, and through this book I would soon discover why.

Carol shared that one of her hopes for me was that I'd use my time at Microsoft as a way to see the world. I had admitted that while I loved my work at the company, I found Seattle to be gloomy (once clouds move in, they never seem to move on), insular and a tad self-satisfied. She and Rick had lived in both Japan and France, and during that time I'd been homebound in the US. 'Maybe someday that growing company you work for will need you in China?' she suggested with a mischievous and encouraging smile.

* * *

Our joint bookstore excursions were about so much more than just the books. It was partly the thought that went into an hour spent selecting *that one perfect read*, but even more so the signals sent by each selection. Each title chosen could express a dream for our dear friend, fire their creativity or push them to expand their horizons. It could be an invitation. Or a dare.

And, of course, it could be a portal to a new world that would shape our lives in ways we could not have predicted. *City of Joy* had deeply touched me with its descriptions of poverty and the sense of endemic hopelessness across such a wide swathe of India. So is it any wonder that shortly after we founded Room to Read we committed to making India – a country that has 35 per cent of the world's illiterate people – our largest country of operations? After reading *China Wakes*, I devoured any book on modern Chinese history that came into my orbit, and since leaving Seattle I've lived for seven of those years in Beijing and Hong Kong. The lessons learned from *Fire in the Lake* were integral to my decision to make not just Vietnam, but also Cambodia and Laos, a major focus of my post-Microsoft life, because you can't fully rebuild civil society if young people are not learning to read.

Books played such a role in shaping my adult life. Little did I know that one day they would play a role in finding my bride.

* * *

Amy walked into my life shortly after she read my first book, *Leaving Microsoft to Change the World* (yes, I admit in retrospect it was a grandiose title). I had published this 'early down-payment on a memoir' just six years after we founded Room to Read. It was my attempt to nail my proclamation to the church door, to declare that our humble little organisation was going to change the future for millions of children across the poorest parts of the world through the power of education. I invited readers to view us as an 'open source movement' that they could immediately join.

Fortunately, Amy was one reader who took me up on the offer.

I met her at the first Room to Read fundraising event hosted by the Los Angeles chapter that she had co-founded. It was – and I hope this will always be a trivia question in the history of Room to Read – the night that Michael Jackson died. LA being LA, this caused *epic* traffic jams even worse than the usual world-class standard. 'What kind of city is this?' I joked. 'Your response to a celebrity death is to clog the freeways?' 'What?' she replied. 'You don't want to run to Cedars-Sinai Hospital with flowers and a teddy bear?'

Not that I minded the delayed start – there were worse

fates in life than talking to a young woman who was beautiful, well-educated, tall and athletic – all combined with a fifty-megawatt smile and killer sense of humour. Over a post-event nightcap, I learned that one of her hobbies was 'going to the beach alone on the weekends to catch up on back issues of the *New Yorker*'. Amazing, I thought as I flew home the next morning – I have met a beautiful nerd. And she might even be into me.

Several weeks later, an invitation to visit gorgeous Manhattan Beach ('Do I have to bring my own back issues?'). Upon arrival at her apartment, the first thing I noticed was the well-stocked bookshelves. One particular title – electric yellow letters against the spine's blue background – immediately caught my eye.

'I so loved *Any Human Heart*.' This was my opening ante.

'I did too. If I ever have a son, I am going to name him after the Logan character.'

'William Boyd was actually at our last Room to Read event in London. I got to hang out with him.'

'Are you always so eager to namedrop, or is tonight just an exception because you're trying to impress me?' Her eyes, as they do to this day, shining with light as she poked gentle fun at me.

We did not just *talk* books – we were soon also exchanging them. If you're as old as I am, you'll likely remember mix tapes – those cassettes we'd make, early in a relationship, to make a statement to our potential mate about the kind of music we liked. I decided to do something similar with books. What did I want to tell Amy, even if only indirectly, and could a book help to share those messages?

JOHN WOOD

One bookstore visit later, I presented Amy with *Mountains Beyond Mountains: The Quest of Dr Paul Farmer, a Man Who Would Cure the World*. Tracy Kidder had written this biography of an idealistic young man who, on his first trip to Haiti, was in shock that a nation just 100 miles offshore from the richest nation on earth could have a healthcare system that resembled that of a war-torn African backwater. He refused to accept that in our modern world people could have a life expectancy of only fifty-seven years.

Fortunately for Haiti, Farmer did not let the inconvenient fact that he was just embarking upon medical school (at Harvard, no less) prevent him from starting a new NGO. Getting Partners in Health off the ground was such a Herculean task that his fellow medical students often referred to him (not always kindly) as Paul Foreigner. He'd walk for hours in 100-degree heat and a bazillion per cent humidity to visit a single patient. He was as focused as a dog with a chew toy, even when it meant not showing up for class, or having to justify long absences and missed holidays to friends and family.

This book was clearly the perfect conduit for my 'Buyer Beware' message to Amy. It would send the signal that life with me, should we work out, would be far from predictable. That I would continue to travel extensively, and that she'd suddenly hear from me from a remote corner of the earth – a school-opening ceremony in rural Cambodia, a girl scholar graduation in Zambia, or while dashing off to a fundraising event in New York, Tokyo or Zürich.

And just to leave nothing to chance, I also put a copy in her mother's Christmas stocking.

In retrospect, I realise that I was sending a signal not about absence, but inclusion. I deeply hoped that we would work out, and that one day I'd no longer be flying off alone on these peripatetic adventures. As she read *Mountains Beyond Mountains*, would the prospect of a life like this attract or repel her?

* * *

Attract – thankfully, she chose the right answer! We were soon adjusting our lives to allow us to each tag along on the other's business trips, ranging from Portland to Portugal, Jo'burg to Jakarta. As we prepped for each trip, one of the best parts was deciding on 'the book stack' and researching the best bookstores in each destination.

I realised we had become an item when the first question asked by old friends was 'Why is Amy not here?' This came up one night in London over dinner with our friends Maura and Guy. Maura and I were following the age-old rule of always letting the Frenchman choose the wine, so as Guy talked to the sommelier Maura dove right in. 'I reread one of my favourite poems this weekend and it reminded me of you and Amy. Have you read Whitman's "Song of the Open Road"?'

I admitted the truth – that I was a small-town boy who had never been a big fan of poetry. That did not stop her from pulling out a sheet from her purse and reciting:

> *Afoot and light-hearted I take to the open road,*
> *Healthy, free, the world before me,*
> *The long brown path before me leading wherever I choose . . .*

> *Allons! Whoever you are come travel with me!*
> *Traveling with me, you find what never tires.*
>
> *The earth never tires,*
> *The earth is rude, silent, incomprehensible at first, Nature*
> *   is rude and incomprehensible at first,*
> *Be not discouraged, keep on, there are divine things well*
> *   envelop'd,*
> *I swear to you there are divine things more beautiful than*
> *   words can tell.*
>
> *Allons! we must not stop here,*
> *However sweet these laid-up stores, however convenient*
> *   this dwelling we cannot remain here,*
> *However shelter'd this port and however calm these waters*
> *   we must not anchor here,*
> *However welcome the hospitality that surrounds us we are*
> *   permitted to receive it but a little while.*

And then, the opera's final act, which had me in tears then, and still has that effect as I write this.

> *Camerado, I give you my hand!*
> *I give you my love more precious than money,*
> *I give you myself before preaching or law;*
> *Will you give me yourself? will you come travel with me?*
> *Shall we stick by each other as long as we live?*

I raised the first pour of Burgundy and toasted my dear friends. 'I'm sure this was not your intent. But, thank you. I'm going to ask Amy to marry me.'

* * *

Now I just needed a strategy. On the flight home, somewhere over Greenland, it hit me. My strategy would involve a book.

How could it not? Books had played such an important role in our relationship. We'd visit bookstores in almost every city we travelled to – Daunt Books in Marylebone. Powell's in Portland. Littered with Books in Singapore's hip Duxton Hill neighbourhood. We would travel to buy books, and the books we read would encourage us to travel more. One of the first books Amy ever bought for me was Robert Macfarlane's *The Old Ways* – a book guaranteed to ignite the fires of wanderlust. On a deserted beach in remote West Bali, we decided that Julian Barnes's *The Sense of an Ending* was the perfect length for a novel. We laughed at the absurdities in Murakami's *A Wild Sheep Chase* while trekking in China's Yunnan Province. On our sofa in New York, in front of a roaring fire we passed George Saunders's *Tenth of December* back and forth. On a Utah hiking holiday, we cried serious buckets of tears reading the final pages of Anthony Marra's *A Constellation of Vital Phenomena*.

When books had played such an important role in the development of our relationship, how could I not find a way to include one in the most important declaration of my life?

Back in New York I visited Utrecht Art Supplies and spent fifteen minutes choosing one of the perfect hard-bound artists' sketchbooks full of beautiful blank pages. Plus a dozen brightly coloured markers. Back home they were hidden beneath the sofa, destined to reappear shortly after my bride-to-be had dozed off and as I prepared for a late night of writing.

Making a comfortable nest in front of the fireplace, I counted the number of pages. Seventy-eight.

And so, in freehand, I started by sketching the book's title on the front cover:

The 78 Reasons We Should Be Together Forever

* * *

As Amy and I travelled and enjoyed hospitality from friends around the world, we initiated a system of sending books as a small token of gratitude. The book I've given most often in the last five years is the German novel *One Clear Ice-Cold January Morning at the Beginning of the Twenty-First Century.* Written by the delightfully named German playwright Roland Schimmelpfennig, this book would win gold if there was an Olympic category for 'the best novel you did not know existed'. From the moment I read the review in the *FT Weekend,* it was clear to me that this book had to find its way into my eager hands.

I don't want to give anything away, so let's just say the protagonist is a wolf, photographed on a snowbank right below a sign that reads *Berlin – 60 km.* Social media goes crazy – '*Was ist es?* What does it mean?' – and characters are introduced as their paths cross with that of the wolf. This was a journey I most certainly did not want to miss. Despite the long title, it promised to be a taut novel – all muscle, no fat, and in perpetual motion.

Short of buying everyone in my life a copy, how best to share books like this more widely? Amy suggested that I set up a system to publish my recommendations, and thus was born my annual John Wood's Top Ten Reads list. It's published each Christmas and circulated to my email contact list. Some friends lobby me for a sneak preview in order to help with their Christmas shopping, so in 2019 I also began publishing my annual Holiday Book Gift Guide.

What results is a very fun quid pro quo – more frequent contact with friends. People I rarely hear from otherwise send their comments. 'You were right – the revenge scene in Salter's *All that Is* is one of the best I've ever read in a novel' and 'Had to laugh at your description of *The Sellout* as the most overrated book of the year.'

The best response was from the world's most popular wine writer, Jancis Robinson. She had responded to my euphoric praise and 'Book of the Year' award for Julian Barnes's *The Noise of Time* by inviting me to meet 'my old Oxford friend' over dinner in her home. Once again, the 'gift' was coming back to me.

All this correspondence may not have been as cosy as a conversation in an Amsterdam coffee shop, but during a time in life when our friends are scattered around the globe, it comes a close second.

* * *

Five years after our wedding (at which, yes, Maura did a reading of 'Song of the Open Road'), we decided it was time for a second honeymoon. Amy had recently left a job after five demanding years so we planned five weeks that would take us to Corsica, Slovenia, northern Italy and southern France. As always, we eagerly dove into book shopping before we'd even booked our flights.

Fortunately for me, Eric and Amy had always gotten along well (he was even co-MC at our wedding), and it was rare for us not to get together several times a year. This trip would be no exception, as Amy suggested to Eric that he come down from Paris to join us for a few days of hiking in the French Alps. As the day grew closer and logistical emails were exchanged, we asked for his help. 'It's the tail end of our trip, and we're low on books. We're super rural, so can you hit a bookstore in Paris before you come down?'

Over SMS, he asked us to send him a list. We thought about it for a day, then replied: 'Hey, here's an idea. Let's go back to the old way of doing things. Rather than us telling you what we want, why don't you wander around Shakespeare & Co. and pick a few things out for us.'

Two days later we greeted his arrival at the tiny train station of Bourg-Saint-Maurice. His bags were weighed down with Champagne and Burgundy he'd liberated from his capacious cellar – he'd already made a side deal with Amy that if she played chef, he'd be our personal sommelier.

And also our Book Santa. Over dinner that night he shared how excited he'd been when we'd responded negatively to his inquiry 'Have you read much by Stefan Zweig?' As he poured the first of what would inevitably be several glasses, he said, 'It feels like a gift to be able to introduce you to him.'

He first presented Zweig's *The World of Yesterday*, a love poem to the Europe where he enjoyed his formative years prior to the Second World War. It had been published in 1941, shortly before he and his wife Charlotte committed suicide together, as exiles in Brazil, in 1942.

Every day I learned to love this country more, and I would not have asked to rebuild my life in any other place after the world of my own language sank and was lost to me and my spiritual homeland, Europe, destroyed itself.

But to start everything anew after a man's 60th year requires special powers, and my own power has been expended after years of wandering homeless. I thus prefer to end my life at the right time, upright, as a man for whom cultural work has always been his purest happiness and personal freedom – the most precious of possessions on this earth.

We paused, staring into the inky centre of our wine glasses. Contemplating what challenges we would all face as we grew older, and whether we'd be there for each other.

This would not be the only Stefan Zweig book in our lives. Perhaps as a subtle reminder that I had not read enough French history – or maybe because he knew Amy was a fellow Francophile, he also gifted us Zweig's biography (all 600 pages of it!) of Marie Antoinette. Later that summer, I'd purchase *Journeys*, a highly readable collection of his memories of train travel across Europe between the world wars.

Over the following days amidst snow fields high above the village of Val d'Isère, we enjoyed long hikes and leisurely lunches. We discussed books, travel, our careers, France's yellow-vest movement and American politics. While Amy cooked each night we joined her in the kitchen to discuss Eric's impending second marriage. The ceremony would take place in Paris in two short months. He asked me to be 'chief witness' and Amy promised that she'd teach me enough French that some of my toast could be in the mother tongue of his bride.

We were eager to spend time with Alexandra. We also

wanted to invite her into this really cool club we've always enjoyed. Alas, her priorities for the wedding weekend did not include hanging out with us in bookstores. But this did not stop us from our own shopping trip. Their wedding gift not only included *One Clear Ice-Cold January Morning*, but also Ann Patchett's *This is the Story of a Happy Marriage*.

© John Wood, 2020

MARKUS ZUSAK

'Maybe books are both everything and part of something.'

Markus Zusak is the internationally bestselling author of six novels, including *The Book Thief*, *Bridge of Clay* and *I am the Messenger*. His books are translated into more than forty languages, and have spent more than a decade on the *New York Times* bestseller list. They have also been adapted into films, plays and musicals throughout the world. He lives in Sydney with his wife, two children, and a constant raft of animals.

The will of stories

MARKUS ZUSAK

There's something that happens all the time round here:
A boy asleep on a book.

My son is nine years old, and he's always been our reader.

To be honest, my first version of this story was submitted with actual photos of him reading (in bed, in the bath, in the car, on the subway in New York, and so on)... But that's the thing – I didn't realise most anthologies don't allow for illustrations, or visuals. I just wish you could have seen him! Never mind how lovely, easy and beautiful kids are when they're asleep – it's even better when they've collapsed on a book.

Having taught English, History, and almost every other subject a casual / substitute / fill-in is required to teach in high school, I don't really dread the teenage version of my son. When you've walked down chaotic high school corridors, you soon discover the sudden *hairiness* of them, and the compost smell of *exponential growth*. But you also learn that you *will* get the odd hello, or a calling-out. Sometimes you'll even get a smile, a joke, or both.

For now, though, my son remains my nine-year-old – part feral, part innocent, full reader.

When he reads, you see him glow.

Usually, when I find him asleep, he's on, or under, a book.

I photograph it every time.

Another thing I wish you could have been there for:

It's the countless nights of reading – and you know those nights when you're chanting to yourself: 'Please, anything but _____' [*insert book title*] … because you've read it at least a thousand times. (And no, that is *not* an exaggeration.)

Of course, they're still books we love, but after work, dogs, kids, kids' arguments, laughter, more kids' arguments, the sheer *barbarism* of dinner, then scrubbing a rug out in the garage after it's been desecrated by a pair of thuggish cats (we all know that *never* comes out), the thought of one more rendition of _____ [*insert book title*] can be the straw that breaks the camel's back.

If you're really lucky, at some point your son or daughter might even whisper something to you, right when you think you've finally nailed it…You've exclaimed an exclamation so perfectly at the critical part of the story – and then comes the delicate, kid-fingered tug on your sleeve. In my case, as I finally pulled off the full-throated portent of another road spillage – the pure *disaster* in a particular book – my son pulled at my wrist and said, 'Hey, um, Dad…' Such a quiet working-up of courage. 'I don't really like it when you do that…'

What can you do but laugh a giant laughter?

Then hug the kid, and say, 'I'm sorry!'

We laugh about it to this day, and it's a favourite family story.

Which brings us to a bathroom scene.

Do you have any idea how many books there are in our bathroom?

It's ridiculous.

And don't get me started on how many have been *dropped* in the bath, and in some cases, *returned* to the bookshelf. In one of the myriad photos of my son reading, there's a healthy ground coverage of books on the bathroom floor. It's a leaf litter of titles and words.

On nights when that bath stretches on and on, we end up shouting down the hallway.

'Hey, Noah, are you finished in that bath yet?!'

No answer.

'Noah? *Are you finished in that bath*?!'

Finally, a reply. 'I'll get out at the end of this chapter!'

Pure bullshit.

He has no intention of getting out. At all.

We could kill him every time.

As for the photo I have of my son reading on the subway in New York?

He's reading the subway magazine, abandoned by someone at Penn Station.

In the photo he is utterly engrossed.

Next to him sits his sister, equally, utterly frustrated.

(I think I'm getting that one framed.)

In the end, what does it all mean?

Why take you on a small tour of a boy in the act of reading?

Why write about it?

I remember my dad staying a few nights with us, back when my daughter was five and my son had just turned one. When he saw me reading to them on the couch, my dad said, 'Geez, you're a better father than I ever was. I never read to you – not even once.'

I said, 'But look, Dad – I turned out to be a writer.'

It got me thinking all those tumultuous thoughts, like, 'Maybe if my dad *had* read to me, I wouldn't have become a writer at all...' But then again: 'Maybe if he had, I'd be a *better* writer.' Also, on top of that, what both my parents did was *tell* me stories, of their lives and childhoods, in Germany and Austria – and those stories were stepping stones to *The Book Thief.* Sometimes I'll tell people that my parents had no idea when they were telling me those stories that they were actually teaching me how to write...

So maybe my point has shifted.

Maybe it's that books are both *everything* and *part of something*.

My mum grew up in a house with not a single book in it.

Not one.

And she's the greatest storyteller I know.

When she came to Australia, unable to speak English, she vowed that she would live in a household of books, so that her kids wouldn't feel how she had felt.

As the last of her four children, I was never thought of as gifted.

No one ever singled me out as a talented writer.

My own children aren't gifted either, nor considered anything but pretty smart, happy and bright. I've talked more about my son in this piece, mainly because he's the one we find under blankets of pages and books – but my daughter could be the outlier, who finds exactly the right book, at exactly the right time.

Speaking of which, at the time of writing – 2019 – it's been one of the tougher years.

We lost family and friends we loved and looked up to this year.

We lost a beautiful, wild, intelligent dog.

We saw a tough year for the planet, too, and our country, culminating in some of the worst bushfires in living memory.

But even when I'm wrapped up in all of that, I can still have a girl telling stories at a table – reminiscent of my parents and their instinct for perfect timing.

Then later I'll find a boy in bed – asleep on, or covered by, a book.

Talk about the will of stories.

And talk about the gifts of reading.

No matter how hard a day has been, or how deep the troubles of the world.

Night for night, they give me *them*.

© Markus Zusak, 2020

THE
GIFTS

෴

Robert Macfarlane believes that books 'possess an exceptional power to transform, to heal and to inspire'. In the essay which inspired this anthology, he shares the names of the five books he most often gives as gifts, and we have invited all of our contributors to do the same.

ROBERT MACFARLANE

Cormac McCarthy, *Blood Meridian*
Vladimir Nabokov, *Lolita*
Patrick Leigh Fermor, *A Time of Gifts*
J.A. Baker, *The Peregrine*
Nan Shepherd, *The Living Mountain*

WILLIAM BOYD

Anton Chekhov, *The Complete Short Novels*
Vladimir Nabokov, *Pale Fire*
Muriel Spark, *A Far Cry from Kensington*
Charles Dickens, *Our Mutual Friend*
Elizabeth Bishop, *The Complete Poems*

CANDICE CARTY-WILLIAMS

Courttia Newland, *The Scholar*
Nicole Dennis-Benn, *Here Comes the Sun*
Anna Jones, *A Modern Way to Eat*
Kei Miller, *Augustown*
Claudia Rankine, *Citizen*

IMTIAZ DHARKER

William Blake, *Songs of Innocence and of Experience*
Angela Carter's Book of Fairy Tales
Naguib Mahfouz, *Arabian Nights and Days*
Marina Warner, *Stranger Magic: Charmed States & the Arabian Nights*
Most often Carol Ann Duffy's *Rapture*, but the gifts of poetry can change from day to day

RODDY DOYLE

Geoff Dyer, *'Broadsword Calling Danny Boy'*
James Baldwin, *I Am Not Your Negro*
Isabel Colegate, *The Shooting Party*
Richmal Crompton, *Just William*
E.L. Doctorow, *Ragtime*

PICO IYER

Graham Greene, *The Quiet American*
Zadie Smith, *Changing my Mind*
Rohinton Mistry, *A Fine Balance*
Shunryu Suzuki, *Zen Mind, Beginner's Mind*
Emily Dickinson, *The Letters of Emily Dickinson*

THE GIFTS

ANDY MILLER

W.N.P. Barbellion, *The Journal of a Disappointed Man*
Penelope Fitzgerald, *The Beginning of Spring*
Stephen Sondheim, *Hat Box: The Collected Lyrics of Stephen Sondheim*
Elizabeth Taylor, *The Devastating Boys and Other Stories*
Geoffrey Willans and Ronald Searle, *The Compleet Molesworth*

JACKIE MORRIS

Maurice Sendak, *Where the Wild Things Are*
Matthew Francis, *The Mabinogi*
Thi Bui, *The Best We Could Do*
Wendell Berry, *Stand by Me*
Letters to the Earth: Writing to a Planet in Crisis (introduced by Emma Thompson)

SISONKE MSIMANG

Jamaica Kincaid, *A Small Place*
Zadie Smith, *Swing Time*
Arundhati Roy, *The God of Small Things*
Bessie Head, *When Rain Clouds Gather*
Panashe Chigumadzi, *These Bones Will Rise Again*

DINA NAYERI

Marilynne Robinson, *Housekeeping*
John Williams, *Stoner*
José Saramago, *Blindness*
Saul Bellow, *Seize the Day*
Anton Gill, *The Journey back from Hell*
Rainer Maria Rilke, *Letters to a Young Poet*

CHIGOZIE OBIOMA

Amos Tutuola, *The Palm-Wine Drinkard*
Richard Wright, *Black Boy*
Virginia Woolf, *The Waves*
William Golding, *Lord of the Flies*
Cormac McCarthy, *The Road*

MICHAEL ONDAATJE

J.L. Carr, *A Month in the Country*
Mavis Gallant, short stories
Lucia Berlin, short stories
Janet Lewis, *The Wife of Martin Guerre*
Denis Johnson, *Train Dreams*
Brenda Hillman, poetry

DAVID PILLING

A.A. Milne, *Winnie-the-Pooh*
Fyodor Dostoyevsky, *Crime and Punishment*
Jared Diamond, *Guns, Germs, and Steel*
Chinua Achebe, *Things Fall Apart*
Walt Whitman, *Song of Myself*

MAX PORTER

Wendell Berry, *Why I Am Not Going to Buy a Computer*
Alice Oswald, *Dart*
Kieran Larwood, *The Legend of Podkin One-Ear* (with
    three children and a lot of parties, this is our
    default book to give keen early readers)
Denise Riley, *Time Lived, Without Its Flow*
Neil Astley (ed.), *Staying Alive*

ALICE PUNG

Jeanette Winterson, *Why Be Happy When You Could
    Be Normal?*
Rohinton Mistry, *A Fine Balance*
Amy Tan, *The Kitchen God's Wife*
Emily Dickinson, *The Complete Poems*
Toni Morrison, *The Bluest Eye*

THE GIFTS

JANCIS ROBINSON

Any book by Elizabeth Taylor
Tom Rachman, *The Imperfectionists*
Simon Hopkinson, *Roast Chicken and Other Stories*
Nicholas Lander, *The Art of the Restaurateur*
Jancis Robinson, *The 24-Hour Wine Expert*

SF SAID

Richard Adams, *Watership Down*
Ursula K. Le Guin, *A Wizard of Earthsea*
Philip Pullman, *The Subtle Knife*
Malorie Blackman, *Noughts & Crosses*
Jason Reynolds and Chris Priestley, *Long Way Down*

MADELEINE THIEN

Joe Brainard, *I remember*
Italo Calvino, *Invisible Cities*
Ma Jian, *Red Dust*
Hannah Arendt and Mary McCarthy, *Between Friends: The Correspondence of Hannah Arendt and Mary McCarthy 1949 - 1975*
Cees Nooteboom, *The Foxes Come at Night*

THE GIFTS

SALLEY VICKERS

Beatrix Potter, *The Tale of Squirrel Nutkin*
Philippa Pearce, *Tom's Midnight Garden*
Joseph Conrad, *Lord Jim*
Sylvia Townsend Warner, *Lolly Willowes*
Penelope Fitzgerald, *The Blue Flower*

JOHN WOOD

Robert Macfarlane, *The Old Ways: A Journey on Foot*
Roland Schimmelpfennig, *One Clear Ice-Cold January
    Morning at the Beginning of the Twenty-First Century*
Tracy Kidder, *Mountains Beyond Mountains: The Quest of
    Dr Paul Farmer, a Man Who Would Cure the World*
Jeffrey Toobin, *American Heiress: The Wild Saga of the
    Kidnapping, Crimes and Trial of Patty Hearst*
Anthony Marra, *A Constellation of Vital Phenomena*

MARKUS ZUSAK

Eric Carle, *'Slowly, Slowly, Slowly,' said the Sloth*
S.E. Hinton, *Rumble Fish*
Pat Barker, *The Silence of the Girls*
Zadie Smith, *The Autograph Man*
Kurt Vonnegut, *Complete Stories*

Acknowledgements

৪৯

In my introduction to this book I wrote that it had been born out of two defining moments – but actually there was a third, the day I received an email from Robert Macfarlane's literary agent, Jessica Woollard at David Higham Associates, with the news that enabled me to launch this project: 'I have the go-ahead from both Robert and his publisher Simon Prosser.'

I would like to thank Jessica and Simon for their crucial support. I would also like to thank other colleagues and friends in the publishing world including Catherine Drayton, Julia Eccleshare and Patsy Irwin. I would especially like to thank Kelly Falconer, Founder of the Asia Literary Agency, and her husband Graeme Falconer who were particularly generous with advice at a critical time.

Yet one more memorable milestone was the email from Weidenfeld's Lettice Franklin, making an offer to publish and telling me she wanted to create an irresistible package of a book. It has been a delight to work with Lettice but also to reconnect with a much valued friend and colleague, Alan Samson, and to work with the rest of the team at W&N including Anne Goddard, Sarah Fortune, Virginia

Woolstencroft, Kate Moreton and Helen Ewing. In Australia, my thanks to Bella Lloyd at Hachette.

Colleagues at Room to Read who have contributed significantly to the development of this project include Geetha Murali, Julie Sims, Sarah Levine and Laurie McMahon. My sincere thanks to them all.

In Sydney, since the very beginning of Room to Read's Australian operation, I have worked with a stellar team of volunteers. Many of those who contributed to the early fundraising successes later became involved with the writer ambassador initiative. I would particularly like to thank Mihiri Udabage, Margaret Wilcox, Wendy Rapee, Pam Cook and Sarah Farmer. I also owe Jodi Mullen a great debt of thanks for all of her work on the Students Helping Students program and the writer ambassador initiative, in Hong Kong as well as Sydney.

As for the writer ambassadors themselves, they have offered support in so many different ways and I can't thank them enough:

In Australia: Deborah Abela, Tristan Bancks, the late Jesse Blackadder, Maxine Beneba Clarke, Pamela Cook, Sarah Davis, Stephanie Dowrick, James Foley, Kate Forsyth, Susanne Gervay, Gus Gordon, Jacqueline Harvey, Libby Hathorn, James Knight, John Larkin, Frané Lessac, Zanni Louise, Paul and Beth Macdonald, Emily Maguire, Christine Manfield, Melina Marchetta, Sophie Masson, Belinda Murrell, Pauline Nguyen, Oliver Phommavanh, Alice Pung, Sally Rippin, Dianne Wolfer, Susan Wyndham, Markus Zusak.

In Hong Kong: Sarah Brennan, Bhakti Mathur, Nury Vittachi.

This anthology would not exist were it not for the generosity of each and every one of our contributors. Alice Pung and Markus Zusak in Australia, and David Pilling and Jancis Robinson (part of the *Financial Times* team) in London, are all long-time Room to Read supporters. William Boyd, Candice Carty-Williams, Imtiaz Dharker, Roddy Doyle, Pico Iyer, Andy Miller, Jackie Morris, the late Jan Morris, Sisonke Msimang, Dina Nayeri, Chigozie Obioma, Michael Ondaatje, Max Porter, Philip Pullman, SF Said, Madeleine Thien and Salley Vickers all embraced the cause and contributed magnanimously. It has been such a very great pleasure to work with them.

My thanks above all to Robert Macfarlane, the literary inspiration for *The Gifts of Reading* and to John Wood, inspirational Founder of Room to Read and source of boundless enthusiasm for this anthology, also to John's wife, Amy Powell.

I would finally like to thank the many loyal and caring friends who have listened and provided encouragement over the past few years, and Ivor, my husband and trusted adviser, always supportive of all my endeavours in the literary and non-profit worlds.

Acknowledgements for material quoted in *The* Gifts of Reading

Jennie Orchard / Introduction
With thanks to Jan Morris and also to Caroline Dawnay at United Agents for permission to reproduce Jan's email.

The quote by Alberto Manguel comes from *A History of Reading* (published by HarperCollins, 1996). The quote by Ben Okri comes from his 'Ten and a Half Inclinations', written for the Royal Society of Literature. The quote from Anna Quindlen is from *How Reading Changed my Life* (Ballantine Books, 1998).

Robert Macfarlane / The gifts of reading
The extract from Gary Snyder's poem 'Riprap', Copyright © 1965 by Gary Snyder, from *Riprap and Cold Mountain Poems*, is reprinted by permission of Counterpoint.

Imtiaz Dharker / All spaces change
Extracts from Nissim Ezekiel's poems, 'The Professor' and *Latter-Day Psalms*, are reprinted by kind permission of Nissim Ezekiel's daughter, Kavita Ezekiel Mendonca.

Extracts from *Invisible Cities* by Italo Calvino, Copyright © 2002, The Estate of Italo Calvino, used by permission of The Wylie Agency (UK) Limited.

The quote by Pablo Neruda comes from *The Book of Questions* (Copper Canyon Press, 1991).

Andy Miller / Andy Miller and the Brain of Terrance Dicks

The extended quotes by Terrance Dicks are taken from an interview with Billy Smart, recorded in front of an audience at Royal Holloway, University of London, Egham, on Friday 24 April 2015.

The quote by Terrance Dicks, pp 100 – 101, is taken from *The Target Book: A History of the Target 'Doctor Who' Books* by David J. Howe, first published by Telos Publishing Ltd, 2007.

Doctor Who and the Brain of Morbius by Terrance Dicks was first published in 1977 by Target Books.

Andy Miller's book, *The Year of Reading Dangerously*, was first published by Fourth Estate, 2014.

The opening quote by Terrance Dicks and quotes by Mark Gatiss are taken from a BBC Radio 4 documentary he [Gatiss] wrote and presented in 2009, 'On the Outside it Looked like an Old-fashioned Police Box'.

Sisonke Msimang / The solace of Sundays

The first quote from James Baldwin (pp 146-7) comes from an article by Jane Howard, 'Telling Talk from a Negro Writer', *Life* magazine, 24 May 1963. The second quote (p 153) comes from a National Public Radio program recorded in 1961, 'The Negro in American Culture', a group discussion including James Baldwin.

Ntozake Shange's poem 'For Colored Girls who have Considered Suicide when The Rainbow is Enuf' is reprinted by permission of Russell & Volkening as agents for Eudora Welty, copyright © 1974 by Ntozake Shange.

Nikki Giovanni's poem 'Nikki-Rosa' is reprinted by kind permission of the author (from *Black Judgement*, first published by Broadside Lotus Press, 1968).

Dina Nayeri / A life's work
The passage from Marilynne Robinson's novel *Housekeeping* is reprinted by kind permission of Marilynne Robinson and Ellen Levine at Trident Media Group.

The quotes from *Stoner* by John Williams are used by permission of Frances Collin Literary Agency.

Seize the Day by Saul Bellow was originally published by Viking in 1956.

Michael Ondaatje / The voice and craft of Toni Morrison
With sincere thanks to Laurie Graham, publisher of *Brick* magazine, which included this essay in its summer 2020 edition.

Michael Ondaatje quotes from 'The Site of Memory' in *Inventing the Truth: The Art and Craft of Memoir* (Houghton Mifflin, 1995); 'Rootedness: The Ancestor as Foundation' in *What Moves at the Margin: Selected Nonfiction* (University Press of Mississippi, 2008); *Toni Morrison: Conversations* (University Press of Mississippi, 2008); and *The Source of Self-Regard: Selected Essays, Speeches, and Meditations* (Knopf, 2019).

The excerpt from *Jazz* by Toni Morrison, copyright © 1992 by Toni Morrison, is used by permission of Alfred A. Knopf, an imprint of the Knopf Doubleday Publishing Group, a division of Penguin Random House LLC. All rights reserved.

Permission courtesy of the Toni Morrison Estate c/o ICM Partners.

Madeleine Thien / Spinoza's rooms
Material quoted in this essay comes from the following publications:

Spinoza: A Life, Steven Nadler (Cambridge University Press, 1999)

Waste Not: Zhao Ziangyuan & Song Dong, Wu Hung (Tokyo Gallery + Beijing Tokyo Art Projects, 2009)

Spinoza, Roger Scruton (Orion Books, 1998)

The Human Condition, Hannah Arendt (University of Chicago Press, 1998)

Betraying Spinoza, Rebecca Goldstein (Schocken Books, 2006)

All possible care has been taken to make full acknowledgement in every case where material is still in copyright. If errors have occurred, they will be corrected in subsequent editions if notification is sent to the publisher.

Room to Read®

World Change Starts with Educated Children.

Room to Read extends its heartfelt thanks to all the contributors to this book and, in particular, to Jennie Orchard for her creativity and passion in developing the idea for this anthology and seeing the project to fruition, and Robert Macfarlane for his generosity in lending his essay and title to the project.

At Room to Read, we know books have the power to expand the boundaries of one's world, allowing us to take a few steps in somebody else's shoes and, in doing so, to recognise our shared humanity. By providing relevant books in local languages, Room to Read strives to help children do just that and become lifelong independent readers. So far, we have published more than 1600 titles in forty-two languages and distributed more than twenty-eight million copies of these books in low-income communities around the world.

Room to Read's programs provide support during the two most critical periods in a child's education: primary school for literacy acquisition and secondary school for girls' education. In addition to publishing books in local languages, our Literacy Program trains and coaches teachers, creates high-quality curricular materials and establishes libraries filled with diverse children's books that can be enjoyed at school or home. Our

331

Girls' Education Program helps girls build skills to succeed in secondary school and make key life decisions by providing life skills curriculum, opportunities for mentorship and peer support, and family and community engagement. Room to Read collaborates with local communities, partner organisations and governments to test and implement innovative models that can be integrated into the education system to deliver positive outcomes for children at scale.

To learn more, join a chapter near you or subscribe to our Book Club, visit www.roomtoread.org.